Jonathan Belcher, Colonial Governor

His Excellency JONATHAN BELCHER *Esq*
Captain General & Governor in Chief of His Majesty's Provinces of
Massachuset's Bay & New Hampshire *in* NEW ENGLAND *and*
Vice Admiral of the same

R. Phillips Pinx.   J. Faber Fecit 1734.

Jonathan Belcher, Colonial Governor

Michael C. Batinski

THE UNIVERSITY PRESS OF KENTUCKY

*F
67
B45
B38
1996*

Frontispiece: Jonathan Belcher, portrait engraving by John Faber. Courtesy of Special Collections at Princeton University Library.

Copyright © 1996 by The University Press of Kentucky

Scholarly publisher for the Commonwealth, serving Bellarmine College, Berea College, Centre College of Ketucky, Eastern Kentucky University, The Filson Club, Georgetown College, Kentucky Historical Society, Kentucky State University, Morehead State University, Murray State University, Northern Kentucky University, Transylvania University, University of Kentucky, University of Louisville, and Western Kentucky University.

Editorial and Sales Offices: The University Press of Kentucky 663 South Limestone Street, Lexington, Kentucky 40508-4008

Library of Congress Catalog-in-Publication Data

Batinski, Michael C., 1943-
Jonathan Belcher, Colonial Governor/Michael C. Batinski.
    p.   cm.
Includes bibliographical references (p.) and index.
ISBN 0-8131-1946-4 (cloth : alk. paper)
    1. Belcher, Jonathan, 1682-1757.   2. Governors—Massachusetts—Biography.   3. Governors—New Hampshire—Biography.
4. Massachusetts—History—Colonial period, ca. 1600-1775.   5. New Hampshire—History—Colonial period, ca. 1600-1775.   I. Title.
F67.B45B38   1996
974.2'02'092—dc20
[B]   95-32666

This book is printed on acid-free recycled paper meeting the requirements of the American National Standard for Permanence of Paper for Printed Library Materials.

Manufactured in the United States of America

For
Jason
and
Ginny
and
Peter
with love

Contents

Preface

New England's Puritans expected their leaders to be modeled from the Book of Nehemiah. It was common fare on election days for the Puritan ministers to retell the story of Nehemiah and his labors to rebuild the walls of Jerusalem. In 1690, for example, Cotton Mather recalled the dark days of the "Babylonish Captivity," when many Jews had been driven from their homes and forced to live in exile.[1] During that time Nehemiah won the favor of King Artaxerxes and was appointed royal cupbearer. One day news came to Nehemiah that the Jews who remained in the homeland were suffering grievously. The wall that once protected Jerusalem had been broken down, the people were naked to their enemies, and the community was slowly dying. Nehemiah wept. He went to his master begging that he be allowed to return to his people. The king consented and made Nehemiah governor of Judea. On returning to the homeland, Nehemiah summoned the people to rebuild the wall and then gathered them to hear the reading of the laws of their fathers and to rededicate themselves to the covenant. Thus, he expelled the heathen from the city, cleansed it of injustice and corruption, restored the proper observation of the Sabbath, and rejuvenated God's people.

Nehemiah stood beside Jeremiah in New England's political thought. With the passing of the founding generation of Puritan settlers, ministers berated the people for their sins, their backsliding ways, their neglect of the covenant. Speaking like latter-day Jeremiahs, they warned that unless the people reformed their ways they were sure to fall under God's judgment. Jonathan Mitchel spoke as a Jeremiah when he delivered the election sermon of 1667. Troubled times required good rulers, men who could stand like "Nehemiah on the Wall" protecting this covenanted people. Cotton Mather picked up that motif in his election sermon and later elaborated on the theme in his *Magnalia Christi Americana*. For Mather, John Winthrop became the "Nehemias Americanus." So too, Jonathan Edwards employed the Book of Nehemiah to press his cause for spiritual awakening. And during the struggle for independence from Great Britain, New England's divines fashioned the biblical leader to fit their quest for liberty.[2]

One son of New England, Jonathan Belcher, became the embodiment of the Nehemiah. When Benjamin Colman delivered the election sermon of 1718, he recommended the young Belcher as a Nehemiah who deserved to be elevated to the governor's Council.[3] Belcher, in turn, sought to make himself into the good ruler. As governor of Massachusetts and New Hampshire in the 1730s, he labored to protect the Puritan legacy, its institutions and its faith, from assault. The ministers responded by giving thanks for his government and praising him from their pulpits as a true Nehemiah. The role brought him fulfillment. Later, when appointed governor of New Jersey, he faithfully pursued that ideal. He was one of the few royal officials who enjoyed the confidence of leading evangelicals such as George Whitefield and Jonathan Edwards. They mustered their political influence to support his administration, and they mourned his passing. Aaron Burr, Edwards's son-in-law, delivered the governor's funeral sermon. In summing up Belcher's life, the minister praised him as God's true "servant" who had conducted himself like "that pious Governor Nehemiah."[4]

Nehemiah standing at the walls of Jerusalem—that image dominated the imaginations of New England's Puritans because it fit their sense of themselves. Like the biblical ruler, their leaders labored to protect a special people in covenant with God. Massachusetts's magistrates, like their biblical counterpart, derived their authority from two sources, from a God who called them to stand watch over this "city on a hill" and from a king who cared nothing for that vision. Massachusetts had become a "wilderness zion" protected by two "hedges" or walls, the covenant with God and the king's charter. It was the task of the good ruler to keep both walls intact.[5]

The first charter had been granted by King Charles I and brought to Massachusetts-Bay by John Winthrop in 1630. It became the legal foundation for planting a Puritan government. This royal charter enabled the saints to elect their own magistrates from legislators to the governor. It secured self-rule. Yet, ironically, the charter came from a king who despised this experiment in Puritan utopia. In the days after the Puritan revolution and the restoration of the English monarchy, Massachusetts struggled valiantly, heroically, defiantly to preserve its charter, but in the end the colony buckled to the royal will. Succeeding generations remembered that moment in 1684 when King Charles II revoked the charter. The next year James II, a Catholic, succeeded to the throne and appointed men to govern New England who were outspoken enemies of the Puritans. Those who witnessed these dark days never tired of recounting the train of tyrannies that followed and that glorious event in 1688, when England overthrew its Catholic king and installed William and Mary. New England's Puritans rose up against their oppressors. They rejoiced to learn that the new government in London had secured a Protestant succession to the throne, and they pledged their loyalty to the monarchy.

When Cotton Mather delivered the election sermon of 1690, he declared that "The People of New-England are a People of God" and the "most Loyal People" of all the king and queen's subjects.[6] The next year, when Massachusetts received a new charter, he and his cohorts celebrated. The charter of 1691 became a new "hedge" or wall protecting God's covenanted people. But the political settlement did not restore the New England way to what it had been. Under the new charter, the franchise was tied to property not church membership. While the voters chose a House of Representatives, which in turn elected a Council each year, the king appointed the governor. The governor remained in office at the king's pleasure. And governors appointed in England came to America with instructions to support the Church of England as the established church. They were expected to promote English economic interests even when they collided with the colony's welfare.

These latter-day Puritans thus entered a whiggish world. The Board of Trade, the Bank of England, the House of Commons stood at the center of this world, imposing their influence upon the peripheries of the empire. New vocabularies were gaining currency. While New England's caretakers still thought within the conventions of the jeremiad and perceived themselves as a people covenanted with God, they were now compelled to wrestle with constitutional issues and legal forms, with questions of currency and finance. Increasingly, as they looked to London, they became conscious of themselves as provincials on the periphery of civilization. The descendants of John Winthrop self-consciously imitated the latest styles of English gentility. They listened to their ministers deliver their jeremiads, but they were also paying attention to the latest prints from London's bookstalls. While they chose to think of themselves as Puritans, they felt embarrassment by their fathers' intolerant ways toward Quakers and witches. Keeping the faith of the fathers in this whiggish world was becoming difficult. The lures of the cosmopolitan were unmistakable. Some provincials were abandoning their fathers' ways. Anglicans were growing in number. Their leaders did not hide their intention to tear down the Congregational establishment and to seize control of Harvard College. Natives who sank their roots deep in New England's history shed their principles for worldly gain. Accusations of apostasy abounded. Few rulers seemed capable of measuring up to the reputations of the founding fathers.

Puritans like Cotton Mather were learning how difficult it was to find the good ruler. They had seen an older generation fall in its uncompromising defense of the first charter and had learned the futility of such histrionics. The times seemed to call for leaders who were at heart Puritans but who also had learned the ways of this whiggish world. They found these Nehemias sitting at the Council table, but they also felt disappointed by the actions of their leaders. New England's self-proclaimed protectors too often proved themselves to be time-servers, opportunists who had become too comfortable with this world and its vanities. The clergy believed that Massachusetts's royal governors did not deserve to be called Nehemiahs. Few were friendly to John Winthrop's legacy and some were downright hostile. Joseph Dudley seemed to represent the times. Though the son of Massachusetts's second governor, Dudley had cooperated in tearing down the old charter government. When he returned as governor in 1702, few could forget or forgive his misdeeds.

While Belcher lived in a world that made it difficult to play the Nehemiah, the role was also appropriate for the times. No one ventured to compare King George with Artaxerxes or to suggest that Massachusetts experienced a kind of captivity. But by using the Nehemiah, New Englanders could address by analogy or indirection their ambivalent feelings toward the imperial relationship. The biblical prototype had gained the opportunity to restore the covenant by being a courtier. While Massachusetts continued to extol the primitive virtues of the "country" patriot and to condemn the courtier, its leaders were coming to own, though grudgingly, that protecting the New England way required the skills of the flatterer and dissembler. Maintaining the proper balance between means and ends became a difficult task. While many failed, Belcher became a consummate master of that art.

Playing the Nehemiah became a means for easing troublesome transitions and for reshaping this New England society. The Nehemiah spoke as a preserver, as a conservator, of Governor Winthrop's legacy. Belcher shared in his society's rituals of filiopietism. But even while he seemed to speak the vocabulary of the fathers, he was revising the meaning of that tradition. Organic community, the just price, equity—these ideas were being forgotten. Belcher and his contemporaries lived comfortably in the marketplace and were coming to speak with new accents. They were asking new questions: What was money? Could the government correct the chronic shortages of money? Could private institutions of banking be allowed? While not deliberately or consciously rejecting the traditional, they were refashioning it to fit the whiggish world of the marketplace. They addressed new issues that came with empire and debated constitutional questions regarding the preservation of rights. They gave new attention to legal forms and institutional arrangements. And Massachusetts's self-styled Nehemiahs began to ape London's latest fashions. The changes provoked controversy, roused impassioned debates, and sometimes caused violent exchanges. By appearing to preserve the fathers' legacy, however, the Nehemiah glossed over the changes, muted the disagreements, and thereby helped to ease the people through important changes.

If asked to characterize this biography, I would begin by placing it somewhere between Bernard Bailyn's *The Origins of American Politics* and Philip Greven's *The Protestant Temperament*.[7] The subject is manifestly political history. To understand Jonathan Belcher, however, I turned to the work of Greven, John Demos, Kenneth A. Lockridge, and the numerous other social historians who have been inspired by their pioneering work.[8] Even while many of these scholars have deliberately turned their backs on political history, they have produced a literature that enriches, even if unintentionally, our understanding of early American political life. Power and authority, conflict and community—these are the very ingredients of politics. While exploring the meanings of these terms in the intimate and private contexts of the family and in the relationship between neighbors, these historians have provided a basis for rejuvenating political history. By building on that work, I have extended the domain of the social historian so that it overlaps the world of politics.

The essential and most perilous task of the biographer turns on the questions: Who was this person? What made him tick? Jonathan Belcher is an illusive subject. His personal papers are at once voluminous and opaque. Belcher was not prone to introspection, and he shied from self-revelation. He was an actor, not a thinker. Unlike many of his contemporaries, he was not by nature a diarist. His letterbooks reveal a man who instinctively grasped for the commonplace. Sometimes he wrote in the style of the most fawning courtier. At other times he indulged himself in what seems to be empty evangelical cant. Indeed, historians who have delved into the letterbooks have dismissed the man as a pompous hypocrite, and perhaps for that reason no one has been moved to write a biography.

On closer examination, however, Belcher emerges as a complicated subject. There are distinct and even contradictory sides to the man. There is the Belcher who was constantly seething with rage and plotting vengeance on his enemies. And there is the Belcher who self-consciously sought to avoid needless contention, and who even slunk from confrontation. There are two faces to Jonathan Belcher. On assuming the government of Massachusetts, for example, Belcher deftly maneuvered long-standing and seemingly irreconcilable rivals toward a political settlement. At the same time, he behaved in a very different manner as governor of New Hampshire, where he recklessly plunged into bitter factional disputes that eventually spelled the ruination of his government. Little by little Belcher begins to reveal himself, sometimes indirectly and sometimes in deeds. There is the moment when he bitterly contested his father's last will and testament over issues that were more symbolic that substantive. And there is that moment when he ordered the destruction of his official portrait. In word and deed Belcher slowly emerges as a man who at heart felt himself surrounded by enemies. Sometimes he acted as the vicious partisan. As often, however, he proved afraid to act. Aggressiveness and timidity—these core traits are essential for understanding the man and his sense of the world.

Jonathan Belcher felt about himself and the world around him in ways that are beginning to be understood by students of that age. Many of Belcher's contemporaries lived in the same constellation of emotions, which were rooted in similar childhood experiences. Belcher grew to adulthood under the authority of a domineering father. His experience, when compared with that of others, does not seem out of the ordinary. Fathers were encouraged not to flinch from exercising their patriarchal powers. Ministers reminded parents of their duty to break the natural "wilfulness" of children; discipline was necessary for turning the child into a social creature and, in turn, for maintaining community.[9] "Well-ordered Families," preached Cotton Mather, "naturally produce a Good Order" throughout society, and the rules that applied to good family government also applied in the larger spheres of local and provincial government.[10] Fathers were the governors of their families in much the way that magistrates ruled the province. To countenance the fractious child was to raise a factious adult and a contentious neighbor.

New England's Puritans believed they were molding their children into good neighbors who would live together in harmonious communities. In one sense they succeeded. People like Belcher grew up without the emotional stamina to stand against their fathers and, in turn, lacked the reserves for conflict with neighbors or with civil authorities. Though their disagreements were substantial, they shied from acting on them. New Englanders succeeded in creating "peaceable kingdoms," but they may have produced unexpected results.[11] What they called breaking the child's natural "stubbornness" appears by modern lights to be a critical assault on the child's autonomy that undermines a sense of self-worth. As several historians have noted, these early American parents created children with an innate sense of the world as threatening and of themselves as vulnerable. Children carried these habits of the heart into adulthood. Adults like Jonathan Belcher lived in a world that they saw as dark, foreboding, and threatening. When engaged in conflict, they tended to exaggerate differences and were prone to concoct enemies in their imaginations. They also shied from engaging directly in these conflicts. And so they kept their rage within. Sometimes, when they gave vent to their feelings, they directed their anger from the original source of danger to other and less threatening objects. Perhaps compliant children made for peaceable neighbors, at least most of the time. But when they expressed themselves, they were likely to explode volcanically.

It seems understandable that Belcher was drawn to Cotton Mather, for both seemed to understand the world in similar terms.[12] Belcher was moved when he listened to the minister fulminate against the enemies of government. It was more than the content of Mather's sermons that stirred him. The two men spoke with the same emotional vocabulary. Conspirators, both real and fantastic, seemed to be ever prowling in the recesses of their imaginations. Both men, the sons of powerful and domineering patriarchs, concocted fantasies of retribution and at the same time sought to suppress them. They both swung from aggression to passivity and meekness. To read Mather's diary is to enter a world not unlike that found in Belcher's letterbooks. Thus, in time of crisis, when Belcher felt himself the innocent victim of his political adversaries, he turned to Cotton Mather. Like the minister, he grappled with disappointment by assuming the martyr's role. While both men professed resignation, meekness, and even forgiveness, neither could conceal his seething rage.

These feelings made Belcher a sensitive interpreter of his times, perhaps in his own way as important as Mather himself. Public life not only provoked great fears but also provided fulfillment. Belcher craved the public arena. It was there that he found satisfaction at playing the Nehemiah. He needed an audience, and like an actor he played his part always with one eye on the public. Thus, he was drawn to put himself in a position that simultaneously provoked deep insecurities. While playing the Nehemiah, he could hear in his imagination the people mocking his performance. He was ever attending to the details of staging appearances before the public. And most important, he always strove to deliver a performance that met what he believed were the expectations of his audience. Because his interpretation was self-consciously commonplace, it illuminates his age.

This biography focuses on the mentality of a doer not a thinker. It places ideas in the context of the public arena as they were used by a decidedly commonplace thinker. By doing so it bridges prescription with action and, thereby, grapples with the complexities of Belcher's world. Distinctions between ideologies that in the abstract seem clear, distinct, and even contradictory begin to dissolve. "Country" and "court" become different interpretations of the Nehemiah. Belcher's life illuminates the complex process of change. While Belcher and many of his contemporaries strove to maintain the legacy of the Puritan founders, they were in fact remaking their world. While they had not rejected the founders' fears of the marketplace, they thrived in the world of commerce. And if they still subscribed to the founders' ideal of a well-defined hierarchical social order in which the people deferred to their superiors, they were playing with new and democratic styles of behavior. Words changed in their meaning; accents shifted. Positions that might seem contradictory from a broader historical perspective seemed to co-exist. Thus, Belcher could simultaneously embrace both Jonathan Edwards and Thomas Hutchinson, even though the two men were emotional and intellectual opposites.

This biography takes its cue from Cotton Mather, who reminded New Englanders that family and provincial governments were inextricably tied together. It is in childhood, he argued, that people acquire the dispositions that will determine what kind of political creatures they will become as adults. For some time social historians have heeded Cotton Mather's words, but only partially. While they have focused on the inner workings of family life and even extended their inquiry to the relations between neighbors, they have not fully applied their investigations to the realm of provincial politics. This biography seeks to do just that.[13]

It is a pleasure for me to acknowledge the numerous debts I have incurred while pursuing Jonathan Belcher through numerous libraries on both sides of the Atlantic. I first wish to thank the staffs of the state historical societies of Connecticut, Massachusetts, New Hampshire, New Jersey, New York, and Pennsylvania, of the state archives at Connecticut, Massachusetts, New Hampshire, and New Jersey, and of the Suffolk County (Massachusetts) Probate Court. In addition, I wish to thank the librarians and staffs at the American Antiquarian Society, the Boston Public Library, the Clements Library at the University of Michigan, the Library Company of Philadelphia, the Library of Congress, the Newberry Library, the New York Public Library, Northwestern University, the Libraries of Princeton University, the Presbyterian Historical Society, Rutgers University, the University of Virginia, and Yale University. I also wish to give special notice to the staff at Morris Library at Southern Illinois University, Carbondale, which has consistently rendered invaluable and cheerful assistance. I am especially appreciative of the always friendly assistance rendered by James W. Fox, Walter R. Stubbs, and the late Charles Holliday. Finally, my research in Great Britain was aided immeasurably by the staffs at the Public Record Office, the British Museum, Friends House, Fulham Palace, and Guildhall.

My travels were also assisted immeasurably by grants from the American Philosophical Society, the National Endowment for the Humanities, the New Jersey Historical Commission, the Woodrow Wilson Foundation, and the Graduate School at Southern Illinois University, Carbondale.

I wish to thank the following for permission to quote from their manuscript collections: the American Antiquarian Society; the Library Company of Philadelphia; the Massachusetts Historical Society; the New Hampshire

Historical Society; the New York Public Library and the Astor, Lenox, and Tilden Foundations; the New Jersey Historical Society; and the Princeton University Libraries. All quotations have been kept in their original form as much as possible. Spelling and punctuation have been changed only on rare occasions for the sake of the modern reader. I also wish to thank the Princeton University Libraries for permission to reproduce John Faber's portrait engraving of Governor Belcher.

Several readers have read this work in various forms. I am most grateful to Clarence L. Ver Steeg and Robert H. Wiebe, John Y. Simon and Howard W. Allen, David Sloan and Stephen H. Coe, and David L. Wilson and Peter N. Carroll for their time and their helpful observations.

After completing the writing of this manuscript, I was fortunate to discover the staff at the University Press of Kentucky. I quickly came to appreciate the suggestions for improvements that were made throughout the process of review and production. Equally important, I have been impressed by the always cheerful and generous spirit with which I was treated throughout this long and sometimes difficult process. I wish to thank the entire press for making the experience almost pleasant.

Finally I wish to thank Ginny Hoffman and Peter Carroll, whose encouragement and advice came at a critical point in this project's progress. I cannot forget.

1

The Puritan in a Whiggish Age

On the morning of August 10, 1730, Jonathan Belcher stood on deck the HMS *Blandford* surveying the familiar sights of his native Boston and clutching in his hand the commissions that made him the king's governor of Massachusetts. For the past two days, he had been waiting anxiously aboard ship in the harbor so that his arrival might not disturb the Sabbath and that his fellow townspeople might have time to prepare for his reception. As he took his seat in the long boat, he could hear the town's church bells peeling in celebration and the batteries of Castle William booming their salute. He neared the town's Long Wharf. Nearby lay Belcher Wharf, where he and his father had made the family's fortune. In the distance he could make out the spire of Old South Church, where he had faithfully attended all his life. Waiting to receive him were the lieutenant governor, councilors, and the elected representatives from the towns of the king's oldest province in New England. He knew them well and had served with many of them in government. He received their congratulations graciously and then proceeded in their company up King Street.

It was a grand procession led by a company of militia. The governor was pleased as he proceeded past the cheering crowds and the homes decorated gaily in his honor. On arriving at the Town House, the dignitaries escorted him upstairs to the Council chamber. The king's commission was read, and then Jonathan Belcher swore the oath of allegiance to King George and to the Protestant succession. He stepped out onto the balcony, the crowd cheered, the militia company fired three volleys in salute, and the harbor batteries once again boomed their approval.

Boston celebrated for the next month.[1] Delegations of the town's selectmen, merchants, and clergymen came to congratulate Governor Belcher and to wish him well. The Congregational ministers confessed that ever since they had heard of his appointment they had been like "Men that dream": "The Cloud that hung over us scattered in a moment, and as the Sun breaks out in a dark Day, so was the Face of GOD, and the Light of the King's Countenance upon Us." For this "We adore the WISE PROVIDENCE that has led in every step to so great an Event."[2]

Two days later, the governor attended the Brattle Street Church to hear his old friend Benjamin Colman expound on the divine foundations of government and the blessings to be expected from a ruler born of New England. Directing his remarks to Belcher, he prayed that "the Lord GOD of our Fathers, who hath spread our Heavens, and laid the Foundations of our Earth, make you a PILLAR to Us both in the State & Church." Another clergyman praised God for choosing to raise Jonathan Belcher up "from among the Sons of New-England." The administration promised to shine "like the light of the Morning, when the Sun riseth after a darksome Night," and no doubt the people would flourish just "as the tender Grass" springs "out of the Earth by clear shining after Rain."[3]

Jonathan Belcher savored these moments. For the celebrants linked his appointment to the symbols of good government that dominated this world. The people of Massachusetts, especially Boston, took every opportunity to demonstrate their affection for the king, to pray for the welfare of the house of Hanover, and to give thanks for the security of the Protestant succession. King George sat at the apex of this political universe, and the anniversary of his birth was cause for public celebration. Belcher prized his connection to the throne. He methodically gathered the symbols of royalty unto himself, and he took special pleasure in playing at the role of "his majesty's loyal servant."[4]

New Englanders gave meaning to monarchy within another and broader context. In the same breath that they paid homage to the king, they celebrated their Puritan heritage. They had spent the summer marking the centennial anniversary of the Bay Colony's settlement. That heroic moment when the founders had come to plant this covenanted society, this wilderness Zion, remained at the heart of their collective imaginations. They revered that legacy of the covenant, and they preserved the memory of the leaders who, like the Old Testament's Nehemiah, had built and maintained the walls and hedges that protected this special people from adversity. It was within that framework that they celebrated the royal connection, for it was the king and his charter to Massachusetts that protected their liberties. For Massachusetts those liberties meant security for the Congregational churches. Thus, Belcher took pride in his connection to the royal family. It elevated him in his society, and it enabled him to play the role of a latter-day Nehemiah.[5]

"Ye are my Brethren: Ye are my Bones and my Flesh." With these words Governor Jonathan Belcher first addressed the Council and House of Representatives of Massachusetts. "The first thing I would recommend to you, is a Regard to Virtue and true Religion, for which *New-England* has (a long Time) had the Honour to be distinguished." He reminded the lawmakers of the "early Care our Fathers took for a liberal and pious Education of their Posterity" and assured them that he would "gladly embrace every Opportunity you'l put in my Power of nourishing that Seminary of Religion and Learning" at Cambridge. Taking his cue from Colman's sermon, he promised to preserve the Puritan heritage. The words came easily. As a child, he had learned to revere the founding generation and its achievement. He had read Cotton Mather's biography of New England's first Nehemiah, John Winthrop. And he remembered the founders as "men of Religion, good Knowledge, and Substance."[6]

Belcher took special pride in his descent from that first generation. But when he joined in the rituals of remembrance and filiopietism, he also felt discomforts. New Englanders gave special notice to those who were descended from the first leaders. Winthrop, Hutchinson, Cotton, Mather— these were names that were remembered and respected. The descendants of these men commanded special notice and deference. New Englanders took note of these genetic connections, and they congratulated themselves that they were still led by the same families. Belcher, however, was not one of these names. While perusing his copy of Cotton Mather's magisterial *Magnalia Christi Americana*, he found no mention of his forebears.

Family reputation and origins fascinated Belcher. Since his youth he had spent much time researching his ancestry. The records were skimpy. He could with some imagination claim descent, albeit indirect, from English gentility. The connection entitled him to use a family crest and motto *Ad Mortem Fidelis*. But his researches also reminded him that his immediate ancestors were weavers from England's eastern counties.[7] His grandfather Andrew left England sometime in the 1630s, settled in Sudbury, and later removed to Cambridge. In 1652, he was living in Cambridge and had secured a license to "sell beer and bread for the entertainment of strangers and to the good of the town." Other than the records of Andrew Belcher's marriage to Elizabeth Danforth, the sister of the colony's deputy governor, of the births of five daughters and a son, and of titles to land, little evidence of his life remained. Perhaps he died in 1680. Jonathan left that date blank on the family tree. The only remembrance that he deemed worth keeping was the record of the lands he inherited.[8]

Nor could Jonathan Belcher find much to say about his own father Andrew. What he did tell was significant in its brevity. When Belcher was an old man, he received an inquiry from his friend Thomas Prince requesting his recollections of his father. Jonathan understood the intent of the query, for Prince was compiling material for the completion of his *Chronological History of New England*. He knew the work well. The first volume had been dedicated to him. Yet Belcher replied that he found the task too "difficult," and wrote only a few lines describing his father's piety and his acumen for business.[9] There seemed little worth the historian's notice, for Prince was interested in New England's saints and God's task assigned to them, and Andrew Belcher was an adventurer who spent much of his life turning the bounties of the land to profit. Sometime in the 1660s, young Andrew had left Cambridge as a peddler, wandered westward toward the Connecticut Valley, and opened a tavern at Wallingford. In 1670 he married Sarah, the daughter of Jonathan Gilbert, a Hartford merchant. He chose well. His father-in-law conducted a flourishing trade with Indians and settlers that extended up the Connecticut River to Springfield and along the southern coast of New England. Gilbert's knowledge of Indian languages recommended him as the government's negotiator with the local tribes. He served in local government and on occasion was elected to the legislature. In sum, the young Andrew Belcher had gained entrance into the region's economic and political leadership.[10]

Andrew Belcher was twenty-seven when King Philip's Indians rose up against the Puritan colonists. New England suffered such afflictions that its leaders concluded that it had fallen under "God's Dreadful judgement." When victory came, it signified that God had not forsaken his people. The war quickly became part of a collective historical consciousness that was passed down by way of sermons and histories from one generation to the next. If Jonathan Belcher had searched those histories, he would have found that his father appeared for only a fleeting moment. Captain Benjamin Church recounted that when New England's troops were sorely besieged by the enemy, Andrew Belcher arrived with much needed supplies.[11] If the story were to be told, it would be gleaned from the records of government accounts. Aided by family connections, this young adventurer was becoming a major engrosser of Connecticut grain and in turn a critical supplier to the forces of that colony and of Massachusetts. At times his ventures clashed with the public welfare. Food shortages during the winter and spring of 1676 forced the Connecticut government to set restrictions on exports. Belcher resented the embargo: in the spring his ship was stopped at Saybrook and the grain on board confiscated. But, no doubt, he benefited from his father-in-law's political connections. Usually the General Court granted him special exemptions from the rule; in May 1676 he received permission to load his ships with corn "before the order granting liberty of transportation be published."[12]

Connecticut was already too confining for Andrew Belcher. Sometime after the war, he moved his family, which now included one son, Andrew, and three daughters—Sarah, Elizabeth, and Mary—to Charlestown, Massachusetts. Soon after, he was living in Cambridge, where in 1682 his wife gave birth to a second son, Jonathan. Shortly after, the family moved to Boston. By this time the family had increased by two more daughters, Ann and Martha.[13]

Jonathan saw little of his father during these years and even less when at the age of seven his mother died, and he was sent to live with relatives in the country. Andrew's fortunes were rising rapidly. In concert with his brother-in-law, Thomas Gilbert, he was emerging as Boston's major supplier of Connecticut grain and pork. Soon he was extending his trading network southward to New York, Philadelphia, Virginia, and the Carolinas and across the Atlantic to London, Glasgow, Holland, and Portugal. His ships carried whatever promised profit, be it slaves, tobacco, naval supplies, fish, or wines. The returns were great, and a few cargoes made a fortune. But the risks were terrifying; a storm or pirate could bring swift ruin. And there also was Edward Randolph, the king's aggressive new customs collector, who was becoming a scourge to American merchants. On occasion Belcher's ships were seized for violating the English acts of trade. How far he ventured beyond the law, of course, escapes precise answer, but the evidence clearly points to illegal dealings. In 1688 he appeared on the Rhode Island coast purchasing booty—fifty hides and forty elephant teeth—from a band of pirates.[14]

Again, New England's misfortunes turned to Andrew Belcher's profit.[15] When he settled in Boston, the Massachusetts government was losing its struggle to ward off the intrusions of a hostile English authority. In 1684, the colony's reputation for disloyalty, largely corroborated by the reports of Edward Randolph, persuaded the king to revoke the charter and to establish a new government presided over by Joseph Dudley, the son of the colony's second governor. Massachusetts, now vulnerable to the avowed enemies of the Puritan experiment and governed by an apostate to that tradition, shuddered in anticipation. The very pillars of that experiment—Congregational church government and the town meeting—teetered precariously. Titles to lands granted under the old charter were declared invalid. These were dark days, long remembered in sermons and histories as the time when Governor Winthrop's "City upon a Hill" seemed destined for destruction. For some, however, the old government's demise opened new opportunities. Many merchants, some Puritan and others not, had been nursing their resentments against the old political establishment for denying them access to power and quickly offered their services to the new Dudley government. Opportunity suddenly opened for the obscure adventurer on the make. William Phips, a poorly educated and rough merchant adventurer, was appointed provost marshal. Andrew Belcher was made his assistant.[16]

But the new regime was fragile, built on opportunism and conflicting interests. Merchants who had once encouraged Randolph in his opposition to the Puritan establishment, but who now had gained power, had no intention of supporting him in the enforcement of English trade laws. Moreover, in 1686 King James II ordered the consolidation of his northernmost colonies into the Dominion of New England. The Dudley government was absorbed into this new administrative agency; the seat of power was shifted to New York; and Sir Edmund Andros was appointed the new governor-general.

Andros, the complete Cavalier, openly displayed his loathing for New England's Puritans and his contempt for the merchant community. Massachusetts's Puritans shuddered: while Andros had decreed that Boston's churches were subject to seizure for Anglican services, his royal master seemed bent on reestablishing Roman Catholicism. Boston's merchants saw their expectations for power dissolve as the government in New York consolidated its power. They grew restive as the new government pressed its prosecution of smugglers and challenged the legality of land titles. So when news of a "glorious" revolution arrived from England in 1689, New England's merchants readily joined in the provincial revolt. Dudley and Randolph were both arrested and sent to England in chains. Andrew Belcher was among the first to volunteer his services. When the revolutionaries offered him a seat on the interim committee of safety, he accepted and served until the arrival of the new charter in 1691.[17]

As if to demonstrate its loyalty to the new monarchs, William and Mary, and to the Protestant succession, the interim Massachusetts government prepared a force of nearly two thousand men for a seaborne assault against the French at Quebec. The expedition failed with heavy loss of life, including Belcher's elder son, Andrew. In 1691, however, the crown granted a new charter to Massachusetts with Phips as the new governor. The province celebrated its escape from Catholic tyranny and the appointment of a native son as governor. But it was also struggling to adjust to a new political world. Many, stunned by Andros's government, embraced the charter as a protective hedge for New England's Protestantism. Others, who had hoped for a restoration of the old charter, felt uneasy that the governor was no longer appointed by the legislature but by the king. A new agenda that turned on constitutional issues and that was argued with a new and whiggish vocabulary of rights and liberties was introduced into the public discussion. For a generation Massachusetts's leaders, both clerical and lay, would struggle to make the adjustment to this whiggish world.

Andrew Belcher was not one to be distracted by such niceties, especially when there were profits to be made. While Massachusetts prepared its expedition against Quebec, he outfitted the *Swan*, an English-built vessel of one hundred tons with nineteen cannons, and placed it under the command of his brother-in-law, Thomas Gilbert, with instructions to prey upon enemy shipping. Captain Gilbert scoured the North Atlantic and even the gulf of the St. Lawrence River and returned rich in prizes. In the meantime Belcher was securing contracts to supply English naval vessels that put into Boston Harbor. His wealth increased steadily, and his standing in the community grew apace. He had acquired the reputation as an expert on Indian affairs, and the government turned to him for his advice on frontier policy. The governor appointed him a captain of the militia. Soon after gaining admission to the Old South Church, he was made a deacon. And in 1698 the town's voters sent him to the House of Representatives.[18]

Sometime in 1691, Andrew Belcher summoned his son Jonathan from the country and soon after enrolled him in Boston's Latin School in preparation for admission to Harvard College. With the death of his brother, Jonathan had become his father's sole male heir and the object of his ambitions. As Andrew Belcher scrambled into the inner circles of government, he was reminded daily that there were limits to his success. While Massachusetts expected its rulers to be men of piety and virtue, it also esteemed those who were distinguished for their education and their descent from the colony's first leaders. On both counts Belcher remained a parvenu. Andrew Belcher understood that he fell short. His son understood too when he remembered: "My Father was as great a Genius as his Countrey could boast of but wanted an Education to improve and polish it."[19]

In the spring of 1695, Jonathan had mastered enough Latin and Greek to satisfy the college authorities and was entered on the freshman class list second behind Jeremiah Dummer. Class rankings were for the most part determined by a student's social station and only in outstanding cases by his academic abilities. There seemed little reason for the college to take note of Jonathan's intellectual achievements. According to the records, he broke a few windows. It was Jeremiah Dummer whose performance quickly caught the faculty's attention. Jonathan did well enough in his studies of the Bible, the classics, and logic. Later in life he remembered enough to quote from the classics, though with an occasional error in attribution, and he demonstrated a passing command of Latin composition. He read widely and eventually assembled an impressive library. But he never displayed keen intellectual curiosity or passion. He wrote letters constantly but principally on practical matters of business and politics. When his thoughts turned to other realms, such as religion, he demonstrated an ingrained penchant for the platitudinous and conventional. He never felt the urge to compose even a pamphlet on any subject, and when he was compelled as governor to address a legislature, he instinctively resorted to the mundane and commonplace.

Jonathan, like his fellow students, came to Cambridge to fulfill his father's ambitions.[20] He studied with the sons of ministers, like John Bulkley, who planned to follow their fathers' vocation. Others—such as Moses Hale, a carpenter's son, and Nathaniel Eells, the son of a shopkeeper—were preparing for the ministry, as was Jeremiah Dummer. Indeed, eight of Belcher's twelve classmates became shepherds of New England's congregations. But prospective clergymen were increasingly coming from the lower end of the class lists. There were other students whose fathers would not allow their sons, especially first sons, to pursue a vocation that paid so poorly. Some were descended from New England's venerable and ancient families such as the

Winthrops, Hutchinsons, Dudleys, Bradstreets, and Saltonstalls. Others, like Belcher, valued the college degree as a badge necessary to consolidate the family's position.

Jonathan was seventeen when he received the bachelor's degree (not an unusual age for the times) and returned home. Andrew Belcher was a commanding figure, at the height of his powers. His shipping fleet increased steadily each year. He seemed always in need of additional warehouses to store his goods and was laying plans to build his own wharf. Within a decade he had emerged as one of Boston's most prominent merchants. The home he had built on King Street was among the town's finest. He ordered expensive coaches from England to impress the community with his achievements. He had taken a new wife—Hannah Frary, the widow of a wealthy merchant and the sister-in-law of Samuel Lillie, perhaps the town's wealthiest merchant. When Jonathan came home, Andrew was laying the foundations for a dynasty. He had arranged the marriages of his daughter Sarah to Joseph Lynde of Charlestown, of Elizabeth to Daniel Oliver of Boston, and of Mary to George Vaughan of Portsmouth. Soon after, he agreed to Ann's marriage to Oliver Noyes of Boston and to Martha's to Anthony Stoddard also of Boston. All were merchants, two were Harvard men, and all became prominent in business and politics during Jonathan Belcher's life.

In May 1702 the General Court elected Andrew Belcher to the governor's Council. A week later Joseph Dudley returned to Boston with Queen Anne's commission to govern the province. Many, who could not forget the loss of the old charter and had not yet come to terms with the new imperial relationship, could hardly hide their horror at Dudley's return. Some, like Andrew Belcher, who had packed Dudley off to England in chains, were embarrassed by the reversal of fortunes and scrambled to accommodate themselves with the new administration. Everyone knew that Dudley was determined to settle old scores. The following May the governor rejected the election of five councilors who had participated in his earlier downfall. Andrew Belcher, however, kept his seat. While old adversaries were moving toward confrontation, Belcher maneuvered deftly to distance himself from his earlier rebel associates and to ingratiate himself with the new government. Moreover, Governor Dudley had announced the outbreak of war with France, and Belcher was calculating that there were great profits to be reaped. He had already begun to supply the English navy, and he knew that government contracts were sure to increase. Belcher convinced Dudley that his knowledge of finance and supply and his experience on defense and frontier policy made him indispensable for the war effort. Dudley nominated Belcher commissary general in charge of supplying provincial forces.[21]

Meanwhile Jonathan began to learn the intricacies of trade under his father's stern tutelage. He spent his days at Belcher Wharf keeping account of pork, fish, and barrel staves bound for the West Indies and of wine due from Portugal. His father's trade extended throughout the North Atlantic. To minimize losses, which were frequent and sometimes devastating, merchants preferred to buy a partial share in a ship and spread investments over several vessels. Thus, Andrew Belcher purchased shares in fourteen ships from 1700 through 1703 but registered sole ownership of only four vessels during the same period. Each ship was a separate investment with a different group of investors. He usually joined with men like Samuel Lillie, Jeremiah Dummer, Sr., and Benjamin Alford of Boston or Jonathan Dowse and Nathaniel Carey of Charlestown. His partners also included Edward Shippen of Philadelphia, Edward Cordivant of Barbados, John Lewis of Jamaica, and Richard Haynes, Nicholas Duval, and John Lloyd of London. The risks were always frightening. One day Samuel Lillie was Boston's most prosperous merchant; the next he was a pauper. With Lillie's fall, Andrew Belcher owned the largest share of Boston's merchant fleet. In 1699 he had registered shares in seven ships; in 1704 he added another thirteen.[22]

At first the business must have seemed to be a bewildering tangle of partnerships and ventures. Soon Jonathan understood that there were a few simple principles to be mastered. As his father explained, a merchant's livelihood depended on the cultivation of trusting associations and the establishment of a network of reliable correspondents. Each time Andrew invested in a ship, he joined with a different combination of partners. But he turned repeatedly to the same men in Boston and environs and throughout the Atlantic world. He had nurtured trusting correspondences that established vital connections to distant ports. He depended on them to buy and sell his goods, to extend credit when necessary, and to provide information on local market conditions. Loss of a correspondent could mean the severing of a vital link with a profitable market. As Andrew Belcher explained, Jonathan's apprenticeship would not be complete until he had cultivated these connections himself. Jonathan must visit London to win the trust of his father's friends and to initiate new associations. Moreover, Andrew Belcher realized that with the outbreak of war London would be dispensing more military contracts to American suppliers, and he needed to establish connections with the new government of Queen Anne. He decided to send Jonathan to London in the spring of 1704.

Andrew Belcher expected his son to achieve something in addition to commercial associations. Jonathan's stay in London would complete his education as a gentleman. In 1702 Jonathan had returned to Cambridge to receive his M.A. degree, which was perfunctorily granted to recipients of the bachelor's degree on the third commencement after graduation. In London he would achieve the polish, the bearing, and the manner of a gentlemen that he could not acquire secondhand in America. Provincial New Englanders

looked to London as the center of their cultural as well as political and economic world. Those who visited the cosmopolitan center earned immediate
recognition among their fellow provincials. Sitting at Governor Dudley's
Council table reminded Belcher of the advantages to be gained by cultivating an interest at court. The governor's son Paul had, after completing his
education at Harvard, also gone to England to study the law at London's
Inner Temple. That training had brought immediate prestige before Massachusetts's courts. Later his election to the Royal Society made him the envy
of New England's cultural elite. Benjamin Colman, another Harvard graduate, had made the trip and was serving his apprenticeship preaching from
London's pulpits when he received an invitation from Boston's newly formed
Brattle Street Church. He was only twenty-six when he returned. The benefits to be gained were not always tangible or specific but they were obvious.
Jeremiah Dummer, Jonathan's classmate, returned after studying at the
Universities of Leyden and Utrecht with a Ph.D. in hand and became an im-
mediate celebrity. Increase Mather proposed that a position be made for
Dummer on the Harvard faculty and in the meantime invited him to preach
from his pulpit at Boston's North Church.[23]

Andrew Belcher also knew the hazards of an ocean passage, the fright-
ful storms that might engulf a ship, and the likelihood of an encounter with a
hostile vessel. He worried as well over the welfare of Jonathan's soul. While
London shone as the center of trade, power, and civilization, it also loomed
in the provincial's imagination as a source of luxury, corruption, and deca-
dence. Thus New Englanders were ambivalent about Joseph Dudley. While
they had not forgotten that Dudley's father had come with the first planters
to Massachusetts-Bay and had been chosen its second governor, they also
wondered whether the present governor and his son had achieved so much
power and glory by selling their birthright. At the same time that they looked
to the center with awe, celebrated their allegiance to the crown and the
Protestant succession, and even sought to emulate the urbane style, they also
shrank in dread of London's seducing lures. Jeremiah Dummer's return
raised up those feelings. Jonathan's classmate had arrived the object of adu-
lation, but as Bostonians listened to his learned sermons, they began to suspect his orthodoxy. Soon Dummer realized that he could not remain in New
England, and he made plans to remove to London. Thus, Jonathan Belcher's
trip assumed dramatic meaning for a people who read John Bunyon's
Pilgrim's Progress. London became a Vanity Fair and his mission something
of a pilgrimage.

While composing letters introducing his son to friends and associates
in London, Andrew Belcher called upon the minister of Old South Church,
Ebenezer Pemberton, to share his fears. Pemberton listened with sympathy
and decided the subject was worthy of a sermon. He spoke to Jonathan di-

rectly, warning him to take heed that he was entering upon a "dangerous Stage." The "Tryals," "Temptations," and "Snares" he would encounter in the "Enemies Country" would make the godly tremble. The righteous parent shrank at the prospect of sending his son into the company of "Hells Factors." Well might a father pray that his son would "be safely piloted thro all these dangers, so as not to split on this Rock, or be founder'd in that Sea, nor yet Stranded on these Sands." Pemberton enjoined the young man not to "fall into any indifferency about Religion." Shun "modish" fashion that will make "you to be loath'd by God." "Get therefore your self armed, being now fore-warned to withstand all the assaults that may be made upon you."[24]

Impressed with the gravity of his mission, Jonathan bade his father farewell. On arriving in London and securing lodgings, he first sought out the company of fellow provincials at the New England Coffeehouse and with their aid began his exploration of the city. "Every day," he wrote home, "Affords you something New and diverting." After walking the streets, touring the city's historic sites and cathedrals, and browsing in the bookstalls, he confessed that "so many pleasing objects Continually present themselves to your View" that there was little time left to write home.[25]

The splendor of Queen Anne's London did not divert him from his task. With letters of introduction in hand, he dutifully sought out his father's trading associates. As he spent his days in the company of these men at their counting houses and his evenings dining with them, he was establishing confidences and trusts that would last a lifetime and secure his standing in the Anglo-American trading world. In July, Jonathan left London with letters of introduction to the merchant communities in Rotterdam and Amsterdam. While he took time to visit the principal sites of interest, he wrote to assure his father that he had spent most of his time in the company of merchants and bankers. The Dutch, he observed, were industrious, "Neat and Clean," a people justly proud of their prosperity, but perhaps a bit too obsessed with matters of shipping and rates of exchange. "If a Man," he observed, "Intends to live by trading and Merchandize, travelling gives him the best Opportunity to Settle a Correspondency in those parts of the world, Where he may Come."[26]

Belcher was also traveling to complete his education as a gentleman. Within a few weeks of his arrival in London, he concluded that he had already learned more of the world than could be acquired in a year of study. His horizons were expanding, and, at the same time, he became acutely self-conscious of his provincial origins. Social encounters caused painful embarrassment, prodded him to rid himself of his rude American ways, and made him a careful student of English manners and fashion. And so, following the example of other young English gentlemen, he decided to complete his education with a tour of Europe. He set his itinerary with an objective in mind, to visit the German Electorate of Hanover and to "pay his duty" to his future queen, the electress. Perhaps he followed the example of ambitious young Englishmen like Robert Walpole. If so, he could not have been as certain as his English counterparts how the trip would translate to his gain. But he could expect his reputation to improve markedly when he returned home and that somehow, in the future, when a Hanoverian sat on the English throne, the trip would translate into more tangible rewards.

In preparation for his trip, Belcher had purchased a bound volume to keep a record of his travels. His "Journal My intended Voyage, & Journey to Holland, Hanover etc." opened with the channel crossing, recounted his travels through Holland and Germany and back to London, and concluded with a short essay on "the Advantages & Disadvantages of Travelling." Belcher did not keep this journal for himself. He wrote with an audience at home in mind. His accounts of Europe's splendid palaces and lofty cathedrals, the historic sites, religious customs, and social life were intended to provide several evenings of pleasant entertainment and conversation among his family and friends in Boston. He also wrote as if to give practical advice to others, but in fact he composed the journal to convey an impression of himself. While advising the reader on matters of transportation and itineraries, currencies, lodging, and clothing, on social customs, and on places to see, he consciously posed as the urbane and self-assured gentleman.

During his stay in Holland, the young traveler visited the home of Erasmus, the palace of William of Orange, and the college grounds at Leyden, where his classmate Jeremiah Dummer had studied. He wondered at the splendor of the palaces and cathedrals and as often speculated on the great expense incurred in their building. Bedlams, orphanages, prisons, and poorhouses piqued his curiosity. After an afternoon inspecting Rotterdam's bedlam, where the inmates were confined in close dark cells with a "little hole made just fit to put their heads out," he left satisfied that they received adequate treatment. In Amsterdam he visited a prison for prostitutes. The women knew little English, but enough to speak "all manner of Lewdness and debauchery Perfectly. And they are not only Impudent in their discourse but in their Actions."[27]

Wherever he went, Belcher sought out local religious services. He found the synagogues beautiful, but the services "Most hoggish & indecent" and the Jews' incessant talk of money equally offensive. He spent a Sunday morning in Amsterdam at the Church of England and in the afternoon went to observe the local "Calvinists way of worship." The service was "much after Our Presbyterians in England"; the organ played "very delightfully"; but he was disappointed that the "form of prayer [was] not altogether Unlike that of the Church of England."[28]

It was mid-summer when he set out for Hanover. "The flies are very troublesome and bite One's legs Most intolerably." The German diet was too rich: the meat was "all Spoil'd in dressing & Saucing." The Germans, unlike the Dutch, were a slovenly people; and the traveler came to expect wretched accommodations. While the people lived in filth and desperate poverty, a handful of princes spent lavishly and ostentatiously on themselves.[29] In mid-August, Belcher arrived at Hanover and quickly gained an audience with the electress. He recorded the moment in his journal.

> [I] made a Very low Reverence to her, then going up to her kneel'd and kiss'd her hand. After this Ceremony was over, I told her; Thus, Madame, The Respect and good affection which the Queen of Great Britain's Subjects (in N England) have for the good Settlement of ye Succession made me Ambitious of doing my Self the honour to Come and pay my humble duty to your Royal Highness.

She received him "as if she had been my Mother" and spent much time questioning him about New England, its people, and its trade. Later he met the rest of the family. The young prince George seemed taciturn and withdrawn, but Belcher was assured that he would make a wise king.[30]

Belcher spent his days at court, dining with the royal family, attending concerts, and strolling in the gardens or playing cards with the electress. He became an assiduous student of court customs. On occasion his Puritan sensibilities were pricked. When accompanying the electress at chapel, he noted the display of a crucifix but refrained from comment. Sometimes he met with embarrassment. On observing that "the ladies here all Affect to have black hair & Eyebrows and for that End are forc'd to grease it," he explained that "the Indian Women in our Country do so too." The electress "lookt very grave" and then refused to own the comparison.[31] Court routine was interrupted when news arrived that the Duke of Marlborough had vanquished the combined French and Bavarian forces at Blenheim. The electress ordered a spectacular celebration ending with an awesome fireworks display. After ten days, Belcher prepared to take his leave. The electress presented him with her portrait and letters of introduction to the court of Berlin.

Bidding farewell to Hanover, Belcher proceeded to Berlin at a leisurely pace, stopping to see the local curiosities on the way. While touring a Benedictine "convent," he came upon a gallery of portraits of the Stuart kings. That Charles I was not among them seemed confirming evidence that he had not been a papist. Belcher was not surprised to learn that the monks lived self-indulgent lives. The maidservant was "free & familiar" with the monks. And they "were often Merry Among themselves & have dancing and other diversions." Each day disclosed fresh reminders of desperate squalor and lavish wealth—of princes who lived in awesome splendor and spent their days in idle self-indulgent pleasure and of the poor peasants who labored for a pittance and squandered their earnings on drink, dice, and cards.[32] On arriving in Berlin, Belcher presented himself to the court. While awed by the splendor of the palace, its well groomed gardens, and the numerous fountains, he could only think that he was at the court of the "Queen of Sheba." The queen received him well enough, but the king would not deign to speak to anyone below noble rank. Belcher found him vain, tyrannical, and a shameless Francophile and observed that his son was a rude and slovenly boor.[33]

On his return to London in early October, Belcher sat down to put the finishing touches to his journal. "A Man without traveling Is not altogether Unlike a Rough diamond, Which Is unpolisht and without beauty." He remains "ignorant of Many points of good breeding." Belcher wrote self-consciously, to convey an image of himself to his fellow New Englanders. One who has traveled, he had learned, acquires a "Civil, Courteous behaviour" and "Confidence & Assurance Enough to talk with those of the greatest quality." The experience "Changes his humour from Sower, pevish & fretful, to pleasant, affable & Most Agreeable, his frequent Conversing with the ladies Moulds him into a flexible & Compliant Temper, and his being often oblig'd to others, Makes him ready to oblige all In his Turn." Too often, he reflected, "We Are Apt to fancy One of Another Religion, that we are prejudic'd at, has something in him that makes him Monstrous or odious." Not so. He had encountered "people of very different Religions" and could discern "no difference in their living and Conversation." Indeed, he had to lay aside his "prejudices Against Countries & Religions" and to see that "Mankind Is much the Same" throughout the world.[34]

The gentleman, polished in manner and urbane in outlook, self-assured with courtiers and kings, adept at moving within the inner corridors of wealth and power—this self-portrait that emerged from the journal pleased him, and he would work for much of his life to make improvements on that image. He made etiquette and fashion a lifelong study so that he might convey in clothing, speech, and manner the impression of an English gentleman stripped of provincial rudeness. He savored those moments that allowed him to demonstrate his knowledge of English social conventions and his familiarity with aristocrats, prime ministers, and courtiers. Twice in the next decade he would return to London to cultivate his interest at court and to nurture his connections in trade. Each time he returned home with his reputation and standing improved. Later, when governor, he credited his success to this first trip. And so he later insisted that his sons follow his example.

Belcher delighted in sporting a waistcoat tailored according to London's latest style and in recounting the dignitaries he had met, the patrons whose favor he had won, and the friendships he enjoyed at court. But he remained a New England Puritan at heart. Although he acquired the vocabulary of the open-minded cosmopolitan who had shed narrow and parochial prejudices, his observations regarding Catholics and Jews, in fact, confirmed inherited opinions. When attending the churches of other Protestant denominations, he judged them by New England's standard. His travels made him self-conscious of his rude American origins but also impressed him with Europe's vices. The courts were "gardens of pleasure" that could seduce the unsuspecting. The English gentlemen whom he admired for their "Civil & obliging" manners were also fops and wastrels. "Dressing and diversion Is all their Care & Concern. And they live in Entire oblivion of Religion and will (I fear) insensibly fall into Atheism." He had seen Europe's arbitrary governments and the stark social contrasts between the rich and poor. The "Princes are all very absolute, And the people Not much better than Slaves." If he seemed to exempt Hanoverian society from critical comment, he did so out of patriotism and loyalty to the Protestant succession and not because he failed to observe the blemishes. Above all, he had come as a New Englander, and he left with his preconceptions confirmed. When he observed Europe's stark social contrasts, especially the miseries endured by the poor and the tyrannies inflicted upon them, he wrote as a New Englander convinced of his native land's special blessings. When he noted the vice, superstition, and Sabbath-breaking run rampant among all social ranks, he confirmed his impressions of the hardy and independent New England farmers who lived simple and virtuous lives and prospered in their covenant with God.[35]

While completing his travel journal, Belcher wrote home: "I take a great deal of Satisfaction, in the Revolution of my Thoughts." No doubt, traveling had broadened his horizons. He expected that his audience with the electress would turn heads in Boston. His manners would set him apart from his peers. But throughout the journal he assured his readers that his travels had not worked so thorough a "Revolution" in his worldview that he had forgotten his father's fears. Indeed, he wrote to answer the prayers of his father and of Ebenezer Pemberton. While recommending the advantages of travel, he was also quick to warn that it bred indolence and laxity in "the duties of Religion." Thus, he presented himself as the gentleman stripped of provincial roughness but still the New England Puritan. As if to assure his father, he made arrangements for a London printing of Pemberton's sermon. Like the pilgrim in that sermon, he prayed "To God almighty who preserv'd me from many hazar[ds] in my travels": "I desire for Ever to Render thanksgiving & praise; & May he grant That I may hereby be made the More Capable of Serving my Generation, When Ever opportunities offer, Then will my desires herein & the End of this My Enterprise be Enterly gain'd."[36]

Early in 1705, Belcher was back home. He presented his journal to his father for his approval. After a few days spent regaling family and friends with his adventures, he delivered the portrait of the electress to Governor Dudley, who ordered that it be hung in the Council chamber. Soon after, Jonathan received the governor's invitation to join with the Council on the Queen's birthday to "drink her Majesties & Royal Highness health." Jonathan seemed ready to assume his maturity, and his father thought it time for him to marry.[37] Andrew Belcher had found a suitable prospect in Mary Partridge. Her father Richard was New Hampshire's former lieutenant governor and had on occasion sold Belcher a shipment of timber. The fathers agreed that it was a good union, and, in early January 1706, Andrew and Jonathan Belcher rode north to Portsmouth for the marriage. Determined to make Boston take notice, Andrew left instructions that a salute be fired from Belcher Wharf on the hour of the wedding. A week later the wedding party returned to Boston escorted by a procession of "20 Horsemen, Three Coaches and many Slays." That evening Jonathan and Mary sat down to a lavish dinner with the lieutenant governor in attendance.[38]

The next month Jonathan and his wife were admitted to membership in Old South Church, and the following November the church recorded the birth of a son, Andrew. In the spring of 1707, Jonathan was elected constable by the Boston town meeting, but he declined the office and paid the fine instead. Perhaps his father thought the office beneath the family's station. Certainly, Andrew continued to direct his son's entry into society. In July 1705, Andrew registered ownership in the *Austrian Eagle* with his son and John Lloyd. It was the first such record and, no doubt, reflected approval of his son's achievements.[39] But Andrew was sparing in his recognition. His son did not appear with him on every registry of ownership.

Though impressed by his own achievements, Jonathan was expected to remain in his father's shadow. While Andrew spent much of his time with the governor, Jonathan attended to cargoes of fish, tobacco, rum, and pork. As Andrew became enfeebled by the ravages of gout, he grew increasingly dependent on his son's energies and talents. He admitted his dependence, but like many a New England patriarch was loath to surrender his control over the family's business. Gradually, grudgingly, he allowed his son's name to be entered on more shipping registries. But the core of the business—warehouses and ships—remained in his hands. While Andrew acted according to society's conventions, so too Jonathan behaved according to the model of a dutiful son. Youthful expectations were postponed. He served compliantly and gave no sign of impatience, resentment, or rebellion. While Andrew spent his evenings in the company of Boston's leading lights—the governor, fellow councilors and representatives, and clergymen—Jonathan remained at home.[40]

During these years father and son were preoccupied by the war with France.[41] When Jonathan had left for London, the Massachusetts government had been working feverishly to repair fortifications that had been allowed to decay, to negotiate treaties with the Indians, and to raise and supply scouting parties and troops. The French and their Indian allies attacked the frontier settlements in Maine at will. In the west, they laid waste to Deerfield and struck at Northampton. The settlers at Marlborough, only twenty miles from Boston, skirmished with the enemy and frequently turned out in alarm. Enemy vessels were sighted regularly off the coast, and Boston's merchants suffered heavy losses. No matter how dismal the situation, however, Governor Dudley was determined to launch an offensive. In 1706, he could claim a modicum of success in checking the enemy's movements on the frontier and persuaded the legislature to undertake an assault on Port Royal in French Acadia. The action failed miserably, but the governor was already discussing an even more ambitious scheme. Samuel Vetch, a merchant recently arrived from Scotland, had visited Quebec under a flag of truce and had surveyed its fortifications. He convinced the governor that the city could be reduced by a joint Anglo-American expedition. In late 1706 he set out for London with Dudley's blessing to persuade the imperial authorities of his plans.

At the outbreak of hostilities, Andrew Belcher had once again outfitted a privateer under his brother-in-law's command to prey on enemy shipping.[42] He had soon demonstrated that his services were indispensable to the war effort. Each year the government raised one thousand and sometimes more troops. Annual military budgets soared to £30,000. Few could rival Belcher's abilities in supplying the military. He had become a major carrier of fish from the north and of pork and grains from the Connecticut River Valley. He had established a relationship with Boston's millers and bakers that gave him a commanding influence over the supply of bread. Recognizing his importance, the governor and his opponents joined to elect Andrew Belcher the province's commissary general. Each year Belcher supplied one thousand troops and sometimes more. Moreover, English warships that were regularly putting into Boston Harbor turned to him for provisions. His appetite was whetted as he conferred with Dudley and Vetch on the "grand enterprise" against Quebec and on the problems of supply. The governor estimated that the campaign would cost £50,000. Andrew decided that his son must return to England.

In March 1708 Jonathan, accompanied by his "Indian boy, Io," booked passage with a convoy bound for England.[43] After sixty-three days at sea and several encounters with the enemy, his ship weighed anchor at Kinsale, Ireland. The "long and tedious" voyage had strained his patience. "My affairs pressing me to be in England, I thought it would be but time lost to await

the motion of our Fleet, so [I] went next morning aboard Frankland packet."
After narrowly escaping capture, his ship arrived on the Welsh coast the next
morning. There he "took post horses and rid 150 miles without sleeping" to
Gloucester, where he found a coach on the way to London. Acquaintances
were to be renewed, accounts to be settled, and shipments to be dispatched
to Boston at once. Most important, there were government contracts waiting
to be won. Belcher submitted a bid to the Admiralty and soon after obtained
a lucrative contract. He was establishing influential connections. The Massachusetts legislature thought so and wrote requesting that he represent the
province's interests during his stay. Though flattered, Jonathan declined the
invitation explaining that he was so preoccupied with his own "Affairs" that
he could not take time to serve his "Countrey" even if he were offered "the
gratuity of 500£."[44]

Once his affairs were settled, however, Belcher crossed the English
Channel and set out to "pay . . . my duty to the Court of Hanover." On the
day of his arrival, Belcher gained an audience with the electress. "Her Royal
Higheness," he wrote home, remembered him by name, "which was indeed
wonderful for a lady of 78 years of age." He spent the evening walking with
her in the palace gardens, and the next day he received an invitation to dine
with the royal family. That evening Belcher arrived with Io, dressed in his
"native habit," and gave him to the electress. His gift "wonderfully pleased"
the royal family. Everyone "took a great liking to the boy," especially the
electress, who gave instructions that he be kept dressed in his native attire,
be taught to "speak and write high Dutch and French," and that he be
trained as her personal servant. No doubt, Belcher reflected, "his fortune is
made for this world." The gift had also improved his standing at court.
During the next week he spent the evenings dining with the royal family. On
the eve of his departure, the electress summoned him to her private cham-
bers. "She talked to me with all imaginal freedom" for nearly an hour and
before parting presented him with "a pretty pocket piece with her face on
one side." She was "sorry she had nothing better to give me," but she "told
me in these words, 'perhaps it may some time be in my power or some of
mine to do you some service.'"

In the meantime, Samuel Vetch had persuaded Queen Anne's government to support his proposal for the conquest of Canada. When Belcher returned to London in November, he recognized at once that Vetch's proposal
was truly a "Glorious Enterprise." Anglo-American forces would launch a
two-pronged invasion—one by land from New York and the other by sea
from Boston. The several colonial governments from Pennsylvania to New
Hampshire would raise twenty-five hundred troops, and England would contribute four thousand regulars and six men-of-war. The supply contracts
would be immense, and Belcher worked feverishly to place himself in an

advantageous position. He seemed to be in a "constant hurry" in his efforts to secure bids to provision the English contingent and to insinuate himself into Vetch's inner circle of confidants. In March he joined Vetch aboard HMS *Dragon* and after nearly seven weeks at sea arrived in Boston.[45]

Soon after, Jonathan and Andrew Belcher registered the *George*, a captured Frenchman, and invited Samuel Vetch to take a share in the vessel. Father and son had positioned themselves well. Years later, Jonathan recalled that Governor Dudley "used to say Mr. Commissary Belcher would make a good Minister of State to any Prince in Europe Especially in the Article of Finances." Andrew could not imagine a limit to his ambitions. Not only was he commissary general for Massachusetts and a major supplier to the English navy, he also reached for the contracts to provision both the Boston and the New York expedition. That summer Andrew and Jonathan Belcher scoured the New England countryside in search of pork, grain, and other necessities.[46] By October Massachusetts had spent nearly £30,000 when news arrived that London had decided to postpone the "Glorious Enterprise" and to try a more limited venture against Port Royal.

Though dispirited for the moment, Governor Dudley and Samuel Vetch soon plunged into making preparations for the campaign. In the summer of 1710, a joint force of four hundred British marines, nine hundred troops from Massachusetts, and another five hundred from Connecticut and Rhode Island assembled at Boston. Massachusetts had strained itself. Ammunition supply had required the government to strip Boston's own fortifications bare. Providing food and clothing had sorely taxed the Belchers' abilities and even more so the provincial economy. More than six thousand bushels of wheat lay in their storehouses, and the city of Boston faced a critical shortage of bread. As the price of bread rose, voices of discontent were heard in the streets against the house of Belcher. The expedition set sail in mid-September. Six weeks later Boston celebrated an easy victory. With Port Royal in English hands, Dudley and Vetch pressed for the complete reduction of Canada. The following June, Colonel Francis Nicholson, Vetch's military adviser and confidant, arrived from London with orders to raise a force against Quebec.[47]

Nicholson was to lead the expedition from New York; and Samuel Vetch, General John Hill, and Admiral Hovenden Walker were to command the force from Boston. The plans called for more troops and ships than what Vetch had originally intended. England would contribute five thousand troops and a fleet of sixty vessels; the colonial governments from New Hampshire south to Pennsylvania would raise a combined force of twenty-two hundred. The prospects for profit were immense. Although the Port Royal campaign had sorely strained their resources, the Belchers readied themselves to provision the English military in both New York and Boston as well as to meet their obligations to Massachusetts's own. While preparing to supply the Massachusetts contingent, they also gained a contract to provide Nicholson with 50 butts of wine, 10,000 gallons of rum, 150,000 bushels of rice, and over 70,000 pounds of fish. When Admiral Walker sailed into Boston Harbor, he expected to be provisioned by the house of Belcher. But father and son had overextended themselves. They wrote agents and correspondents urgently pressing for supplies and for payment of debts outstanding. They had borrowed heavily—£1400—from the Massachusetts government. Commissary Belcher informed Admiral Walker that he could not supply the fleet and bluntly explained that the provisions he had at his command would fetch higher prices in New York than in Boston. Walker turned to another merchant, Andrew Faneuil, but was enraged to learn that the Belchers not only dominated the town's grain supply but in collusion with the towns bakers controlled bread production. The admiral had no recourse but to appeal to Governor Dudley, and orders were issued requiring Andrew Belcher to supply the fleet. Finally, the expedition set sail on July 30.[48]

Six weeks later, Boston was stunned to learn that Walker's fleet had foundered at the mouth of the St. Lawrence with losses of nearly one thousand. Governor Dudley set aside a day of fasting so that the people might reflect on the "Rebukes of Heaven" and search out their "provoking Sins." Already burdened by the costs of war, now dispirited by the defeat, Massachusetts prayed for an end of this "long Calamitous" conflict. The war ended a year later.[49]

Peace required the province to attend to the consequences of war. The conflict had brought prosperity for many. Boston's shipyards had doubled production; shipwrights, caulkers, and blacksmiths had enjoyed full employment; bakers and distillers had benefited from military contracts; and the port's seamen had no trouble finding berths on merchantmen and privateers. But many had suffered. Prices had risen, especially for food. The disparities between rich and poor were growing more visible. Boston's widows increased at an alarming pace; Cotton Mather estimated that they made up one fifth of his church's membership. Then, with peace came a precipitous decline in trade, a depression in shipbuilding, unrelenting inflation, and the prospect of increased taxes. The public debt seemed staggering. After first doubling taxes to finance the war, the government had issued over a quarter million pounds in paper currency, and the public was in no mood to redeem these notes with added taxes.

Bostonians listened to Cotton Mather as he thundered against a "detestable Hobbsianism" that infected the community. Early in the war, he pointed to the merchants who swarmed like "Sharks," preying upon their neighbors and devouring the poor.[50] He spoke to a communal ideal rooted deeply in the public imagination. The vocabulary of "Christian Charity" that

John Winthrop had employed aboard the *Arbella*, the image that he invoked of a society in which the rich and powerful and the poor and helpless lived in community bound by a spirit of love and equity—these ideals continued to resonate clearly, powerfully in Mather's Boston. His audience understood when he bore witness against commerce's corrosive influence, the instincts that were born of the marketplace, and the lustful selfishness that rent organic harmony. The spirit of avarice, Mather noted, set the tone of the Dudley government. The predators who lurked in the marketplace had intruded themselves into public office and were now grasping for power even at the Council table of the governor.

Mather painted a dismal picture of a grand conspiracy concocted by Governor Dudley and joined by men of little "Courage or Conduct," bereft of social conscience, and obsessed with the engrossment of offices and profit. Elections were rigged and offices were dispensed for profit. Money ruled. This court conspired to establish a tyranny and "Ruine" the country. What more proof of the governor's intentions was needed, Mather asked, than his infamous collaboration with the Andros government? And now the governor had appointed his son, whose contempt for the charter was notorious, as the province's attorney general.[51] Mather spoke for many who suspected that Samuel Vetch had gone to Quebec under a flag of truce for the purpose of trading with the enemy. Suspicions grew that Dudley and many of his favorites including the commissary general were accomplices in the illegal trade, and the General Court began its own investigation.

Vetch was found guilty. Andrew Belcher escaped indictment but remained the object of resentment. Provincial troops accused him of supplying them with rotten food. The people of Boston came to resent this engrosser of their grain supply, especially as their dependence on him grew more acute during the war. Grain prices doubled and the town sought to control exports. The governor was sympathetic with the town's predicament. Councilor Samuel Sewall, though a merchant himself, was disturbed by what seemed to be the commissary general's unbridled lust for profit. Neither government nor public opinion seemed to affect Belcher.[52] In early 1710, the town learned that the Belchers were loading a cargo of bread and more than five thousand bushels of grain for export. In the dead of night, a band of outraged and desperate townspeople slipped aboard the ship, cut the rudder, and attempted to run the ship aground. Belcher, however, was able to rouse enough townsmen to salvage the cargo. He pressed for prosecution, and Judge Sewall assembled a grand jury to hear the evidence. Although Sewall, like many in the government, could not countenance an assault on private property, he also believed that Belcher had given the rioters just cause. The grand jury listened to the charges and then returned a finding of *ignoramus*.[53]

Andrew Belcher met hard disapproving stares when he sat down at the Council table. His son Jonathan was once beaten on the streets of Boston. On occasion a window was broken. In the spring of 1713, the townspeople turned out again. The Belchers were loading a shipment of grain bound for Curacao. The selectmen visited Andrew in hopes of dissuading him from this venture. When they argued that the shipment would deprive the town of bread, he curtly responded that he was simply acting according to his calling. Simply put, he could fetch a higher price for grain in Curacao than he could in Boston. The delegation pled that his action would drive the price of bread beyond the reach of many of his less fortunate neighbors. Andrew had had enough. He ordered the selectmen to "Fend off!" Before they left, he warned them that he would not tolerate the repetition of the earlier assault on his ship. If the mob were to move against this cargo, he promised that he would prevent the importation of three times that amount to the city. Later that night a crowd of two hundred descended on Belcher's warehouses, ransacked their contents, and smashed several windows before disappearing into the darkness.[54]

According to Ebenezer Pemberton, the Belchers were the victims of immorality and levelism run rampant. When the minister awoke to the report of the attempt against Belcher's ship, he was composing the election sermon that he had been invited to deliver to the General Court. In his mind he was already enumerating the signs of disorder, and he was determined that his sermon would move the lawmakers to defend the moral order. This assault upon a prominent member of his congregation roused his sympathy and indignation. A few days later, when the minister encountered Samuel Sewall on the street, he sought to impress the judge with the gravity of the crime. Sewall agreed that the violent attack on property could not be countenanced but added that the people had suffered provocations. "He that withholds Corn, the people will curse him." The rioters were God's people too; they deserved pity and understanding. Pemberton could not contain himself. Bread was not scarce. Those who pretended to be in need squandered their money on rum. The rioters were not God's chosen; they were the devil's own.[55]

Three weeks later, Pemberton carried his message to the General Court. "Levelism" had raised its head; this distemper flourished in "open Defiance to GOD, his Wisdom and Will, as well as the Reason of Mankind." Property was "exposed to fatal Invasions." As he revealed a deep moral crisis, he invoked traditional images of the good society. When he raised up the ideal of a social hierarchy with a few given "Superiority, and Power" and the rest placed in "Inferiority and Submission," he presented himself a caretaker of John Winthrop's legacy. His first concern was the widespread disrespect for the authority of government. The people had forgotten that their rulers were like "Gods, whose dwelling is in flesh." The habits of obedience and deference were being forgotten. Everywhere he heard the "Murmurings, Discontents, Evil Surmisings and Jealousies" growing in volume. While he owned that submissiveness might turn to slavery, he thought that in balance the greater danger came from anarchic forces. Rulers erred, but they were "GOD's Vice-gerants." He spoke with the unmistakable accents of a spokesman for the administration. When he proposed that "all favourable Allowances" be made for "the Infirmities and Defects" of rulers, everyone knew that he addressed the lawmakers. It was no surprise when he later praised the governor as a "Favour of Heaven."[56]

Dudley's enemies countered that it was the governor and his allies who threatened to undermine the Puritan legacy.[57] Cotton Mather would not allow the people to forgive Dudley for his complicity with Sir Edmund Andros. Nor would Elisha Cooke, Sr. This Boston merchant had been in the forefront of the revolution that had sent Dudley to England in chains. He had served in the Council for eight years before Dudley returned as governor. The next May, after the governor rejected his reelection, Cooke quickly established himself as the center of the opposition in the House of Representatives. He began to train his son Elisha, Jr., to follow in his footsteps.

As long as the war lasted, the opposition had proved itself nettlesome but disunited and, therefore, ineffective. On the one hand, Cooke spoke for many who resented the Mathers for abandoning the old charter and accepting the new imperial presence. He spoke effectively to lawmakers from the backcountry who distrusted the urban and cosmopolitan. On the other hand, he gained support from merchants and entrepreneurs in Boston who were becoming increasingly jealous as they watched the friends of the governor tighten their hold on the government. These disaffected merchants included John Colman, brother of the minister Benjamin and sometime business associate of the Belchers; Oliver Noyes, merchant, land speculator, and brother-in-law of Jonathan Belcher; Nathaniel Byfield, a long-time adviser to the governor who had fallen out with Dudley most likely for personal reasons; and William Tailer, Byfield's son-in-law.

While Massachusetts was at war, however, the Dudley administration seemed impervious to its critics. Eventually even Mather attempted to reach an accord with Dudley. But peace brought depression that inspired a new agenda. In early 1714 Colman, Tailer, Noyes, Byfield, and Elisha Cooke, Jr., joined to create a private bank that would issue notes to subscribers as loans that were secured by land mortgages. The Dudley administration sprang to the alarm and sought to check the project by proposing that the government erect a bank that would issue paper money at loan. Debate erupted with each side charging the other with factious intent to undermine the traditional moral order. When the private bankers argued that their measure would meet the growing need for currency and thereby reinvigorate a sagging economy, the Dudleians countered that the depression was largely a moral issue. The common people "especially the ordinary sort" had been seduced by profit hungry merchants to squander their livelihoods on useless luxuries. Each side accused the other of constructing a tyrannous conspiracy. The private bankers warned that a government bank would put an intolerable power into the hands of government officials. The public bankers retorted that the private signified the triumph of the vices of the marketplace over the virtues of community or the victory of faction over the public welfare. It would, warned Paul Dudley, become an "absolute Independent Government, which like a Fire in the Bowels, will burn up and Consume the whole Body."[58]

The private bankers, realizing that they could not survive the government's assault, were preparing to petition the queen for a charter when news arrived in mid-September that she had died. Governor Dudley's commission would expire in six months. A desperate scramble for power followed with Nathaniel Byfield sailing to London to secure the commission for himself, Jeremiah Dummer successfully outmaneuvering his opponent but failing to recommission Dudley, and the king lighting on an unknown Colonel Elizeus Burgess to govern Massachusetts-Bay. Disturbing reports followed: the new governor was a notorious dueler who preferred the profane and violent companionship of his army comrades. The Dudleians were doubly dumfounded when they learned that Byfield had wormed his way into Burgess's confidence and had won him to the land-bank cause and that William Tailer had been made the new lieutenant governor. While Burgess dallied in England, Tailer immediately demanded to assume the executive. And though Governor Dudley desperately employed bluff, intimidation, and clever legalist arguments to forestall the transfer of power, Tailer could not be denied. On taking office in November 1715, the new lieutenant governor immediately began to sweep the "disaffected" from government and to replace them with his allies.[59]

Jonathan Belcher had already departed for London. With the Hanoverian succession, the young man suddenly rose in reputation. His father had decided that he must employ his connections with the court. Andrew felt an urgency to keep the Dudley family in power. In part, he was inspired by self-interest, which was intensified by bitter factional rivalries. But he was able to turn his private motives into concern for the public welfare. Burgess's character had horrified many. Cotton Mather, Ebenezer Pemberton, and even John Colman joined to support the old governor. Provincial morality, good government, the charter itself seemed to hang in the balance. Andrew echoed these concerns when he instructed his son. He sent Jonathan out of "tender Concern for the good of this people." "You [must] improve all the Interest you can possibly make." "Spare no Money." Do whatever is necessary to "secure our Charter Privileges." "And if Providence should Honor you to be an Instrument to lengthen out the Tranquillity of this people, you will upon a Just reflection never repent it. And what ever the event may be, I shall lay down my head in the Grave, in greater peace under this sense, that I and mine have laboured to our utmost in this critical juncture to secure the Prosperity of our Country."[60]

Once united with Dummer, Belcher realized that the new governor was every bit as venal as he had expected. When Burgess awakened to the dismal prospect that his commissions carried meager cash rewards, he was eager to resign, providing he received suitable compensation. His price was £1000. Dummer and Belcher accepted. Dummer raised half largely from the sale of South Sea Company Stock, and Belcher drew on the family's credit in London for the rest. Their more pressing problem, however, was to find a suitable successor. Soon their searches discovered a likely candidate in Samuel Shute. Though a military man like Burgess, Shute came from a family of notable English dissenters. His grandfather, an English Presbyterian minister, was remembered in New England for his commentary on the Book of Job. His brother Lord Barrington was a prominent leader of the dissenting interest in Parliament. In sum, Shute represented the model of piety and character that Massachusetts expected of its rulers.

The two Americans—aided by Shute's brother, friends in the city's commercial community, and even Burgess's patron Lord Stanhope—moved their candidate's name through the government offices. In late April 1716, they celebrated their achievement. The people of Massachusetts, they wrote home, cannot imagine "the unspeakable happyness they will Have by this Change" in governors. Belcher wrote to Benjamin Colman recounting his struggles against Massachusetts's "Many Enemies" who are "Continually Watching to Rob us of our Charter." He and Dummer had "spared No pains or Application . . . to Serve the Countrey." Though they had endured a "great deal of difficulty," they had prevailed. "We knew of No person, In whom the Countrey Could be so Very Easy & happy." Massachusetts could rest secure in its liberties and property; it could count itself the "happyest people in the World."[61]

There were also scores to settle and preparations to be made for the new government. Lieutenant Governor Tailer was dismissed, and Jeremiah Dummer's brother William was appointed in his stead. Belcher and Dummer spent the summer months in London preparing the governor for his administration. They explained the issues, with special attention to the intricacies of the provincial currency crisis and the evils of the land bank. They enumerated the friends and enemies he would encounter and made arrangements

for Shute to take up temporary quarters at the home of Paul Dudley. With
their triumph complete they bade farewell to one another. Dummer confi-
dently waited in England to be reinstated as provincial agent. And Belcher
returned home expecting to assume a new and elevated rank as Governor
Shute's principal adviser.

By celebrating Massachusetts's deliverance, Belcher was promoting himself
as its deliverer. He was playing a role that was deeply embedded in New
England's political culture. By preserving God's people from iniquity and tyranny and by keeping the protective walls of charter and covenant intact, he
was playing the Nehemiah. The clergy regularly turned to the Old Testament leader as a model. Cotton Mather had raised up the Bay's first governor as an American Nehemiah. Mather's father Increase had in his own
way played that Nehemiah when he went to England to intercede with the
king in behalf of the people. The charter he secured was now becoming the
second hedge that preserved the people's welfare. So too Jonathan Belcher
returned not just as a successful politician but as his generation's Nehemiah.
    The Nehemiah preserved, conserved, the legacies from the past. He
played his part before a filiopietistic audience. Yet the role was undergoing
changes in interpretation. The actors were performing with accents that fit
the changing times. They played in a whiggish world. Belcher and his contemporaries were becoming more comfortable with the cosmopolitan center
than were their predecessors. Though they revered their forefathers, they
preferred to forget the intolerance and bloody persecutions of the last century. The Salem witch trials and the execution of Quakers had become an
embarrassment. Their generation, unlike its ancestors, was coming to accept
the presence of imperial authority and was employing the whiggish vocabulary of rights and privileges. They lived in the marketplace comfortably and
were beginning to accept its rules. Thus, while they continued to think of
themselves as inheritors and protectors of the past, they were also refashioning that inheritance. They still spoke of social justice and equity, but less of
the wickedness that lurked in the marketplace and of the injustices inflicted
by the rich upon the poor.
    The role was difficult to play. It was best played with conservative and
traditional accents. Yet it was performed before audiences that were reinterpreting New England's traditions. While it required the proper emphasis on
Puritan and provincial themes, it also came to embrace cosmopolitan and
whiggish styles. But the Nehemiah that was played before an audience of
Boston merchants seemed flat and often roused suspicions when performed
before a backcountry audience. Jeremiah Dummer served as reminder of
how difficult it was to play the Nehemiah in a whiggish world. Belcher, on the

other hand, would not become the expatriate. He could not let go the New England heritage. The role he played became a well-crafted model of the conventional, designed to please his audience at home. If it was fraught with platitudes and conventions, it was an interpretation that was rendered with an eye toward approval. At heart it was a performance intended to reflect or become an interpretation of his world.

2

The Perils of Public Life

Jonathan Belcher returned home to find his father in declining health. Nearly seventy, afflicted with gout and the general infirmities of age, Andrew Belcher found it increasingly difficult to take his seat at the Council table. A generation was passing from the scene. The former governor, Joseph Dudley, also nearly seventy, lived in quiet retirement in the country. His long-time adversary Elisha Cooke, Sr., had died in 1715. Of the twenty-eight members of the governor's Council who were elected in 1716, eight had begun service before the turn of the century. Three—Samuel Sewall, Wait Winthrop, and Elisha Hutchinson—had been sitting since 1693, when the new charter had been introduced. Six councilors were over seventy and another five were over sixty-five.

In October 1717, Andrew Belcher took to his bed, dictated his will, and summoned his son. Years later Jonathan vividly recalled that moment as his father took his hand to give his blessing: "May the Blessing of the God of Abraham and the God of Isaac and the God of Jacob rest upon you and your seed for Ever. Amen. Farewell." Andrew lay quietly for a moment. Then he wrapped himself in his winding sheet and shortly after expired in peace. "Neither the Patriarchs nor Apostles could have done it better," Jonathan remembered. The funeral was a grand event. A splendid tomb had been erected under Councilor Belcher's supervision. The new lieutenant governor, William Dummer, with four of the most senior councilors—Samuel Sewall, Elisha and Eliakim Hutchinson, and Addington Davenport—served as pall bearers. The customary mourning gloves, rings, and scarves were presented, and a lavish dinner was prepared for the funeral party.[1]

Jonathan Belcher's account of his father's death is in itself not remarkable. It is significant, however, in broader contexts. During the weeks immediately following his father's funeral, Jonathan was overcome with conflicting emotions of loss and rage. One of his first acts was to challenge his father's last will and testament. The issue at contest was small, indeed trivial. Although he had been named the principal heir, Jonathan was outraged to read that a small amount had been set aside for the maintenance of his stepmother. Jonathan insisted that she make concessions, and Judge Sewall was

called in to mediate. A settlement was reached, but Belcher could not let go
the issue. Within a week he bullied the widow into making more concessions.
She relinquished an annual payment of £30; although she was allowed to
keep her present residence, Jonathan would have use of the cellar. What was
at stake seemed insignificant for a family of Belcher's wealth. Sewall thought
Jonathan mean-spirited. The widow believed Jonathan resented her. Perhaps
she was right. When she confronted him, he protested that he had no ill
feelings toward her or toward his father.[2]

Perhaps Belcher volunteered too much. The ugly scene is also revealing in light of Belcher's later silence regarding his father. In his voluminous
correspondence with friends and family, he often discussed family affairs but
rarely mentioned his father, even when the subject seemed germane. When
he did refer to Andrew, he did so in a parenthetical fashion. He recounted
the death-bed scene in response to Thomas Prince's interrogation, but even
in that letter was studiously reticent. Except for that letter, the only other
concrete recollection of his father was a moment in his early childhood when
Andrew came to visit him in the country and directed his relatives not to
flinch from disciplining him. The overall habit of silence suggests that he
tucked his memories deep in the recesses of his thoughts rather than confront Andrew Belcher's commanding presence.

Andrew Belcher was indeed a distant and dominating figure, but there
is nothing to suggest that he exercised his authority more sternly than other
New England patriarchs. Fathers were enjoined by the clergy to break their
children's willfulness and to mold them into cooperative and compliant
adults. If fathers were derelict in their duty, warned Cotton Mather, they
would raise a generation that would later tear apart the social order, dis-
obey government, and foment faction. Andrew Belcher exercised his authority without flinching. Slowly and grudgingly did he let loose his reins of
authority and grant to his son a measure of independence. In turn, Jonathan
learned from his father how to dominate his own sons.

Jonathan's outburst against his dead father was striking in light of his
previous behavior. He had been a compliant son until that moment. His
marriage was arranged for him. For the next ten years, even while he was beginning to raise his own family, he remained in his father's shadow. Although
he proved an able apprentice at Belcher Wharf and a worthy heir to his
father's fortune, he received little recognition for his achievement. As Queen
Anne's War drew to a close, Jonathan's name appeared more frequently, but
not always, alongside his father's on the shipping registries. While Andrew
still invested on his own, Jonathan did so rarely. Even though declining health
required Andrew to rely on his son, he remained loath to relinquish control
of the family business. While Jonathan had found the means to invest on his
own in several Connecticut mines, Andrew kept critical Boston properties in

his own hands. Although Jonathan had ventured several Atlantic crossings at his father's bidding and each time had met or exceeded his father's expectations, he remained in the shadows. He rarely appeared in his father's social circles with the governor, councilors, representatives, and clergymen.[3]

Historians have seen this relationship in other contexts. Like many a New England son who felt the heavy weight of patriarchal authority, Belcher entered the adult world with a deep-felt sense of vulnerability. Society was filled with perils. He exaggerated the threats that were real and sometimes conjured up others that were not. In his imagination he heard voices mocking him and spied conspirators plotting against him. Moreover, his sense of vulnerability weakened his ability to confront these threats directly. For Belcher and for many like him, the prescriptions against factious discord, selfishness, and insubordination that were heard from the pulpit touched the heart as well as the mind. Community harmony and deference to authority— these were ideals that sank deeply into Belcher's world. When disagreements arose with others, Belcher lacked the emotional reserves to express them. Thus, he often raged, but in private. He seemed forever devising schemes of retribution, but he also hesitated to act on these impulses in public. When he did, however, he often acted impulsively and volcanically.

At the moment of his father's death, Belcher felt adrift. Feelings of loss and anger welled up in him. During one church meeting, he stood up before the congregation to recount a recent religious experience. With tears flowing, he recalled that moment when suddenly he had felt God's presence come upon him with a force and an immediacy that he had never known before. It was not in character for him to display such emotion.[4] Later his evangelical friends reproached him for his emotional coldness, but at this moment he could not keep his feelings in check. At the same time he was bullying his stepmother. Above all he could not restrain his impatience to step out of the shadows and take his place at center stage.

On the day he bullied his stepmother into additional concessions, he called upon Samuel Sewall. Wait Winthrop, the chief justice of the Superior Court had died, and Sewall, who had sat on the court for more than a quarter century and was its senior member, seemed the most likely choice for the position. Sewall assumed so.[5] But Belcher thought otherwise, and he had come to press the aging judge to step aside in favor of Paul Dudley. Massachusetts "had yet done little" for Dudley, he argued. He offered Sewall a second appointment on the Suffolk County court, which was nearly as profitable. Belcher was eager to demonstrate his influence, and he spoke as if he had the governor's ear. Sewall was dubious. When Belcher continued to press him, Sewall replied that he would need time to consider the matter. Belcher realized that he might have presumed too much. Lest he lose face, he proposed that the governor, the judge, and he meet to confer on the matter.

Belcher had presumed too much. He had acted rashly in part from eagerness to appoint Paul Dudley. The Belchers had looked to the Dudleys as their superiors. They had depended upon the former governor's favors. By playing a hand in elevating Dudley's son, Jonathan expected to turn the relationship around. Yet Governor Shute apparently ignored Jonathan Belcher's plea. Instead, he promoted Sewall as chief justice. Nonetheless, when the governor did appoint Dudley to the court later that year, Belcher considered it his personal achievement. Perhaps, he played a part in the governor's decision. Belcher always liked to think so. More important, he expected acknowledgment from Dudley.

Belcher was also determined to take his father's seat at the Council table. It was not uncommon for the sons of councilors to succeed their fathers. New Englanders congratulated themselves when they noted such dynastic continuities linking past with present. But filiopietistic sentiments were not enough for Belcher. On learning that Benjamin Colman had been chosen to deliver the sermon customarily given on the eve of the councilor elections, Belcher went to the minister and persuaded him to promote his candidacy.

Colman chose to speak to the idea of the Nehemiah. Massachusetts, he said, needed rulers, councilors, who, like the Old Testament leader, would build and maintain the wall that protected the covenanted people. On this day of election, the lawmakers must seek out the man who had the "weal of his People at heart," who loved true religion and the college, and who protected the just and scourged the evil-doer. Such a latter-day Nehemiah must be ever vigilant in preserving both the charter and the covenant, which served as hedges shielding the people from danger. Colman's description of the good ruler was conventional. His application of principle to practice seemed unexceptional. The spirit of faction must be shunned, he argued. He called upon the lawmakers to beware those who would act from private motives to tear down this wilderness Zion and its government. When he gave thanks that Massachusetts had escaped an iniquitous governor and now enjoyed the beneficent rule of Samuel Shute, he studiously chose his words lest he rouse lingering factious resentments.[6]

Then Colman summoned the lawmakers to reflect upon their recent losses: four councilors had died during the last year. One was Andrew Belcher. The minister recalled the dark days when the province learned of Burgess's appointment and Andrew Belcher had summoned his son to defend the province from this reprobate. Then he read Andrew's letter instructing Jonathan to protect the charter against its enemies in London. Colman exhorted the lawmakers: "Your Winthrop, and your Hutchinsons were sincere & hearty lovers of this People, & prov'd themselves so in the Evil times as well as the Good which have pass'd over us. And the Name of BELCHER ought also to be endear'd to us in all future times, for that one generous Order which he sent to his Son in London, when a black cloud was gathering over us which threaten'd our Charter." It is to this man that "we very much owe the satisfactions we enjoy to day."[7] Later that day Jonathan Belcher was elected to the Council on the first ballot. No matter Colman's impact on the election, his sermon defined the meaning of the moment for the young councilor.

During his recent mission to London, Belcher had also won election to the Boston council of the Company for the Propagation of the Gospel in New England.[8] Since its establishment by prominent English Puritans in 1649, the company had provided financial support for the conversion of the Indians. Its governing board in London, composed of leading English dissenters and friends of New England, voted funds for missions, the establishment of praying towns, the erection and maintenance of schools, and the translation and publication of the Bible for the native peoples. It appointed a board in Boston to dispense its moneys, to oversee its projects, and to report on whatever progress had been realized. The company stood as an embodiment and reminder of Massachusetts's historic position in the vanguard of the Protestant Reformation. When commemorating the first planters, Massachusetts still gave thanks to the almighty for opening the wilderness by visiting plague upon the native peoples and in the same breath renewed its dedication to gospelizing the survivors. Without pausing, New England's leaders memorialized both Captain Benjamin Church and his slaughters and John Eliot and his missions. The caretakers of that tradition—such eminent clerics as Increase and Cotton Mather and Edward Wigglesworth and senior councilors as Samuel Sewall, Adam Winthrop, Penn Townsend, and Eliakim Hutchinson—sat on the company's Boston council. Jonathan Belcher proudly joined this company.

His days were filled with new responsibilities. There were church committees to attend for the assignment of pews, the audit of accounts, and building maintenance; there were the meetings of the New England Company at the home of Cotton Mather or at the Council chamber to discuss the most effective strategy for gospelizing the Indians. The Council proved most demanding with meetings called nearly every week for a total of between 100 and 150 days a year. And as councilor, Belcher sat *ex officio* on Harvard College's board of overseers. In the evenings he dined with the governor and the Dudleys, with the town's clergymen, and with his new colleagues on the Council.[9]

Belcher still tended to his business, but his ventures, diverse and numerous though they were, did not require him to budget his time. The pace of business and of communications was slow enough so that he could transact his affairs, meet with associates, and write whatever letters were required by noon and spend the rest of the day in public service.[10] Indeed, he savored those moments when he sat with the pillars of his society to conduct church affairs, to oversee the college's curriculum and attend its commencement ceremonies, and to consider more effective means to convert the natives. His attendance at the Council was outstanding. Eighteen of the twenty-eight councilors usually attended during the legislative sessions with the House of Representatives, but in the interim periods attendance fell to nine and sometimes lower. Belcher's attendance rate, however, stood at 90 percent and in some years higher.[11]

The Massachusetts Council acted as a lawmaking body with the House of Representatives, as an advisory body to the executive, and as a judiciary body. It met with the House of Representatives to set fiscal policies, such as the levying of taxes, the printing of paper money, and the appropriating of funds for defense and salaries. Belcher's reputation earned him appointment to committees to determine the market value of paper money and to make recommendations for preserving its worth, to investigate Connecticut's currency policies, and to establish some sort of intercolonial cooperation on monetary affairs.[12] The frontiers and their defense required a vigilant eye even during peace. Forts were to be surveyed and kept ready. The Council received reports of attacks on provincial shipping and fishing. To the north in Maine, Father Sebastian Rale was rousing the natives. Belcher sat on committees to treat with the Indians or to attend to such small details as the repair of Castle William's boat. Much of the Council's time was spent reviewing accounts. Officers in the provincial forces submitted their muster rolls enumerating the troops to be paid. When vacancies on the civil list occurred, the governor asked the Council for its advice. And there was the constant flow of petitions from individuals and towns asking that an injustice be corrected or that a local dispute be settled. Samuel Mayo of Harwich, for example, prayed that he and his neighbors be allowed to separate themselves and create a new town; John Hayes, who served as lighthouse keeper at Beacon Island, wanted a higher salary; and Samuel Smith, who had been moldering in jail under charges of murder, requested that he be given a speedy trial.[13]

While the office of councilor was established by the new charter, the role acquired meaning within the context of the Puritan tradition. Each May, the General Court invited a local minister to expound upon the principles of good government and the qualities necessary for good rulers. Councilors were the "Shepherds of Israel," the caretakers of the Puritan legacy, the "nursing Fathers" of Massachusetts's churches and the college at Cambridge. As God's anointed, they stood vigilant, protecting the institutions of this "wilderness zion." Councilors were "Fathers and Benefactors to their People" according to Peter Thacher. They were distinguished by their "Prudence and Holiness" and they governed as much by example as by deed. "They do a great deal with GOD, to keep off Judgements, and to procure Publick Blessings. They have great Power with GOD *by their Prayers*, to open his Infinite Stores." It was their task as fathers to preserve the people in their special relationship with heaven.[14] Accordingly, the Council met with the governor each spring to set aside a "day of Solemn Fasting and Prayer" and to issue a proclamation calling upon the people to gather in their churches to "Acknowledge our Manifold Sins and Unworthiness" and to "seek the Favour and Blessing of GOD . . . as the Church and People of GOD throughout the whole World."[15] And at harvest time the government summoned the people again to give thanks for the divine bounty. Sometimes, as in 1721, when the small pox ravaged the people, the Council responded to God's displeasures and issued a special day of fasting.

In 1725 Cotton Mather, perhaps the most prestigious clergyman in the province, submitted a petition to the Council requesting the government to sponsor a synod so that the province's ministers might devise a strategy for combating the "visible Decay of Piety in the Countrey." Approval came at once and so did controversy. Boston's Anglicans protested that they were the established church, not the Congregationalists, and therefore the government had no warrant under the charter to extend official recognition to a gathering of dissenters. The protest offended the councilors' sensibilities, and they summarily voted to dismiss it. But they were, no doubt, relieved that Mather's movement for a synod came to naught.[16]

The times were changing, and New England's Nehemiahs were being forced to make difficult adjustments to empire. The controversy regarding the position of the Congregational churches prompted the councilors to stand, just as their predecessors had, at the protecting wall that sheltered the covenanted people. But while they revered the first American Nehemiahs for their heroic resolution, they also celebrated the charter of 1691 as a second hedge that reinforced the covenant. When they had embraced the Protestant succession, they had also welcomed royal authority and by that fact the Episcopalian establishment. Thus, they were compelled to speak a new vocabulary of toleration, albeit in a faltering manner. While they continued the rituals of ancestor worship, they were obliged to separate themselves from their fathers' bloody persecutions. Everyone knew that the synod had been called in response to the Anglican challenge. But silence was best. Thus, New Englanders spoke of themselves as a special covenanted people, but by embracing the crown they implicitly had accepted an authority that turned themselves into tolerated dissenters.

Soon after taking his seat at the Council table, Belcher realized that New England was besieged. In February 1719, Paul Dudley informed his fellow councilors that John Checkley, an Anglican minister, was preparing to publish a tract that condemned both deists and Congregationalists in the same breath. The Council appointed a special investigating committee, which included Dudley, Samuel Sewall, and Cotton Mather, and soon after it ordered Checkley not to print the book. Later that autumn, another Anglican was accused of defaming the Congregationalist clergy for not praying for the king's welfare. Five years later John Checkley appeared before the Council again to answer for a recent publication. The Council found that the tract contained "many vile and scandalous passages . . . reflecting on the Ministers of the Gospel . . . and denying their sacred Function & ye holy Ordinances of Religion as administered by them." Attorney General Dudley was directed to initiate prosecution in the Suffolk County Court. Checkley was only one of many new voices challenging the Congregational establishment. Not all were Anglican. The councilors were especially alarmed as they read each week's installment of Boston's newspaper *The New-England Courant*. Soon they were convinced that the newspaper's attacks on the clergy and government were intolerable, and orders were issued for the printer's arrest.[17]

Before Belcher had completed his first year at the Council table, he could see that the political settlement that he had secured in London was rapidly disintegrating. When Governor Shute recommended that the legislature comply with the king's instruction to establish a permanent fund for the payment of his salary, the House of Representatives responded that "fixt and stated Salaries" were incompatible with "our Constitution." Soon the governor was accused of assembling a court of favorites that conspired to bend the government to its selfish interests. As each session of the legislature passed, debate became more heated. The governor and house were locked in controversies over the salary, the right to elect the speaker, and the control of treasury funds. In addition, the growing economic depression sparked renewed calls for paper money, which, in turn, collided with the governor's position.[18]

Massachusetts politics exploded. Observers, no matter which side they took on the issues, expressed amazement as they witnessed the spirit of faction and discord spread like an infectious delirium throughout the land. They all agreed that the controversies were fanned by long-time contentions between two parties, one led by Elisha Cooke, Jr., and the other by Paul Dudley. Like their fathers before them, each accused the other of plotting to undermine the social order. Cooke explained to his Boston constituents that Dudley and his cohorts had made Governor Shute into a tool to advance their selfish and tyrannical designs against the people's liberties. Warning that public virtue was at stake, Cooke prevailed at the Boston elections. By speaking effectively to a country persuasion or temperament that scorned the contaminations coming from the cosmopolitan center, he quickly assumed a leading role in the legislature against the administration. Against the country persuasion stood Dudley, who countered that Cooke and his adherents indulged in demagoguery to advance their selfish interests. He warned that public order and respect for authority were at stake.

Both sides indulged in histrionics. Indeed, their rhetoric has sometimes seduced historians into believing that there was a confrontation between court and country. Though the specific issues were substantive, they were debated in an ethereal realm. First, the differences between the two positions were not as great as the antagonists made them out to be. Though they were loath to admit it, both sides measured themselves by a common standard. The image of the well-ordered society that John Winthrop had revealed on board the *Arbella*—with rank set over rank, rich over poor, rulers over ruled, and with all bound together in organic community and in covenant with God—remained at the center of the public imagination. When both sides bewailed the decline of public virtue in government, they raised up a traditional image of the good ruler that was contained in the ideal of the Nehemiah. Their differences were, in fact, a matter of accent or interpretation of that ideal. On the one side was Cooke, who stressed the country or traditional and restorative side of the Nehemiah. On the other was Dudley, who did not reject the traditional but was more willing to embrace the courtier side of the Nehemiah.

The genteel Nehemiah was more comfortable with London's presence. He stressed the ideals of hierarchy and subordination, and bewailed the breakdown of character that led to disrespect for authority. By his lights Elisha Cooke seemed a reckless agitator of the people's passions in order to advance his own interest. The primitive Nehemiah also lamented moral breakdown but focused his concern on the ranks of the elite. Massachusetts's fathers, he argued, no longer attended to the obligations that went with their station. Gentility turned into corruption and tyranny. Primitiveness, on the other hand, meant unstained virtue and public-mindedness.

But neither Nehemiah explicitly rejected the cosmopolitan center. Both revered the charter, the Protestant succession, and Winthrop's legacy. The primitive Nehemiah spoke to provincial sensibilities, specifically a deeply felt ambivalence toward the cosmopolitan and an equally passionate regard for local authority. His genteel counterpart did not reject that position. Instead, he responded that his primitive opponent gave free rein to nature's destructive impulses. New England, he warned, still stood on the edge of the wilderness. The cosmopolitan center provided the civilizing influence necessary for preventing the people from descending into a beastlike condition. Yet, while the genteel Nehemiah stressed the anarchic tendencies within the primitive, he did not deny that too much of the urbane converted the gentleman into the effete and depraved courtier. Ebenezer Pemberton had said as much when he advised the young Belcher of the perils as well as the benefits of a trip to London.

The country and court were temperaments rather than distinct ideologies or contending party organizations. Men moved easily from one position to another. What appeared to be high political drama at one point dissolved soon after in petty squabbling. Cooke's so-called party included a disparate lot. Some like Nathaniel Byfield and William Tailer were once Dudley men. Those who joined with Cooke against the administration did not always agree with him on priorities. John Colman joined Cooke in opposition to the government's conservative fiscal policies. But while Colman remained an advocate of private banking schemes, Cooke pressed for liberal emissions by the government instead. Moreover Colman, unlike Cooke, focused his opposition narrowly on fiscal matters and retained good relations with members of the administration, including Belcher. While Cooke engaged in a broad range of constitutional issues concerning the relationship between the House of Representatives and the governor and his Council, Colman became increasingly sympathetic with the governor. And when Cotton Mather joined in defense of the administration, he acted principally from a greater dislike for Cooke than from a new-found appreciation of Paul Dudley.

Ethereal rhetoric and unstable associations made for a politics that might be described as effervescent. Politicians engaged in debate within an institutional and cultural context that nurtured instability. Antagonists struggled for control of a legislature, whose members were largely impervious to political organization. A small group of eastern and urban politicians debated before a majority of lawmakers who were capable of supporting either the court or the country Nehemiah. The ability to move these majorities depended upon certain dramaturgical skills. Each side sought to impose its own scenario upon the political scene, and whichever was successful at controlling the stage in Boston was able to sway the legislature to support its cause.

Independence and indifference characterized a majority of the lawmakers who held the more than one hundred seats in the legislature.[19] These representatives from rural and isolated towns were interested principally in local affairs. They came to resolve issues that could not be settled among their constituents, stayed for only a short portion of the legislative session, were disinclined to return for a second term, and were largely indifferent to the political battles that raged in Boston. This backbencher majority could not be molded into an organization. Cooke's country adherents exaggerated when they charged that the governor wielded his powers of appointment to extend the court's influence into the legislature. There were too few offices under the governor's control, and most of them brought little compensation. Moreover, the governor's appointees were not his creatures. The province's local oligarchs expected to be consulted on local appointments. Political expediency required that the governor accede to their recommendations lest he antagonize them in the legislature.

Cooke's critics also exaggerated the extent of his influence over these localists. Although Cooke and a small cluster of lawmakers from Boston and environs sat on the important committees that drafted messages to the governor and defined the house's agenda, their influence rested more on widespread indifference to provincial politics than on organization. The majority was uninterested in constitutional affairs. Defense, taxation, and currency questions were more likely to prick their interest. But while inclined to join with Cooke on currency questions, they did not constitute Cooke's party. And while these backbenchers accorded the Boston representative so much influence, they were simultaneously predisposed to defer to the Dudley faction.

These backbencher majorities were as likely to support one side as the other. Cooke's influence depended on his ability to speak to a pervasive local and country temperament. As a country Nehemiah, he evoked memories of the old charter, suspicions of the cosmopolitan center, fears of an Anglican assault on the Congregational establishment, and resentments of London's intrusions into provincial affairs. But Cooke's urban style and his passionate confrontation with the governor and the Council simultaneously roused concerns for the social order and political authority. His behavior smacked of democratic excess and demagoguery. Thus, majorities in the House of Representatives elected both Cooke and Dudley to the Council at the outset of the Shute administration. After Cooke's election was rejected by the governor and he returned to the lower house, Cooke quickly emerged as leader of the opposition but could not dissuade his colleagues to reelect Paul Dudley as attorney general and councilor. At the same time Dudley's brother William, who had been elected from the town of Roxbury, quickly assumed a leadership position in the House of Representatives. After prolonged conflict with the Council that stirred anti-Dudley feelings, the House of Representatives elected William Dudley its speaker for five consecutive years.

These legislators also acted within a political culture that encouraged exaggeration and volatility. First, New Englanders employed a manichean vocabulary even before they engaged in constitutional and economic discourse. Indeed, the country ideology was an embellishment on the jeremiad and the rhetoric of declension. Second, New Englanders approached conflict with deep misgivings. Their idea of community left little place for dissent or disagreement. Faction was anathema; it became a sign of impending disorder. This fear sat at the core of the political culture. New Englanders not only spoke against faction, they applied that principle to the raising of their children. In their efforts to root out their children's "willfulness," or incipient factiousness, parents may have succeeded at one level in producing community-mindedness. But in doing so, they nurtured predispositions to see the world as hostile, to exaggerate the malicious intentions of others, and even to concoct enemies in their imaginations. New Englanders lacked the emotional reserves to engage in conflict, but when they did, they exploded volcanically.

They also needed to exaggerate their differences in order to justify their factious behavior. Political conflict was anathema unless the opponent represented grave threat to the moral fiber of the community. By casting his antagonist into opprobrium, the faction leader could deny that he acted on base or selfish motives and thereby succeeded in transforming himself into the public-minded patriot. Thus, Cooke sought to turn Dudley into a craven courtier, while Dudley struggled to make Cooke into a fiend of anarchy.

Finally, the ability to exaggerate became a political skill. To move the backbencher majorities in the House of Representatives, Cooke needed to impose his own dramatic scenario on the political scene. Staging, cues, and a cast of characters were crucial. Oratorical skills became necessary for persuading the backbencher majorities that they confronted a court conspiracy against the New England way. If Cooke failed to frame provincial politics within his scenario, Dudley would be able to impose his own script in which Cooke's patriotic pose turned into demagoguery.

Governor Shute provided Cooke with the cues for enacting the primitive Nehemiah's scenario. A soldier, unacquainted with the art of political maneuver and incapable of tolerating dissent, Shute lacked the sensitivity necessary for governing this contentious people. He delivered his call for an end to faction as if he were giving a command. On his arrival he roused suspicions by taking temporary residence in the home of Paul Dudley. Within a year of his arrival, Governor Shute was charged with distributing favors to a court of friends. He protested but did nothing to correct the impression. Instead, he set out to pursue Cooke and his cohorts with a vengeance and a pettiness that appeared unbecoming to a royal official. The style in which he lived disappointed friends and pricked provincial sensibilities. On the first Sunday after his arrival, Shute chose to attend the Church of England, and soon after it became evident that he regularly observed the church's holidays. He employed his office to support the Anglicans in their efforts to win exemption from paying taxes for the Congregational establishment. Bostonians noted that the governor spent his days racing horses and his evenings holding loud and sumptuous dinners.[20]

Lawmakers found the governor petty, quarrelsome, and weak. When the legislature refused to establish a permanent salary, Shute quickly forsook his royal instructions rather than go without an income. Yet he could not let go his yearning for revenge. In 1720 the House elected Cooke its speaker and appointed a delegation to inform the governor. The lawmakers returned with what seemed to be his approval, but later that day Shute announced that he had received the delegation informally not in his official capacity. Now that he was sitting in the governor's official chair, he would receive the delegation.

When approached a second time, however, the governor rejected Cooke and ordered the House to vote again. Shute seemed to be toying with the lawmakers. A House delegation appointed to present the governor with the list of newly elected councilors was told again that he would receive it only while he sat in his official chair. Twice the delegation had been informed that the governor was sitting in his chair. Each time the representatives approached the chair, they discovered that it was empty. The House was outraged and refused to elect another speaker. The next day, five days after the opening of the session, Shute dissolved the House and called for new elections.[21]

With Governor Shute as his foil, Cooke was able to play the virtuous patriot. He explained to the public that the governor had offered to accept his election as speaker but only in return for a public apology. Boston's representative explained that public honors meant nothing if they were bought at the expense of principles. It has been "My Resolution and fixed Principle" to seek the "Good and Welfare of my Dear Native Country." Constitutional principle was at stake: "The House of Representatives have an Indubitable Fundamental Right to Chuse their own Speaker, & the Governor no Negative Voice in that Election." Acquiescence would open the door for more incursions upon the provincial constitution. Other Boston patriots joined Cooke in warning the public that they could smell the "suffocating Stench of Court-flattery." One predicted that "If we tamely give up one Inch," the people would become prey to a perfidious court conspiracy. And John Colman summoned the people to stand steadfast against rich and powerful predators who had gained control of the administration.[22]

The country was on the ascendant during Jonathan Belcher's first year on the Council. When he petitioned the legislature for compensation for the expenses incurred in securing Shute's appointment, the lower house summarily dismissed his application. Perhaps the lawmakers acted from parsimony, but the counselor was also becoming the target of anti-administration feelings. In the spring of 1721, the Boston town meeting instructed its representatives to stand fast in opposition to the permanent salary and to reject any attempt by Councilor Belcher to seek reimbursement for his London mission. That May, Belcher failed to keep his seat at the Council table. He was returned in 1722 and 1723 but by the slimmest of margins, and he fell short again in 1724.[23]

The Shute administration was in disarray. Cooke and his allies in the House of Representatives had succeded in framing the public debate in their terms. On reviewing the government's accounts, the lawmakers found that the governor and Council had been routinely approving payments to militia officers that were based on fraudulent claims. In 1721 Cooke and his allies argued that since the Council and governor could no longer be trusted with the people's moneys, the House must pass a supply bill that stipulated precisely how treasury funds could be spent and also specified that they could be spent only on approval of the House. The Council and governor accepted what was in fact a significant abdication of power over the public purse. The House persisted in its investigations of the militia officers and concluded that the governor and Council could no longer be trusted with the management of the province's defense, especially while the General Court was not in session. In December 1722, the representatives proposed the establishment of a standing committee of both houses to oversee the executive on military affairs. The Council capitulated again.[24]

Shute was especially provoked by the House's intrusions upon his authority as commander in chief. He had already concluded that neither the dissolution of the legislature nor reprimands from London would bring Cooke and his cohorts to their senses and that peace would be restored only by persuading the king to station troops in Boston and to revise or revoke the charter. He prepared his return to London. But before he left, he delivered his last insult to his tormentors by adjourning the Council over the Christmas holiday. The decision broke tradition and pricked Congregationalist sensibilities. Samuel Sewall was aghast. The Council pressed the governor to reconsider. On the second afternoon of discussion, however, Shute dismissed the councilors' protests and disclosed what had only been suspected—that he was, in fact, a member of the Church of England. He took communion and celebrated Christmas. Two days later, without warning, he left for London.[25]

With Shute's absence, the voices of discord became less audible. Lieutenant Governor William Dummer preferred to placate rather than provoke contending personalities. Unlike Shute, who did not hesitate to purge his critics, the lieutenant governor concurred in the election of Cooke and his allies to the Council. But most important, Governor Shute was now in London, where he was convincing officialdom that the province's behavior required stern discipline. Genteel Nehemiahs like Dudley, who had warned in vain that Cooke's behavior might lead to the revocation of the charter, gained credibility. The House agreed that the province stood at a "Critical Juncture" and began its defense. Jeremiah Dummer, who had been recently dismissed, was reappointed agent, and Elisha Cooke was chosen to join in the province's defense in London.[26]

Two years later Cooke returned in humiliation. All Boston knew that his efforts to rebut Shute's complaints proved ineffective before the Privy Council and that the charter might have been lost if it had not been for Dummer's talents. Massachusetts had kept its charter on condition that the province accept an additional or explanatory charter that affirmed the executive's right to approve the speaker of the House and denied the House's right to adjourn itself without the governor's consent. Cooke had no recourse but to accept. When he arrived in Boston, however, he found that many of his followers were disgruntled. Nearly a third of the House of Representatives voted to reject the charter. Cooke, who had been elected to the Council *in absentia*, tried to recover his reputation by reversing himself and voting against the explanatory charter.[27]

But the country patriot had lost the initiative. Although Cooke was reelected to the Council, his allies lost two of Boston's seats in the legislature. The Dudleys and the Dummers were again on the ascendant. While Paul Dudley sat in Council and on the Superior Court, his brother was elected speaker of the House of Representatives. Dudley's brother-in-law, William Dummer, was the province's chief executive. And Jeremiah Dummer represented the province in London.

Jonathan Belcher's fortunes did not improve, however. He was the most vulnerable of all Governor Shute's allies. While Cooke struggled but failed to remove Paul Dudley from the Council, he was able to block Belcher's reelection. Nor did Belcher's position improve with the relaxation of tensions. In 1724 and 1725, when Cooke and Dudley were both elected to the Council, Belcher was left out. Perhaps Belcher benefited from the conservative resurgence but if so, only slightly. In 1726 and 1727, he regained his seat but on the last ballot. He lost again in 1728.

Disappointments turned to bitterness. Slowly he became ambivalent toward the administration he had helped to create. Belcher was not concerned about the constitutional issues that Shute had provoked. He was largely indifferent to the issues that turned on government by royal instruction even when he was governor. While he seemed to doubt that Parliament's authority extended to the colonies, he stated his position parenthetically. He was not wont to belabor constitutional abstractions, but he did make the moral tone of government his first concern. Like other councilors who labored to shore up government authority against demagogic assault, he felt uncomfortable with Shute's petty quarrelsomeness. Shute's love of gambling and horseracing and his friendly association with the Anglican establishment had roused concerns. Belcher kept these thoughts to himself.

Moreover, he was coming to feel estranged from the Dudleys and Dummers. Belcher had expected to enjoy commanding influence in this government that he had been instrumental in creating, but he soon came to realize that he had to play second to Dudley during the Council's deliberations with the governor. He kept these feelings to himself largely because he saw no other alternative. He had pinned his political future to the Shute administration and had nowhere else to go. He heartily approved its stand against paper money. He dreaded the consequences of Cooke's ascendance. That fear more than his approval of Shute defined his position. When the Council learned that Shute was preparing to leave, however, Belcher could not disguise his ambivalent feelings. Dudley moved that the Council appoint a delegation to visit the governor aboard the *Seahorse* to wish him well. Belcher declined to support the measure.[28]

Belcher was forty when the governor left. He was approaching important transitions in his life, which he expected to bring fulfillment but which seemed to turn to disappointment. His children were growing to maturity. He had enrolled Andrew at Harvard in 1720 and Jonathan in 1724. His daughter Sarah would soon be married. Belcher was laying dynastic plans. He expected that one son, most likely the eldest, would complete his education in England. Perhaps the young man would take an advanced degree at one of the universities. Perhaps he would study the law at the Inns of Court, settle in London, and pursue a career at the bar. There was no question that the other son would go on to Belcher Wharf in preparation for a life in commerce. At the same time, Belcher began to contemplate retirement from commerce and to lay plans for buying property on the outskirts of Boston, where he would build his country estate.[29]

Like many of Boston's more prosperous merchants, Belcher was drawn to the Horatian ideal of pastoral retreat far from the vulgar crowd. By laying aside the mundane cares of commerce, he would more fully embody the ideal of the gentleman. Sometimes he considered retirement from the clamor of politics. But he was posturing. Retirement brought the opportunity to devote himself fully to a public life and to dissociate himself from his entrepreneurial origins.

As he brooded over his disappointments, Belcher began to see himself as the innocent victim of evil-doers. The image came naturally. The culture promoted a paranoid response to adversity. New Englanders who engaged in political debate were forever painting dark pictures of conspirators lurking in "chimney corners" or concocting their designs over "punch bowls." Moreover, there were many like Belcher whose sense of the world derived from primary childhood experiences. For them the world felt threatening and hostile.

Perhaps it was not by accident that Belcher sought out Cotton Mather. The minister's language resonated in Belcher's imagination. In 1719 the councilor listened as Mather warned the government that the province was about to descend into a "dreadful Convulsion." Jerusalem was overcome by the raging spirit of faction. Public harmony was evaporating as the people forgot their respect for authority. Massachusetts was transforming itself into a land rent by sedition, mutiny, and rebellion against God's ordinances. Unless "well-disposed Men" joined in shepherding the people back to the faith of their fathers, God would turn away from his people. Belcher was moved. When he pressed his colleagues at the Council table to subsidize the sermon's publication, he discovered that several were indifferent to Mather's rhetoric. For two generations New Englanders had listened to their ministers preach like latter-day Jeremiahs bewailing the signs of declension and predicting divine judgments. Mather's sermon seemed to be a ritual, a hollow convention not worthy of special notice.[30]

But somehow Mather touched Belcher. Even though he was not a member of Mather's church, Belcher often sought the minister out. Indeed, both men shared a worldview rooted in similar formative experiences of living under the authority of domineering patriarchs. Both men viewed the world as threatening. They were forever concocting hobgoblins in their minds. Mather's tormentors were sometimes the imps of Satan. Belcher's were often faceless; the mocking voices of people who wished him ill echoed through his imagination. Mather and Belcher employed the same emotional vocabulary. They seethed with rage and were incessantly concocting fantasies of retribution. Mather felt guilty and struggled to stifle his destructive fantasies. Belcher denied his vengeful feelings but also often felt unable to act upon them. His core sense of vulnerability made him emotionally incapable of confronting an adversary, either real or imagined. When Mather and Belcher felt especially embittered, they swung from raging avengers to passive martyrs. The injuries they endured became signs of their innocence and virtue. Mather took satisfaction in imagining himself the innocent victim who prayed for the welfare of those who rejected him. Belcher also resorted to this role. Sometimes he drew upon Horace's Roman Odes, which raised up the ideal of the country retreat.[31]

Each spring Belcher looked forward to the elections to the Council with growing apprehension. One year he sought out Mather. He expected to lose his position but professed contentment. He longed to retire from the tumults of public affairs, to "leave the Factions to themselves," and to seek the "Solace" of the "Study." He continued in a manner that echoed the minister's own response to adversity. Though a victim, he would always take "a particular, Secret pleasure" in "indeavouring to do my Countrey all the good in My power, in the Most Silent Wayes & Manner." Belcher also unburdened himself to John Colman. "How Easy is it," he reflected, "for the Inveterate malice of private [per]sons to Veil & Cloud the highest merit. For my part I am Sick of all Our publick Affairs." Belcher braced himself for rejection. He promised that no matter the injuries that he might suffer, he would work in private ways for the good of the people. "I shall always pray for the peace of Jerusalem."[32]

In later years, Belcher liked to remind his children that this was a fruitful and rewarding time when he labored to plant a "vineyard" for their benefit.[33] He forgot the disappointments and the bitterness. Although he professed contentment with the prospect of retirement from politics, he could not still his ambitions. Each year he anxiously awaited the outcome of the councilor elections. That he sometimes won half as many votes as Dudley served to remind him of the distance separating him from his ambitions. Benjamin

Colman's sermon that had promoted Jonathan Belcher as a New England Nehemiah became a bitter memory.

As he brooded, Belcher began to focus his resentments, but not upon Elisha Cooke, who was the obvious source of his troubles. Instead, he fixed on the Dummers and the Dudleys, especially Paul Dudley. As he contemplated his troubles, he turned Paul Dudley into his chief antagonist. What Belcher dwelt on was Dudley's demeanor, which, he became convinced, revealed malevolent intent. Perhaps Dudley had taken offense at the aggressive manner in which Belcher had pressed his opinion during the early days of the Shute administration. There is no evidence, not even in Belcher's correspondence, of a concrete or specific issue that caused him to turn against his ally. Nonetheless, Belcher was working his resentments into what would become a lifelong obsession. Equally significant, he confronted his adversary in his imagination but felt too vulnerable to risk confrontation.[34]

While Belcher anguished over his tribulations, news arrived from London in May 1727 that the king had died. Massachusetts wondered whether the succession would bring a new administration or simply the renewal of existing appointments. Rumors abounded that Shute would return. While all waited, Belcher made plans for a trip to London. That autumn, he visited Connecticut, ostensibly to inspect his estates and mines. He called upon the governor and lawmakers to propose that he be appointed the province's agent in London. He reminded them that he was a Connecticut man through his mother's family. Moreover, he noted that the present agent, Jeremiah Dummer, was so incapacitated by illness that he had been forced to surrender his duties as Massachusetts's agent to Francis Wilks. The officials listened skeptically. They had been well-satisfied with Dummer's services and proposed to consider Belcher not as a replacement but as an associate of the present agent.[35]

What Belcher intended is not clear, in part because of the paucity of manuscript material from this period of his life. But he was also by nature loath to reveal his ambitions before they were realized. He had made it his life's maxim that "Secrecy is the Soul of Business." Experience had taught that "Mankind is wicked, full of ill nature & Envy and when a Man misses his aim they are full of Sneer & Ridicule."[36] No doubt, he did not intend to settle permanently in London; the agent's salary provided him with the means to pursue his interest. Most likely he had little idea what to expect. But his earlier missions to London had always redounded to his favor. Thus he proceeded, driven by unfulfilled ambitions and haunted by fears of failure. On the eve of Belcher's departure, however, news arrived that the new king, George II, had chosen William Burnet, the Governor of New York, to govern Massachusetts. In addition, the king had reappointed William Dummer as his lieutenant governor.

Massachusetts awaited the new governor and wondered how his administration would affect long-standing political rivalries and unresolved constitutional debates. Once Burnet arrived in mid-July, he quickly plunged into controversy. He pressed the permanent salary in a high-toned and elaborate manner that had not been heard before. Unlike Shute, he would not compromise. He loved debate, and each exchange with the legislature became more elaborate than the last. The House responded in kind with ever longer and more intricate arguments. While the lawmakers shared the governor's reverence for England's balanced constitution, they argued that the principles that applied to England were not necessarily suited to conditions in Massachusetts. Executive independence meant arbitrary government and the breakdown of the provincial constitution.[37]

While the Council warned the House that its messages were needlessly provocative, it could not support the governor on the salary. By early fall, Burnet raised political debate to a new plane. Cooke regained his reputation as champion of provincial rights. The government was at deadlock. The House appealed directly to its constituents for support against what constituted a breach of precedent, an attempt to diminish the "Dignity and Freedom of the House," and a blatant violation of Magna Charta and the provincial charter.[38]

When the Boston town meeting convened to discuss the House's appeal, it made Jonathan Belcher its moderator. The choice surprised his friends, especially because Cooke had engineered the election. For the past few months Belcher had been uncertain what to do. In May, he had received word that Connecticut had voted that he join agent Dummer in London, but he delayed making a reply. As he watched the new administration take shape, however, ambition and principle were forcing a decision.[39] He had lost his seat in the Council again. Yet the Dudleys and Dummer remained firmly entrenched. At the same time, Belcher viewed the Burnet administration with growing misgivings. He was never convinced, even when governor himself, of the arguments for a permanent salary. In any event, constitutional issues never moved him. What concerned Belcher, however, was the tone that the new governor gave to public affairs. Burnet was an Anglican and he loved to live lavishly and ostentatiously. Moreover, Burnet seemed to be forcing a significant alteration in the language of public debate. Massachusetts listened as he argued his case in legalistic, constitutional, and essentially whiggish terms. To be sure, the vocabulary of rights and privileges or the principle of a balanced constitution were not alien to provincial New England. But this language was secondary, or peripheral, to that heard in the election sermons and the jeremiads. The governor's language and his style of living signified a change that was too much for many genteel Nehemiahs to countenance.

Many of Belcher's former colleagues in the Council shared his concerns. No doubt Belcher acted from a combination of principle and personal ambition. Desperate and alienated by this government, he cast his lot with Cooke. Soon after the Boston town meeting resolved its support for Cooke's position, Belcher accepted appointment as Connecticut's agent. Then the Massachusetts House of Representatives voted that since Belcher was going to London, he should also be appointed to assist Francis Wilks as provincial agent. The Council opposed the motion. So Cooke established a fund to be collected by private subscriptions to cover the agency's expenses.[40]

When Belcher arrived in London in early April 1729, Wilks had completed his arguments before an unsympathetic Board of Trade and was preparing to go before the Privy Council. The situation was uncertain. Martin Bladen at the Board of Trade and the new secretary of state in charge of colonial affairs, the Duke of Newcastle, were leading a movement for tightening the crown's authority over the colonies. Determined to strengthen the hands of the royal governors, these reformers pressed for permanent salaries. Massachusetts was not their single concern, but they had chosen to make it an object lesson or a test of their intentions. No doubt, Governor Shute's reports had turned opinion against the province. Belcher and Wilks understood the depth of the prejudice.[41] They anticipated that opinion when they met with the Privy Council and vigorously protested that their employers did not secretly yearn for independence. Instead, they argued, a permanent salary gave a governor the license to act contrary to the public interest and to lay the foundation for tyranny. In their efforts to counter the councilors preconceptions of Massachusetts, they sought to awaken whiggish sympathies. They pointed out that the salary instruction was unprecedented, violated the charter, and undermined the foundations of English liberties.

The Privy Council was not moved, however, and recommended that unless the Massachusetts legislature speedily complied with the salary instruction, the matter would be presented to Parliament. Belcher and Wilks, while uncertain what to expect, had convinced each other that the cause of liberty and virtue could not be compromised. In their minds this confrontation had become a reenactment in the drama of whiggish history. Their inspiration came from Joseph Addison's Cato, who stood at the walls of Utica defending the principles of republicanism against Julius Caesar and preferred death to tyranny. The two agents wrote pressing their employers in Boston to stand resolute. "If we must be finally compelled to a fixt Salary, doubtless it must be better that it be done by the supream Legislature than to do it by our selves: if our liberties must be Lost, much better they should be taken away, than we be in any measure accessory to our own Ruin."[42]

Some friends of Massachusetts's charter in London believed the agents were foolhardy. No doubt, Belcher and Wilks were indulging in histrionics, but they also calculated that the London government was not comfortable with the position that it had taken. When Newcastle and his cohorts had committed themselves to establish permanent salaries for colonial executives, they were forced to consider drastic measures such as the deployment of troops to the colonies and the revision of charters. But such proposals raised up memories of Stuart tyrannies. Few imperial reformers, no matter their impatience with the intransigent colonists, dared violate ingrained whiggish sensibilities. Belcher and Wilks gambled that their critics were bluffing and that few of them could endure playing Caesar against their Cato. Several well-placed officials in government listened sympathetically to their arguments. The agents sensed that the government was eager to compromise. Indeed, Newcastle was moving toward a face-saving compromise when he advised Burnet to settle for a temporary salary for a fixed number of years.[43]

During the summer of 1729, while the agents waited for news from Boston, they began to worry that they had gone too far in arguing their case before the Privy Council. They sought to recast the political drama in terms less provocative. Constitutional principle, they emphasized, was not the cause for controversy; rather, it was the governor's irascible and factious personality that had driven Massachusetts to extremes. They relayed to London officialdom recent reports that Burnet had taken to imposing arbitrary and crushing duties on Boston merchants. Lord Townsend, brother-in-law of Prime Minister Robert Walpole and secretary of state for northern affairs, listened sympathetically. But Belcher and Wilks also sensed that this was the time for concessions. They wrote to the House leadership that it consider surrendering its control over the treasury and suggested that it offer the governor a compromise salary that was for more than one year but less than permanent.[44]

But the controversy had assumed a momentum of its own in Boston. Burnet ordered the General Court to move to Salem in hopes of immunizing the independent backbenchers from the infectious atmosphere that seemed to prevail in Boston. The tactic, however, was reinterpreted within the opposition's scenario as further evidence of the governor's oppressive intentions. When the House elected Belcher to the Council *in absentia* and the governor rejected the choice, Cooke appealed to the public and established a "voluntary Collection" to support the agents. In late August the House considered a proposal to establish a salary for the duration of Burnet's term only. The compromise, however, was overwhelmingly rejected by a vote of fifty-four to eighteen.[45]

The governor stood alone. The Council, traditionally an ally of governors, agreed with the House that a permanent salary endangered the people's rights and liberties. But it also warned the House to exercise prudence lest its histrionics provoke another charter crisis. Its counsels for moderation went unheeded. Councilors, including Paul Dudley, withdrew from public life; attendance at the Council table dropped precipitously.[46] By the end of August, Burnet had ordered the legislature moved again, this time to Cambridge. The representatives scolded him for the "Harshness and Severity" of his rule. The government was at stalemate. Then, one week later, on September 7, Governor Burnet died.[47]

The news reached London six weeks later, while Belcher and Wilks were defending their case before the Privy Council. Their cause seemed to hang in the balance. The Board of Trade under Bladen's influence had called for revocation of the charter, and Parliament was expected to begin its own investigation. Immediately the agents requested the government to suspend its proceedings. With Burnet gone they promised that peace would soon be restored to Massachusetts. The Board of Trade and Privy Council agreed. Echoing the agents' argument, they prayed that since the controversy was almost "intirely personal," a new governor would be able to restore peace to the province.[48]

But who was to be the new governor? There were few placeseekers in England so desperate to take this troublesome and unremunerative post. Samuel Shute seemed a likely candidate. Some had thought that London had erred by not renewing his commissions in 1727. Belcher wrote offering his support to the former governor. He was not surprised when Shute refused to consider returning to Massachusetts. His intention was to confirm that the former governor would not oppose his own application for the office. He doubtless hoped to gain the favor of Shute's brother Lord Barrington. Belcher also realized that although he faced no competition for the office, he could expect strenuous objections to his appointment. How could he, as the king's governor, be entrusted with the enforcement of the same instructions that as agent of the colony he had so recently opposed? But to Lord Townsend Belcher explained that as a native of New England he understood the people, enjoyed their confidence, and could therefore restore peace to the province. The argument satisfied the secretary. Newcastle and Bladen, however, could be expected to oppose the application.[49]

Four trips to London had taught Belcher the ways to manipulate the government. Imperial administration was a quagmire of offices and agencies that often worked at cross purposes. Officials not associated with the empire interrupted the process of decision making. Politicians meddled in colonial affairs to advance their interests and, sometimes, to test their influence against their rivals. In spite of Newcastle's effort to consolidate his hold on colonial patronage, Townsend and Lord Wilmington, the president of the Privy Council, were able to name their own candidates to colonial posts. Belcher moved through the anterooms of power, enlisting support from Townsend, Wilmington, Sir Charles Wager, first lord of the Admiralty, and Arthur

Onslow, speaker of the House of Commons. His brother-in-law Richard Partridge exerted his growing influence with London's merchants and with his fellow Quakers. Samuel Holden, a prominent London merchant, dissenter, and governor of the Bank of England, came forward with the support of nearly thirty other merchants. Belcher moved quickly while Newcastle was out of town. He bypassed the Board of Trade and made certain that Martin Bladen was kept ignorant of his application. By the end of November his name was presented to the king. George II remembered Belcher from his trips to Hanover and spoke of him to his advisers in a "Very kind Manner." The ministers reminded Belcher that "If I valued the being Govr of my own Countrey My having been at Hanover Now provd One of the happiest Articles of My Whole Life." On November 27, Belcher joined with friends from the merchant community at the Pontius tavern to celebrate his appointment.[50]

Belcher stayed in London through mid-summer. He tried to placate Newcastle but realized the futility of his efforts. He asked that his instruction for a permanent salary be relaxed but failed to convince the Privy Council. These were pleasant times though. He spent his days at the court in the company of the king. He sat for an official portrait and gave instructions that it be reproduced in a mezzotint engraving for distribution in New England. Since the governor of Massachusetts also held commissions for New Hampshire, New Englanders from both colonies came to court his favor. John Wentworth, the lieutenant governor of New Hampshire, sent his congratulations, and Belcher conveyed his assurances that he would be kept in office. He also gloated when he thought of his enemies in Massachusetts trembling in anticipation of his return. He arranged for the dismissal of Lieutenant Governor William Dummer and then secured the appointment of his one-time foe and new ally William Tailer as his new lieutenant. Then he turned on Jeremiah Dummer. The two classmates had worked under strained conditions on behalf of Connecticut. Dummer could hardly conceal his contempt for Belcher and what he considered an inept showing before the Privy Council. Now Belcher left his papers related to the Connecticut agency with Francis Wilks and wrote to the government in Hartford, recommending that Dummer be replaced by Richard Partridge. The Dudleys, especially Paul, would have to wait until his return.[51]

Jonathan Belcher's transformations from Elisha Cooke's adversary to his ally, from provincial agent to royal governor, from opponent to advocate of the king's instructions bewildered many of his fellow New Englanders. One anonymous observer was inspired to write a short play entitled "Belcher the Apostate." In the opening scenes, Jonathan Belcher establishes himself as the stalwart patriot, resolute in his determination to defend New England against

Burnet's tyrannies. In contrast to Elisha Cooke, who appears irresolute, Belcher forcefully argues against the permanent salary. His arguments are so convincing that he is appointed the provincial agent. But in London, when he receives news of Burnet's death, his soul is suddenly fired by ambition. He applies for the vacancy fully aware that if successful he would be obliged to promote a position that he had opposed. "My greatest difficulty," he confesses, "is to unsay what I have said and support an Instruction so much against my former opinion, but what wont a man do for the honour of being a Governour?" When he returns as governor, he commands his wife to address him as his "Excellency" instead of Jonathan. Driven by ambition, he presses the permanent salary upon his former allies. After conferring with a delegation of representatives led by Cooke, he speaks to himself: "I fear this ambition will ruin me." But he decides that "since rising upon the ruins of our country is at present the fashion[,] I am resolved to follow the mode." In the epilogue the playwright underscores his lesson: beware the self-proclaimed Cato who returns from Caesar's court transformed.

> Be not surprised; sincerity's no more.
> And ancient honesty turned out of door
> The trust reposed, is broken every day
> As you may see by the preceding play:
> We do resolve to make the man repent
> That he to Caesar's Court was ever sent.[52]

Speculation abounded in the months following Belcher's appointment. While one observer thought the choice was reason for celebration, he also prayed that the governor's new "station will not make him doe any thing that is not for the honour & Interest of his Country tho' it seems to us a Parodox that a Gentleman sent by the People to oppose the Imediate orders of the King should be preferred to Execute those orders he went to oppose." Some Bostonians predicted that Belcher could not long endure his unnatural association with Elisha Cooke and that he would soon return to his former allies, the Dudleys and Dummers. Others wondered whether William Dummer's dismissal was a harbinger of a thorough purge. The governor's one-time associates at the Council table "against whom he declared war, when he undertook to go to England as Agent" were "much alarmed" at his elevation. And there were those who hoped that as a native son, the governor would exercise a calming influence upon the contending factions and restore tranquility to public affairs.[53]

Belcher's public career seemed but another illustration of an ongoing political drama that pitted virtue against corruption. New Englanders were wont to spy dark and sinister motives at play in public life. They framed their conflicts within absolute categories of virtue and corruption, of the country patriot vying against the courtier sycophant, and of Cato challenging Caesar. At the same time, they often witnessed these manichean absolutes dissolve. Paul Dudley's allies Nathaniel Byfield and William Tailer suddenly became his enemies; Elisha Cooke and John Colman joined for a moment against the Dudleys and then went their separate ways; and Belcher, who once stood with the Dudleys, aligned himself with Cooke and Byfield. However frequently they occurred, such changes aroused the anxieties of Massachusetts politicians. The motives that were often mundane and petty were quickly condemned as defection from principle and apostasy. And there were those who went off to London to repair the province's protective hedges. A generation earlier Increase Mather had gone to restore the old charter, but when he returned with a new charter, Elisha Cooke, Sr., condemned him for betraying his people. So too, when Cooke's son went to defend the charter in 1723, he came to recognize the wisdom in compromise. But on his return, he too was censured for abandoning his principles.

Exaggeration was endemic to the political culture. Political exchange turned naturally into histrionics. Differences were often slight; two self-styled Nehemiahs—one speaking with a genteel and the other with a primitive accent—faced each other. Both struggled to claim the same symbols of cultural authority, and in the process each sought to expose the other's professions of patriotism as the deceptive and selfish guise of the apostate. In part, the propensity toward distortion came from discomforts with faction and contention that were deep-seated in the culture. To justify action against the other, each needed to cast his opponent into a culturally opprobrious role as the outsider bent on destroying the public welfare. By turning the other into the outsider, one transformed or elevated one's own factious motive into patriotism, virtue, and public-mindedness. In addition, many like Belcher had acquired a heartfelt sense of the world as dark and foreboding, which nurtured a propensity to exaggerate differences, to turn mundane disagreements into grave perils, and sometimes to concoct threats from the material of their imaginations.

New Englanders were predisposed to see their Catos turn into apostates and their country patriots into either demagogues or courtiers. Deviation from professed principles were quickly censured as the symptoms of corrupting selfishness. Pragmatism was the transparent defense of the apostate. While many of Belcher's fellow New Englanders were predisposed to see naked selfishness and ambition in his recent tergiversations, one outsider detected a consistent core of principles. David Dunbar, the surveyor general of the king's woods, was horrified by Belcher's appointment. He wrote to his superiors that Belcher was essentially a latter-day Puritan. Warning that the new governor would compromise and change his position on constitutional issues, would deceive his superiors, and would even betray the king, Dunbar emphasized that Belcher would not abandon his religious convictions. Dunbar understood that Belcher was the Nehemiah who struggled in this whiggish world to act as "intercessor" between king and people. At heart Belcher was the Puritan ruler.[54]

3

Interpreting the Role of Governor

During the summer of 1734, Governor Belcher received the first copies of his official portrait from London (see frontispiece illustration). The mezzotint engraving, done from a painting he had commissioned during his last mission to England, was meant for public distribution in New England. It portrayed the governor according to the latest fashion with an elegant powdered wig and a velvet waistcoat trimmed in gold brocade and the finest lace. Holding his commissions in one hand, he stood before Boston Harbor with an English naval vessel firing its salute. The seal of King George was placed prominently in a lower corner near the Belcher family crest. It was a handsome portrait. As Belcher gazed at the print, however, he convinced himself that it would become the object of public ridicule. And so he wrote his son in London that "Such a foolish affair will pull down much envy, and give occasion to your father's enemies to squirt & squib & what not. It is therefore my order . . . that you destroy the plate & burn all the impressions taken from it."[1]

He could scarcely conceal his pain and anger. In characteristic fashion he accused his son of commissioning the engraving without his permission. Belcher was uncommonly fond of having his portrait done; he commissioned six during his lifetime. This was an especially significant one. He loved being governor. The office put him at the center of his society, and it enabled him to realize the ideals that he had sought for so long and which had become so elusive in recent years. It gave him the opportunity to separate himself from his entrepreneurial origins, to become the complete model of gentility, and to lay the foundation for greater achievement in the next generation. Being governor enabled him to become the good ruler, the father of the community, the Nehemiah. He relished those moments when he stood before the public as the embodiment of its ideals and values.

These moments before the public promised fulfillment but also roused deep fears of exposure and ridicule. Belcher self-consciously played at his public roles. He rehearsed them in his mind always with an eye on his audience. He savored the thought of ceremonies where he stood at center stage, although he could never still the fears that he was subjecting himself to the "sneer & ridicule" of others. His appearances before the public required careful staging, he explained, for he would not allow himself to be exposed to the "Censure of the Staring Crowd."[2] And so he turned to writing letters to friends and associates. It was in this act that he acquired the means to select and control his audience. He became an inveterate letter writer. The pages of his letterbooks became a stage on which he rehearsed and improved upon his roles. It was there that he presented himself, albeit vicariously, to the public.

Belcher's presentation of himself was at heart an interpretation of the beliefs that held his society together. He played to his public for recognition, approval, and affirmation and with a sensitivity sharpened by deep-seated fears of rejection and humiliation. Thus, the interpretation he rendered was deliberately and meticulously crafted to represent the expectations of his audience. His rendering was intended to be conventional, commonplace, even cliché ridden. He thought himself capable of such a performance because he was a native son who knew his audience's beliefs and prejudices intimately, instinctively.

On taking office Belcher announced, "I am now become a perfect stranger to all Trade & Commerce" and have "become something of a Planter in a Small Place I have in the Country." The estate at Milton, where he had once expected to find solace for his disappointments, now signified life's fulfillment. Like other merchants who had the means to realize that ideal of landed gentility that haunted the provincial imagination, Belcher relished painting a picture of himself at his "cottage" set serenely in the countryside far from the tumults of the Boston crowd and the bustle of trade.[3] He seemed always in the process of devising improvements, of ordering materials for his gardens and furnishings for the home, and of instructing his gardener and workmen. According to his plans, he would have his guests make their approach along a broad, smoothly graded drive, lined with oaks and chestnuts. Gardens, well-tended and abloom with carnations and auriculas, surrounded the governor's mansion. Orchards and a vineyard were laid out on either side. Belcher planned meticulously. There were grounds to be prepared for planting his groves of almond, cork, and olive trees. His "cottage" was furnished richly with imported walnut chairs and mahogany tables. The walls were hung with portraits and paintings from England and Holland depicting scenes from the Bible.[4]

Belcher liked to write to friends and associates as if he were a gentleman farmer. But it was a role that he played vicariously. He preferred to live in Boston at center stage, and he rarely made the hour-long ride to his Milton estate. He thrived on public events and required that meticulous attention be given to their preparation. He spent heavily to maintain himself in the style and dignity that was befitting his office, "the King's Honour & my own."[5] His

Boston household was staffed with ten servants and several slaves. He entertained lavishly and took pains to acquire the best Portuguese Madeiras and French clarets. Always attentive to public appearances, he kept one coach and several carriages emblazoned with the family coat of arms. He dressed according to London's latest fashion. After ordering a cane that must be "fashionable, thick & substantial" with his crest engraved on its gold head, he realized that he also required "a very handsome sword-knot, cane string & Cockade all of Orange Ribbon richly flower'd with silver & Crimson." When seeking a new personal servant, he wrote asking friends in England that they find one who was trained to "shave & dress a wigg well, and do everything about a Gentleman."[6]

Belcher expressed his ambitions through his children much in the manner that he had learned from his father. As he watched his children grow to maturity, he prayed that he had cultivated a "good plant" and that they "will bring much more Fruit . . . than I have ever done." On marriage Belcher made it clear to his children that the decision was his and that while he considered their affections, he approached the subject principally as a dynastic arrangement. In 1727 Sarah, his second child, was nineteen when he agreed that she marry Byfield Lyde. It seemed to be a promising union. Belcher had done business with Lyde's father, and he knew the grandfather as a man of considerable wealth. He balked for a moment because Lyde was an Anglican. When the young man gave his assurance that he had forsaken the church, Belcher readily gave his consent.[7] Belcher, however, did not plan to see his two sons Andrew and Jonathan marry so soon. In 1728, he had taken Andrew to London where he expected the young man to make his way perhaps at the bar or in politics. The younger son, Jonathan, Jr., stayed behind to complete his education at Harvard and begin his training at Belcher Wharf.

Andrew, however, proved unsuited for his London assignment and returned to Boston with his father to take his place in trade alongside Byfield Lyde. Andrew seemed incapable of satisfying his father. Belcher watched his son at the family wharf closely; he regularly inspected the accounts, and Andrew always came up short. Belcher appointed him to offices twice but saw him lose both positions. Convinced that his son was a lazy, ungrateful, irresponsible wretch, Jonathan Belcher berated him ceaselessly and mercilessly. "From your entire Sloth & Negligence you have been represented not only as a most indolent but as a crazy Creature." He withdrew his affection; he lavished relatives with favors and rewards in hopes of pricking Andrew's jealousy. Nothing seemed to move the young man.[8]

Since Jonathan, Jr., evinced greater promise, it was decided that he should take his brother's place in London. In the spring of 1731, he set out with a package of his father's letters introducing him to English society. His mission was both vague and weighty. Often his father was uncertain what to expect. Sometimes he changed his mind, but he always aimed high. Most often he thought of his son studying at the Middle Temple and later embarking on a distinguished career at the English bar. He also expected his son's success would not be purchased at the expense of his virtue. Thus, he wrote two kinds of letters for his son. To Richard Partridge, for example, he wrote asking that Jonathan be cared for and shielded from the vices of the city. At the same time he wrote another letter to patrons, well placed ministers, and courtiers requesting them to aid his son's passage into London society. His letters were self-deprecating and apologetic for his son's rude American ways: "You must be so good," he wrote, "as to overlook the oddities in my Son too natural to us raw Americans. . . . I hope he will aspire after, at least, some faint Imitation of you bright Europeans."[9]

Belcher counseled his son in the same vein. Jonathan's speech marked him as a provincial. "When you say His Lordship *resents* such a singular Favor," he wrote correcting Jonathan, "You must observe the word *Resent* is a New England Phrase hardly known in the Polite World where you are, and is by all modern Authors taken in an ill sense, as when a man is angry or provok'd." Belcher pored over each report of his son's progress and composed lengthy letters of instruction. Jonathan must not fritter his time in "ordinary" company. He must dress according to the latest fashion. "When you wait upon Persons of any Distinction you must always take a Chair or Coach—and if not too far a Chair is handsomest." Jonathan must cultivate a proper manner and bearing if he were to make his mark in polite society. "Take care in General that good manners Courtesy & Affability make a proper part of your Character among Mankind." "Observe a just Decorum, & never make yourself mean or cheap to anybody." "Give no just occasion of Offense to anybody." Exercise moderation: "Endeavor after a Steady, Solid Government of your Affections, nothing will give you a greater Advantage, or a more graceful Elocution, than a constant happy Command of your Temper."[10]

Belcher was pleased to read that his son had spent a pleasant evening with the speaker of the House of Commons and that he had been introduced to the Duke of Newcastle, Sir Robert Walpole, the Archbishop of Canterbury, and Samuel Holden of the Bank of England. When Jonathan requested permission to study at Oxford, he agreed that a Master of Arts degree from that "most ancient & famous University" would earn "the most Honour." But he warned Jonathan not to become too absorbed in his studies lest he lose contact with London.[11]

"I am desirous," Belcher reminded his son, "to form you into a Great man" whose accomplishments would "reflect Honour on yourself, your Father & all to whom you are related." Although he did not explain what he expected, he let it be known that his son's achievements should somehow exceed his own. Whatever he became, be it a great lawyer, a judge, or even lord chancellor of the realm, would be realized only if Jonathan were single-minded, patient, and always calculating. Belcher was horrified to learn that Jonathan contemplated marriage. He instructed Partridge to intercede: "should he presume to carry on any Courtship without my Knowledge & free Consent, he will be very short of his Duty to so good a Father, and shou'd he marry without my Approbation, he woul'd at once destroy All my Designs for his Good & Advancement in the World." At any rate, Jonathan was forced to forsake all thoughts of marriage for the time. His father advised that he might wait for five or, perhaps, twenty years.[12]

In the meantime, Jonathan was considering election to Parliament. "Nothing certainly wou'd be more acceptable to me," Belcher wrote, "than to see you in the House of Commons." He encouraged Jonathan to study Roman and English history so that "your Part of all Debates may be wisely conducted." His son in the House would, no doubt, "be of Service for Strengthening" his own standing in London. He counseled Jonathan to seek a vacancy with care lest he fail. Belcher weighed the prospects for success and dwelt on the terrors of failure. If Jonathan stumbled, "It will give Glee & Pleasure to mine & your Enemies." Fearing public contempt and "Ridicule," he enjoined Jonathan to keep their plans secret. "It is much better the World shou'd know a Thing" when it has been accomplished than when it is planned, for "Mankind is wicked, full of ill nature & Envy—and when a Man misses his aim they are full of Sneer & Ridicule." "Secrecy," Belcher counseled his son, "is the Soul of Business."[13]

Eventually the Belchers decided to pin their ambitions on Tamworth. The election, to be held in the spring of 1734, required heavy expenditures: £5000 for the purchase of an estate and another £500 for campaign expenses. Belcher pledged "to Support & forward him all I possibly can in this matter" and called upon his brother-in-law, Richard Partridge, to "Stir up all your Friends, and resolve not to Suffer a Baulk." On learning, however, that Jonathan had placed a distant third at the polls, Belcher reflected that the defeat "will make Father & Son look contemptible, that they fancy'd they cou'd do a Thing that there was no likelyhood of."[14]

Though disappointed, Belcher still dreamed of the day when his son would take his seat in Parliament or when he would have established himself as "an eminent lawyer" at Westminster. While he prodded Jonathan forward, he also worried for his son "so far remov'd from our View & Observations," "surrounded with Snares and Temptations," and alone with only his "good Principles and Resolutions of Virtue." While he expected Jonathan to cast aside his provincial mannerisms, he also required that the young man remain a "true New England Christian." Belcher appealed to friends to watch over and protect the young provincial from the "Lures & Temptations with which he will be continually attackt." Thus, he gave Jonathan a dual message. While advising his son on the proper coffeehouses and encouraging him to seek a seat in Parliament, he warned Jonathan that he would be consorting with men of low principles and morality. These men spoke of virtue without understanding "true Religion." What they called religion was a "heathenish" faith without heart.[15]

While awaiting news of the Tamworth election, Belcher had learned that his son was seen attending the Church of England. Rebuke came swiftly. But the reports continued to arrive that Jonathan persisted. Belcher reminded the errant son that he had known others who had converted but had never observed them grow "in Vertue and vital Piety." They were "trifling with God & their own souls!" Yet argument and exhortation proved fruitless. In 1740 Jonathan was confirmed in the church. This act, his father lamented, "was the greatest folly you could be guilty of, & could I have imagind it, you had never sat your feet off your Native countrey."[16]

With the passing of each year Belcher grew increasingly impatient with his son's progress. Jonathan had taken a degree at Cambridge. He had been admitted to the bar. But he seemed incapable of establishing himself, at least according to his father's standards. His clients were principally Americans, often associates of his father. His income was meager, and he was still dependent on his father's allowance. He began to consider a move to Dublin. When Belcher reviewed his son's accounts, he raged. Sometimes he threatened to summon Jonathan home. But he could not let go his dynastic ambitions, and he continued to press Jonathan to "get forward into business at Westminster Hall." His letters were censorious and unrelenting. Jonathan's expenses had become an unbearable burden; "you know Jonthn with what Straits & Struggles I have encountered to bring you thus far forward in Life." It was time for him to shift for himself. Jonathan kept the wrong company. Once he had been advised not to fritter his time with New Englanders; later he was rebuked for shunning their company. Jonathan failed to write. Why did he neglect his "Duty to so fond a Father"? "Why will you so often stir up my anger on this head." Belcher threatened to suspend Jonathan's allowance; he invoked the Bible's curses upon the disobedient child. Nothing, however, could stir this "monster of ingratitude." "I cannot bear," Belcher raged, "to own him for my son."[17]

Relentlessly, Belcher berated and bullied both his sons. Why, he nagged, did they not exert themselves? Why would they not follow his example? Why did they choose instead to live their lives in sloth? Why did they turn a deaf ear to his instructions? He grew increasingly impatient as he noted the signs of his own mortality, and he prayed with renewed urgency that he might see his labors bear fruit in his sons. A paralysis had begun to afflict his right hand during the late 1730s, making it increasingly difficult to write. "The Shadows of the Evening are Thick upon me." When Andrew turned thirty-four in 1740 and Jonathan thirty, their prospects seemed dismal. Belcher's disappointments turned to bitterness. Nearly sixty, he reflected that he had come to that time in life when a parent might expect discharge from his duties. Increasingly, he played the aging patriarch, ignored, unappreciated, and disobeyed. How long, he demanded, would his children continue to burden him in his old age? When would they be able to stand on their own feet? It was not right, he railed, that "so loving" a father remain a "slave" to his sons.[18]

Andrew and Jonathan had not been raised to become independent adults. They grew to adulthood dominated, bullied, and incapable of freeing themselves. Their father wielded his authority in much the same manner as his own and, indeed, many fathers did. But the expectations imposed upon them were exceptional, if not fantastic. Neither son could succeed in his mission to London. The eldest had come home, already made well aware that he was a disappointment, to live under his father's continuing surveillance. While the youngest stayed abroad, he remained dependent on his father's allowance. Neither son mustered the ability to clash with his father. Andrew simply avoided his father's presence as often as he could, and Jonathan would not write. That both did not marry and establish families of their own until late in life is perhaps the most suggestive testimony of their lifelong subservience. Jonathan had several amorous adventures in England, all of which provoked stern disapproval. He did not marry until the age of forty-six. Andrew was still a bachelor at fifty, when his father found him a suitable mate. At first he balked, perhaps because he had not met the woman. But his father insisted, and he obediently performed his filial duty.

"His majesty's faithful servant"—the words themselves always seemed to resonate in Belcher's imagination.[19] He never tired of discussing the dignity and importance of his office and the duties that required his attention. He was constantly posing, seeking to represent himself as the model governor.

Governor Belcher's performance rested on his association with the symbols of royalty and of the Puritan fathers. Whenever he recounted his accomplishments, he began with his first trip to Hanover. While New Englanders joined to celebrate the monarchy and the Protestant succession, few could claim comparable connections with the royal family. The clergy summoned the people to be thankful for the king who respected the province's charter and liberties. They moved easily from this whiggish rhetoric to the Puritan legacy and the language of the covenant. The charter was prized because it served as another hedge protecting this covenanted people. While Belcher boasted of his connections with the cosmopolitan center, he took special pleasure in his association with the ministers. When he heard them call for rulers who would act like Nehemiahs, he knew that his first task was to stand at the wall protecting that legacy of the fathers.

Massachusetts had prospered from this inheritance. "The Province of the Massachusetts Bay," Belcher boasted, "may be justly esteem'd the Mistress of all North America, tho' but just entered upon its second Century." Since childhood he had heard the story of how the first planters had transformed a foreboding wilderness into a new Canaan. His travels had corroborated what he had learned. New England remained a primitive society. But primitiveness, he believed, was a condition to be cherished. It meant simplicity, the absence of corruption, and a vital and purified religion. To the New England clergy and to Belcher, the people's prosperity rested on a few simple principles: a bounty bestowed by God upon his people and the people, in turn, keeping faith with their covenant. Belcher believed that he governed a people distinguished for their morality and religion and for their enterprising spirit. In his eyes, theirs was a well-ordered society, not unlike John Winthrop's original model, which distinguished rich and poor and rulers and ruled. Unlike the society of Europe, however, New England's social distinctions had not become oppressive. The right to own property was secured by the crown. "No man that will be sober & diligent can fail of living comfortably in this country," Belcher believed. Even the "poorest Beggar among us" lived secure in the title to his land.[20]

With the ministers Belcher argued that the prosperity of the people depended largely on their rulers. He had heard Ebenezer Gay preach that "Rulers are the light of a People." Thomas Prince had used the province's centennial anniversary to raise up the example of the founding generation, and Thomas Foxcroft followed with his own recounting of "our Forefathers" and their heroic "Errand . . . into a waste Wilderness." When a minister turned to the Bible, he was likely to take inspiration from the Book of Nehemiah. All agreed that it was the duty of rulers to tend to the hedges protecting the people. Rulers should be "nursing fathers" of religion and preservers of the covenant. Ministers were also coming to recognize that the times demanded new talents, namely the ability to attend to constitutional matters and the protection of the charter. "The Care & Trust of our valuable, civil Liberties and Privileges" lay in the hands of the province's fathers. But these were whiggish embellishments on what remained essentially a traditional model of the Puritan Nehemiah.[21]

Indeed, the Old Testament governor of Judea provided a model that was especially appropriate to Massachusetts's experience under the new charter. The Nehemiah who rebuilt the walls of Jerusalem held his commission from the king of Persia. When New Englanders sought out Nehemiahs to protect their covenanted society, they refrained from applying their typology completely. No one could make explicit comparison between King Artaxerxes and King George. But New England's Nehemiahs were the builders of the walls protecting a covenanted people. While their authority derived from the king and his charter, their task was to protect the people from intrusions which, in fact, came from the imperial center. The idea of the Nehemiah captured the essential tensions and ambiguities between the cosmopolitan and provincial, the Puritan and the whig. While Massachusetts remembered its governors under the old charter as Nehemiahs standing heroically at the wall, it could not find comparable examples under the new charter. Both Governors Shute and Burnet were outsiders who had threatened to tear down the walls. Governor Dudley provoked ambiguous feelings. In sum, no one of Jonathan Belcher's generation had encountered a living model of a Nehemiah in the governor's office.

The Nehemiah in a whiggish world—the ideal was at once a powerful and an unstable synthesis that endured as long as its contradictions and tensions were left unexamined. Perhaps Belcher sensed that his mezzotint portrait carried too many cosmopolitan associations when he ordered its destruction. That he did not address the tensions directly or consciously was a matter of temperament. But none of his contemporaries seemed inclined to dismantle this consensus. Although Belcher's position as governor forced him to reveal himself, he did so in brief parenthetical remarks. He described his position as if it were free of contradiction and he always refrained from explication. "It has been my standing Care to promote the Interest and honour of the Crown and at ye same time to preserve the Liberties and Privileges of the People." He offered one qualification that caught the inherent tension: "while the king's orders don't interefere with the Charter, there can be no just Ground of Complaint."[22] True to character, he did not elaborate. Although at times Belcher paid his respects to the principle of constitutional balance, he chose not to explain his position.

Belcher's remarks when taken with his behavior reflect certain basic beliefs. He did not hold the king's orders in high esteem. Parliament's regulations such as the navigation acts and timber laws were nuisances. Instructions to protect the Church of England were impositions to be avoided. The laws of England did not necessarily apply to New England. When he stated these beliefs, he made them as parenthetical remarks.[23] On the one hand, he eagerly gathered the symbols of monarchical authority unto himself and took pride in his association with the king. On the other hand, he often read his instructions from his "royal master" as if they were intrusions. On the one hand, he derived his legal authority to govern from the king, but on the other, he viewed his responsibilities in terms of the people's welfare and of himself as their caretaker and protector. In principle there was no contradiction: Anglo-Americans joined to celebrate a king who was a caretaker, a father of the people. In practice tensions emerged. Sometimes the governor had to mediate between imperial and provincial interests. Sometimes he was forced to play the dissembler in order to protect the people. If he had to play the courtier, so too did the archetypal Nehemiah before he became the builder of the walls.

At heart Belcher was a Nehemiah protecting the traditional New England way. He secured special pleasures from promoting the welfare of Harvard College. He used his office to advance the missions of the New England Company. It was in the company of the clergy that he found fulfillment. Writing to a clergyman gave him the opportunity to play the Nehemiah. His letters echoed what he heard from the pulpit. He dwelt upon the Puritan forebears, that "sett of Excellent Persons," "our Forefathers" who came to "this desert" much like God's "Covenant People" and planted a "noble Vine." By doing so he made himself a caretaker of that tradition. When he attended to the present, he echoed the warnings of the self-styled Jeremiahs who preached their warnings. "Luxury and vanity too much swallow up the thoughts of the present and rising generation. . . . Vice and prophaness will (like a torrent) soon carry all. Oh Tempora! Oh Mores!" Still there was hope. There remained a "Remnant" of the saints whose "prayers are daily going up to the God of all mercy."[24]

He responded to the clergy's call for rulers who would act as "nursing fathers" to religion. It was his task, he reflected, to have a "just & proper Regard to the Honour & Glory of God, in upholding his Religion & Worship." Belcher attended to the election sermons that were delivered in Boston and in neighboring colonies. Connecticut's Samuel Whittelsey moved him to reflect: "My Prayer to God is that Rulers & Ruled may more & more devote themselves to seek the Publick Good and more especially by promoting Vertue & true Religion. In this way we may hope to wrestle down a blessing on the present & future Generations." The clergy responded in kind. Samuel Wigglesworth, for one, praised the governor for promoting religion and Harvard College like a "Nursing father." "Your Self shall have an honourable Name to all Futurity with Jehoiada, Nehemiah, and others, who have headed Reformations in most Corrupt and Degenerate Ages."[25]

New England's Jeremiahs, while warning the people of their sins and of imminent judgment, set the stage for the Nehemiah. One was dependent on the other. Jeremiah and Nehemiah joined in single chorus lamenting New England's decline. Their lamentations had turned into ritual, and their rhetoric seemed commonplace. Within these conventions, however, New Englanders were grappling with real, significant, and disturbing changes.

By the third decade of the eighteenth century, the voices of dissent and disorder seemed to be growing louder. Anglicans and Quakers were increasing in numbers and becoming more visible. Congregationalism was under siege. Massachusetts had embraced a royal authority that required toleration for dissent and expected the establishment to be the Church of England. In addition, the traditional conception of a social order articulated by well-defined ranks and classes but bound together by sentiments of community was rapidly evaporating. Distinctions between rich and poor were becoming greater. Classes clashed in the streets of Boston. Rival interests competed for control of government, and factionalism was rampant. Those who were fomenting change often spoke the traditional vocabulary. Some were crafting a new vocabulary to fit the world they were creating. Constitutional questions and economic issues did not fit easily into the inherited way of looking at the world. The currency debates alone caused the caretakers of the New England way to doubt their abilities.

When Governor Belcher delivered his first address to the General Court, he invoked memories of "our Ancestors" and "our Fathers" and, like a Nehemiah, promised to protect that legacy. At the same time, he spoke as a royal servant. The king had ordered him to enforce "all the Laws now in Force against Immorality and Impiety" and to recommend "enacting such others as may best promote and encourage our most holy Religion." He moved smoothly from Puritan to imperial official as if there were no tensions. While taking care to assure his audience that he remained a Puritan at heart, he raised the thorny issue of religious toleration. "One of the shining Graces of His Majesty's Reign" was "that Dissenters of all Denominations in Great Britain, enjoy the Toleration in its full Ease and Extent." Massachusetts should "imitate the Royal Indulgence" and take care lest it pass laws that may "carry in them a Spirit of Rigour or Severity to those who may conscientiously differ from us in the Modes of Divine Worship." Toleration had special meaning for Massachusetts, he reminded the lawmakers, "since our Ancestors (but in the last Century) left their native Country, as not able to comply with any Impositions on their Consciences."[26]

He was glossing over the past and reframing the subject. The issue was not toleration; it was whether the religious establishment would be the Congregationalism of his forebears or the Church of England. Since childhood Belcher had heard his elders recall the days of the old charter when the government protected the Puritan establishment. His generation, which had been raised in the aftermath of the Glorious Revolution, had learned to celebrate the Protestant succession and with it the new charter. By embracing the Protestant revolution of 1688, however, Massachusetts also accepted a new and intrusive imperial authority that required the Puritans to end their bloody persecutions. These were tolerating times. Belcher's brother-in-law, Richard Partridge, was a prominent English Quaker. Tastes had changed so that a gentleman was judged by his open-mindedness. Belcher counted it as one of his accomplishments that he rejected the "stingy narrow notions of Christianity which reigned too much in the first beginnings of this country." Indeed, he knew that he was recommending nothing controversial when he addressed the lawmakers. The controversy turned on his instructions requiring him to promote the Church of England as the establishment. He had crafted his address to assure the lawmakers that he remained faithful to the church of the fathers. While his office prevented him from being explicit, he took care to assure his audience that he would not make the Congregational establishment into a denomination of tolerated dissenters. Thus, he concluded his discussion of religion by turning to the college at Cambridge. Again speaking like a Nehemiah, he assured the lawmakers that he would "embrace every Opportunity you'l put in my Power of nourishing that Seminary of Religion and Learning."[27]

For more than thirty years, the Massachusetts General Court had been struggling to preserve the Congregational establishment.[28] When it passed legislation in the 1690s requiring that taxes be paid toward the support of the Congregational churches, Quakers and Anglicans protested. Quakers claimed protection under the Act of Toleration, and Anglicans asserted that the same act made them into the established church and the Congregationalists the dissenters. The government in Boston was unimpressed. When some diehards refused to pay their taxes, warrants were issued for their arrest. In the 1720s representatives of the Anglicans and of the Friends took their appeals to London. While both opposed the Puritan churches, Quakers also feared Anglican claims to be the true establishment and preferred to act independently. The English government, already predisposed to attend to the Anglicans, had come to respect the Quakers' political organization, especially their influence at the polls. Boston, consequently, could not ignore the challenge. The legislature extended tax relief to the Anglicans in 1727 and to the Quakers in 1728. It made the concessions grudgingly. The standards for exemption from taxation were made so stringent that many could not qualify. The protests resumed, and tax resistors were once again being brought before the local courts.

Many New Englanders, like Belcher, remained contemptuous of Quaker and Anglican beliefs but were willing to tolerate them as long as the Puritan establishment remained in place. It was the Anglicans' determination to overturn the establishment that made them the greater threat. Royal governors came with instructions to promote the church's interests, and Anglicans were building churches and gaining converts. Though the Anglicans remained a minority, Congregationalists like Belcher worried for the future. The Society for the Propagation of the Gospel had come, it claimed, to convert the Indians, but many Puritans suspected that its real intent was to spearhead an assault on the New England way. They spied a conspiracy aimed at Harvard College. In 1723 Timothy Cutler, Yale College's infamous apostate, returned from England, where he had been ordained an Anglican priest and took up his new post at Boston's Christ Church. He became the symbol and champion of the Anglican assault. One day, he expected to see the church install a bishop in Boston and then take control of his alma mater in Cambridge.

Anglicans and Quakers were preparing another appeal to London against the new tax laws when Belcher took office. During his last stay in London, he had listened while his brother-in-law recounted his efforts to seek relief. He could see that Partridge was a leading spokesman for the Quaker interest and that the Quakers exercised a formidable influence with the government. The Friends' protest in tandem with the Anglican appeals made for a serious assault on Massachusetts's church establishment. To diminish the threat required, first, that the Massachusetts government placate the Quakers. In 1731, he pressed the legislature to pass a relief bill for "the People among us called Quakers, who think themselves under soe great Hardships from some of the Laws of this Province." After a month of campaigning and personally courting several lawmakers, he signed a bill into law. As he reported to Partridge, the Quakers "never had a Govr so much of their friend as the present."[29] The Quakers on both sides of the ocean seemed to agree.

The Anglicans were outraged that the relief act excluded them. Belcher was not surprised by their reaction. He knew that they had protested his appointment and that they were writing to church authorities and government officials in London to undermine his reputation. Though concerned, he had resolved not to bend to their demands. He also understood that prudence required him to eschew heroic confrontation and that a successful Nehemiah must engage in duplicity and deceit. Regularly, he wrote to English churchmen and politicians as if he were a friend to the Anglican interest. He volunteered that although he had been raised a Puritan, he accepted many of the church's doctrines. At times he attended Timothy Cutler's church and often entertained leading Anglicans at his dinner table. He listened to them recount their struggles, offered them aid, and on occasion promoted their projects. He appealed to the Duke of Grafton: Dr. Cutler's parishioners were unable to complete the erection of their church and had applied to him "to intercede with your Grace in their behalf." Feigning sympathy for the church's "Infant State," he asked that funds be sent for finishing the building and purchasing prayer books. "The Church of England itself is yet in this country in its infancy and wants all the assistance and Countenance it can have."[30]

Few were fooled. Sometimes Belcher revealed himself. One evening Governor Belcher entertained several of the province's leading lights, including two prominent Anglicans. During the dinner the conversation turned to religion and inevitably to the differences between the Anglican and Congregational churches. Several glasses of port had been poured. Belcher explained that he could not respect a church so notorious for the depravity of its members. Then the conversation turned to the establishment itself. Belcher listened to the Anglicans with growing impatience as they referred to themselves as the official church and the Congregationalists as dissenting sectarians. Suddenly he burst out: "We are the church and you are the Dissenters." One churchman chose to hold his tongue. The other, however, countered that the governor's position violated the Act of Toleration. Belcher became quiet suddenly. Sensing that he had gone too far, he replied that he would not "dispute the matter" longer. Reports of the argument were sent to London. Governor Belcher provided the churchmen with additional evidence confirming their assessment. They were appalled when he endorsed republication of the Cambridge Platform of 1648, which called for the rooting out of bishops and archbishops. When it came time to issue a proclamation for a day of fasting or thanksgiving, he could not resist selecting dates that conflicted with Anglican holidays.[31]

The Congregational Church was not the establishment of Massachusetts, Governor Belcher explained to the Bishop of London. The people of each town had the right to make whatever denomination they chose to be their official church. "Should any Town or Parish in the Province Elect a Clergyman of the Chh of England to be their minister, and he be qualify'd as the Law directs, altho' 9/20s of such Parish should be Dissenters, yet by the Laws of the Province they wou'd be oblig'd to pay to the Maintenance of such a Minister." He had not devised the argument; it was one commonly employed by Congregationalist clergymen. Sometimes he explained that most towns rejected the Anglican church because of the intemperate and offensive manner of its leading representatives. His conclusion that the Church of England was "as much establisht by the Laws of this Province, as that of the Independents Presbyterians or Baptists" could only serve to measure the distance between himself and the bishop.[32]

Evasion and duplicity had become well-established strategies for warding off intrusions from London. Sometimes it was necessary to make concessions. In June 1735 the House of Representatives began consideration of a bill extending tax relief to Anglicans. The initiative had not come from the governor, at least not by way of a message. But both the governor and a majority of lawmakers knew that the Privy Council in London was about to respond favorably to Anglican petitions for relief. The governor signed a relief bill. The provisions were not as liberal as those granted to others, and the Congregational establishment remained securely in place. Moreover the law was scheduled to expire in five years.[33]

Belcher's caring for the covenant, while not heroic, proved appropriate for the times. Most important, the Massachusetts religious establishment endured. Boston's Anglicans, such as Cutler, came to such an assessment. They realized that they could not match his skill and ability to manipulate the imperial machinery. Moreover, Belcher's sponsorship of Quaker relief had earned him impressive allies among powerful English Friends. The Congregational clergy also understood that Belcher was a Nehemiah for the times. Ministers supported his administration from their pulpits. When they learned that his government was under attack in London, they called upon their dissenting allies in England to come to his defense.[34]

Not only did New England expect its rulers to be "nursing fathers" of its churches, it also looked to them as guardians at the frontiers. The wilderness set the context for the Nehemiah. He was protector of a legacy that was rooted in that moment when a covenanted people had swarmed out of England to plant a "wilderness Canaan." The first Nehemiahs were remembered for their labors in caring for that covenant "hedge" that secured the people from the "howling wilderness." They had subdued the land and turned it into a garden. The afflictions they had suffered at the hands of the native "savage" and the triumphs they had finally achieved were remembered as divine providences and confirming signs of their mission. Past encounters with the wilderness merged with the present. The massacre at Deerfield in 1704 and the depredations that the settlers of Maine endured at the hands of Father Rale's Indians during the 1720s were recent chapters in the history of the founders' "errand into the wilderness."

Imperialism, greed, and religion moved this wilderness drama from the beginning. The founders had tamed the land's native inhabitants by the Bible and sword. Their conquest had been made in the name of profit and utopian communalism. Their descendants added their revisions to the drama to fit within the new imperial setting. The frontier wars became skirmishes in the global conflict between the crowns of England and France. Though fighting had ceased when Belcher took office, Americans gleaned the news from Europe, always expecting to find the harbingers of renewed conflict. Reports of frontier violence kept them attentive to the interior. Meanwhile the expansion of Massachusetts continued. New towns were being founded, and land speculators were eagerly laying out their claims.[35]

In August 1735 Governor Belcher set out from Boston to confer with the western tribes, which were assembling at Deerfield.[36] This was the third in a series of conferences he had held to secure the frontiers. During the past two years he had been negotiating with the tribes of the Maine region, which were known French allies. Now he turned his attention westward and to the tribes whose sympathies were uncertain. The Deerfield meeting promised to be a major event in his administration. Even the Caughnawaga Mohawks, who were infamous in Boston for their long time friendship with the French, their conversion to Catholicism, and their participation in the Deerfield massacre, had agreed to come. Elaborate preparations had been made. Presents were purchased. Delegations from the House of Representatives and the Council joined the governor. Dignitaries from the towns surrounding Deerfield assembled to greet the governor's party. Workmen had erected a tent one hundred feet in length for the conference. For five days the governor received the delegations from the Caughnawaga, Housatonics, Schaghticokes, and Mohegans; presented them with gifts; and listened to their professions of friendship and peace. He counted the conference a triumph, especially when the aged Caughnawaga chief Ountaussoogoe drank to the health of King George and the governor. The conference was doubly momentous because it marked the establishment of a mission to the Housatonics.

Belcher, an active member of the New England Company, had long dreamed of making the Indians over into good Protestants. In 1730, after receiving his commissions of appointment and before he left London, he had approached the officers of the company with a proposal to establish a mission. The site was on the coast, north of Portsmouth, in Massachusetts's York County. He knew the area and he assured the company directors that the soil was rich and the prospects for a profitable settlement were enticing. The French, however, had been allowed to cultivate their influence in the area for too long. This was the time, since conflict on this frontier had abated, for the English to seize the initiative. His proposal was simply that the company join with the Massachusetts government to plant a settlement of English and friendly Indians. The Massachusetts General Court, he proposed, would grant the lands. The company would provide the funds necessary for the erection of a schoolhouse and church and for the support of the minister and teacher. The minister and teacher, both conversant in the native tongue, would bring English ways to the Indians. The children would learn crafts from the English settlers. With civilization would follow conversion: "By these means they would soon be Civilized & more easily brought into the knowledge & esteem of the true Christian Religion." The company's directors endorsed the plan and voted to send the funds once the legislature had granted the lands.[37]

The Massachusetts lawmakers responded politely to the proposal but failed to provide the lands. In the meantime, Belcher turned to the Penobscot Indians in the hopes of inducing them to live at the settlement. The Protestant faith, he explained, was far superior to papist superstition. The Indians were not convinced, but Belcher persevered. He applied to Scotland's Society for Propagating Christian Knowledge for aid to support missions on the Kennebec River in Maine and on the northern banks of the

Connecticut River.[38] Encouraged by the response, he began to search for candidates for missionaries. In August 1734, Belcher and the Boston council of the New England Company met to discuss plans for a mission to the Housatonic Indians in western Massachusetts. The leading lights of Hampshire County—"Squire" John Stoddard and his cousin Jonathan Edwards, the powerful Williams family, and Samuel Hopkins—were convinced that the local Housatonics remained unaffected by French influence and were therefore prime candidates for conversion. Initial plans for a settlement had been made. The promoters had already recruited John Sergeant, a tutor at Yale, to serve as minister and Timothy Woodbridge to teach the school. The Boston council was impressed and voted to support the mission. As the governor watched the project's progress, he grew steadily more enthusiastic.[39]

The Deerfield Conference marked the formal establishment of the mission. Belcher received the Housatonics on the second day of the conference: "I look upon you," he assured them, "as my Children, and hope you are good Subjects of King George, and I shall always take the same Care of you as of the English, and take you under my Protection at all times." The Indians remained silent, and he continued. They had done well to accept Sergeant and Woodbridge. "Religion is a serious thing, and it ought to be always born in your Minds." Still the Indians remained silent. The next day they replied that although they were willing to accept Christ, they feared the severity of English laws, especially those regarding debt. Belcher assured them that the laws were good but that if they had need for protection, they should apply to Colonel Stoddard, "who will see you have Justice done you."[40]

The last day of the conference was a Sunday and the occasion for John Sergeant's ordination. Belcher came to church that morning, attended by councilors, representatives, and numerous dignitaries both clerical and lay. He took his seat in the first pew while the Indians were escorted to the balcony. Nathaniel Appleton had come from Cambridge to deliver the sermon. William Williams from the neighboring Hatfield congregation presided over the ordination service. "Hands were laid upon Mr. Sargent." Then Stephen Williams, Springfield's minister, turned to the Indians "Seated in the Gallery by themselves; and asked them if they were desirous of having Mr. Sergent for their Minister. . . . Whereupon: they all rose up by one Consent, and with grave as well as cheerful Countenances signified their full, and hearty Acceptance of him."[41]

The next year Belcher met with the Housatonics to review their progress. Although the government had granted lands for settling a mission at Stockbridge, funds were needed for farming implements and a school building. He summoned the lawmakers to remember the missionary zeal that had guided their fathers and to consider "this poor People." What did not come from Massachusetts he received from the New England Company. Isaac Hollis established a fund that would yield £500 a year for educating a dozen Indian boys, and Samuel Holden gave £100 for the education of Indian women. As he watched the mission's progress, Governor Belcher made himself its protector and patron. Even after he left office, he watched and worried over the mission's welfare.[42]

Gospelizing the Indians was, Belcher reminded the General Court, "the Principal End of our Ancestors in the first Settlement of this Plantation."[43] Although he exaggerated, he captured an important element in New England's sense of mission. Since the days of John Eliot and John Winthrop, New Englanders had acknowledged that by making the natives into good Protestants, missionaries pacified the wilderness and secured the frontiers so that this covenanted people could extend control over the land, plant new settlements, and multiply in numbers. From the beginning religion blended with land hunger to inspire New England's imperial imagination. While the planters of the first towns pledged themselves to the creation of well-knit and loving communities, they also lusted for the gains that came from speculating in the land. Community builders and loving neighbors were also entrepreneurs and profiteers. While Belcher and his contemporaries employed the vocabulary of the fathers, they also spoke with special accent on the acquisitive. In increasing numbers men like Belcher were investing in lands, developing farms for rent, and laying out towns to settle. They were becoming absentee landlords and the proprietors of towns they rarely visited. Since his youthful days as a merchant, Belcher had been developing tennent farms in Connecticut and speculating in properties throughout Massachusetts, which were by his estimate worth nearly £70,000.[44]

On returning from a conference with the Penobscot Indians of Maine, Belcher wrote to Christopher Toppan, the minister at Newbury. The intent of his letter, however, was not to discuss the possibility of winning souls to the Protestant cause. He knew the minister as an inveterate speculator in land especially in the regions northward, and he had returned amazed at the bounty that he had encountered. He had toured the "fine Harbours and Rivers full of Fish," and he had surveyed the "Champion Lands fill'd with noble Timber of all Sorts, . . . which when clear'd will be fit for the Sythe & the Plough." He wrote as one speculator to another, and soon the two men were corresponding regularly. They knew that the profits to be realized were immense but elusive as long as Massachusetts's claims to the region were disputed by rival land companies.[45] Belcher assured Toppan that he would use his influence to the utmost to ward off the challengers. Perhaps he hoped to be compensated.

But his motives included more than personal profit. From Belcher's perspective it was land hunger that provided the driving energy in New England's struggle to subdue the wilderness. He conferred regularly with speculators like himself. The conference with the Penobscots had been undertaken to secure peace, to establish a mission, and to open the region for settlement. Numerous speculators besides Toppan stood poised ready to develop the region. The most influential group was the Mucongas Company headed by Elisha Cooke. The principal obstacle, however, came not from the Indians but from England and a rival land company that argued its claims superseded the grants made under the Massachusetts charter. While Massachusetts pled its case in London, the rival company had taken the initiative. It had found an agent in David Dunbar, the surveyor general of the king's woods and Belcher's recently appointed lieutenant governor in New Hampshire, and with his assistance it was recruiting Scots-Irish immigrants for settlement at Fort Frederick in Casco Bay. Belcher was horrified. It was Dunbar's challenge that prompted him to make the trip to Maine and on his return to appeal to the General Court. Forts must be rebuilt and missions established in preparation for settlement by "good Protestants." The soils were rich, the rivers overflowed with fish, the forests abounded with prime timber, the harbors were naturally suited for commerce. And there were souls to be saved.[46]

Belcher's imagination quickened as he watched the speculators and proprietors devising schemes for subduing the wilderness. Sometimes he considered joining with them, and he did on occasion. Even if he did not invest, he participated vicariously. New England was already in the midst of a powerful expansionist drive when he took office. Massachusetts witnessed the establishment of over a hundred towns during the twenty-five years after the peace of Utrecht. Belcher used his office to champion Massachusetts's territorial claims in the regions of Maine and along the Merrimack River. Sometimes the General Court recognized his services by granting him lands. But always he was known as a friend of the expansionists.

Belcher surveyed the land as an improver and a visionary whose perspective had been formed in the marketplace. The riches of the land translated into commodities for extraction and export. As governor, he regularly urged the legislature to encourage the development of resources. "The Climate and Soil of New-England is well adapted to the raising of Masts, Hemp, and other Naval Stores." He forecast that "Plenty of Iron Mines" awaited investors. He recommended that encouragement be given to manufactures of canvas and potash; their export would bring profits, which in turn would right the balance of trade. The General Court shared his vision. It was quick to grant aid in the form of lands and loans to the entrepreneurs who proposed to build a factory for paper manufacture, to erect casting furnaces, or to start a mining operation. When Thomas Plaisted, for example, set out to manufacture potash, the lawmakers and the governor agreed that the venture deserved support and granted him a loan. Belcher called for the establishment of bounties to encourage the production of hemp, naval stores, and grain for export. In his effort to encourage the production of hemp and flax, he applied to London for seeds and ordered the printing of books on their cultivation to be distributed to each representative and town in the province. The legislature responded by voting bounties on hemp and flax as well as on grains for export.[47]

Governor Belcher liked to think that he knew the people of Massachusetts and that he understood what was in their interest. His understanding was in fact shaped by his experience at Belcher Wharf. What he meant by *the people* was his community of Boston and his fellow merchants. When he spoke of the people's welfare, he thought in terms of commerce. In spatial terms he mapped the world from Boston looking outward into the Atlantic trading community. He had little reason to attend to New England's interior. As a merchant and absentee landlord, he relied on agents to represent his interests and to report on local conditions. These agents and his business with them shaped his understanding of the interior. But he had little firsthand contact with the self-sufficient farmers in the isolated communities. Indeed, the record documents that during his eleven years as governor he made only two trips into the backcountry. Moreover, many of the representatives who came to Boston from these rural communities and were important enough to meet with the governor were entrepreneurs like himself. Meeting with them confirmed his belief that he was of the same flesh and bone as the people.

These entrepreneurs spoke the language of their fathers; they joined in celebrating the ideals of an organic community and the personal virtues of selfless patriotism. Yet these adventurers in the marketplace were transforming the world that they inherited and in the process were refashioning the traditional vocabulary. They spoke of their oneness with the people but with the accents of the land speculator and merchant. They were creating the social distinctions between rich and poor in the town of Boston and in the country towns as well. Yet they spoke the vocabulary of the jeremiad. They considered themselves conservators of tradition, while at the same time they were the advance agents of change. Their ministers, such as Ebenezer Pemberton, spoke less of equity or the moral responsibility of the rich and powerful toward the poor and dependent. They said less against commerce and its corrosive influence on the moral order. When they prayed for good rulers, they turned for inspiration to New England's first Nehemiahs. But the Nehemiah they presented was a man who could attend to the world of trade, the mysteries of money and currency, who understood the world of banking, and who possessed the grace and ability to maneuver through the anterooms of power in London.

Covenant and charter fused, and so too did religion and commerce. Governor Belcher summoned the people and their lawmakers to the protection of religion and its institutions and in the same breath recommended measures for nurturing the province's commercial well-being. He attended to clergymen and merchants alike and often invited both to discuss provincial affairs at his dinner table. Much in the manner that he played the Nehemiah in warding off Timothy Cutler's Anglican campaign, he conspired to curb a zealous official in his efforts to enforce England's economic regulations. He became a dissembler. When writing to London, he presented himself as if he were dedicated to protecting New England's mast trees, which were reserved for the king's navy. At the same time, illegal timber cutters knew that they had a friend in the governor. When Boston's merchants learned that Parliament was considering new customs legislation, they conferred with the governor, who, in turn, assured them that he would employ his influence to protect them.[48]

The times, however, required more than the talents of the courtier. Boston's economy was foundering in depression when Belcher came to office. Trade declined precipitously. Imports fell by ten percent during Belcher's administration. The shipyards were quiet. Trade deficits grew, and the money supply might have shrunk had it not been for government printing. Instead, the economy was awash in a sea of paper currencies. The real value of these currencies grew increasingly suspect and declined as it became clear that the government would not take steps toward redemption. As inflation spiraled upward, wages remained stagnant. The cost of living soared, and the ranks of the poor increased dramatically. The cost of poor relief in Boston doubled, and the town's almshouse could no longer accommodate the needy population. The voices of discontent grew louder, and the wealthy were vilified publicly. As the depression continued, its effects were felt in the countryside. Belcher addressed the lawmakers in alarm. He nagged at them relentlessly to attend to the "decaying state of the Trade of the Province," the mounting trade deficits, and "the low Ebb" to which "our Bills of Credit" have fallen.[49]

The currency question became the focus of discussion. Government notes made as loans to private persons or as substitutes for taxation amounted to nearly £300,000 when Belcher took office. Not only was he personally appalled by government's inability to maintain the notes at stable value but he was also prodded by growing pressures from London to take action. His instructions, which required him to achieve redemption by 1741, would reduce the province's money supply by nearly ninety percent. At the same time, paper money was reawakening longstanding divisions within the province. The government seemed incapable of reaching a solution, and the presses of

Boston burst out with a profusion of pamphlets discussing the economic crisis. The participants confronted a series of issues, broad, profound, and also bewildering. The debate turned on deep-seated problems of trade and Massachusetts's place within the Atlantic economy. Inevitably and recurringly it touched on the nature of the province's colonial status. It provoked discussion of the relationship between government and the people and finally of the nature of this society. Perhaps most disquieting, it required concerned New Englanders to grapple with new and unfamiliar subjects related to the nature of money and the workings of the marketplace. This was an alien territory that strained old vocabularies and required the devising of new forms of thought. Clergymen who entered the foray found themselves floundering and felt their intellectual authority somehow diminished.

Of course, many framed the money question as a traditional issue concerning public morality. The discussion awakened longstanding discomforts with commerce. A wanton trade in expensive and often frivolous English imports worked with the "fatal" and profligate emission of paper money to discourage honest labor, to stunt "the Growth of Agriculture and Manufactures," and to nurture "Extravagance, Vanity and Luxury." Selfishness and slothfulness became commonplace. The people sank into poverty. Debtors defrauded their creditors by repaying loans in depreciated paper money. The enemies of paper money deprecated its advocates as thieves acting on private selfish motives. If one pamphlet writer accused the rich of indulging in luxuries, another blamed the poor for living irresponsibly beyond their means. Whatever their differences, these moral economists saw a society in which predators were free to act upon their rapacious lusts. The catalogues of casualties ranged from widows and orphans to clergymen and officials who lived on fixed incomes. If the causes for an imbalance of trade and dormant industry were moral, so too were the solutions. Sumptuary laws would quash the selfish lust for luxury as would measures to withdraw paper money from circulation. By cleansing itself of this "Dishonest Trash," Massachusetts would enter a "Golden Age" in which the moral order would be restored and agriculture and manufactures would flourish.[50]

Boston's Jeremiahs often indulged themselves in hyperbole when they fulminated against commerce's corrosive influence on the commonwealth. What they objected to was trade run wild. Few, even among New England's original Jeremiahs, could envision a world without trade. Indeed, the debate did not turn on whether a paper currency was necessary. The question was what kind of currency policy was appropriate. Inevitably that discussion prompted inquiries into the nature of wealth, trade, value, and money. What then was this thing called paper money? A variety of answers was offered. One stock reply was that the value of money was based on a universal standard and that that standard was bullion, or gold and silver. But others countered that value was a social convention and that the standard might vary from one people to another. Anything might do. In America the standard might be land. Many entered the debate by addressing the nagging question of inflation or proposing measures to secure the value of money. It was government's responsibility, some argued, to fix the value of money, usually to bullion. Another argument emerged that the value fluctuated according to the marketplace, the principles of supply and demand, and the public's confidence in an issue.[51] The debate was often confused, and the participants expressed themselves awkwardly. In their efforts to understand the world they were creating, they struggled against old vocabularies of the jeremiad and explored new and unfamiliar realms. They were forced to manage calculations of resources and balances of trade. In the process they were coming to own that Governor Winthrop's "city on a hill" could endure only if they learned from the banking capitals of London, Amsterdam, and even Venice.

What moved the debate was the practical question, what to do about the provincial currency. The answers seemed to multiply. But two persuasions emerged from the cacophony of voices. One group of traditionalists, or contractionists, called for strict limits on the amount of paper in circulation. The government had issued money on weak foundation, had printed too much, then had shirked its responsibility to call in the notes, and had allowed them to sink in value. Consequently the colony suffered a decline in trade. Redemption was necessary for economic recovery. Furthermore, the government must limit itself in the future, and it must issue its currency only on gold and silver redemption. Since the contractionist flew in the face of prevailing opinion, he was forced to turn to the agency of royal authority, the governor and his instructions specifically, to restrain the irresponsible democracy in the House of Representatives. Such proposals provoked an outcry. The economy depended on an expansionist paper money policy. Notes based on land values were appropriate for a people struggling with an adverse balance of payments and a consequent scarcity of bullion. Contraction entailed taxation and recalling loans. The burden was too much for a people already overwhelmed by economic hardships. Thus, an expansionist majority in the House of Representatives rejected contraction because it would "bring the greatest Oppressions upon Multitudes, if not utter Stagnation of our Trade and Business."[52]

The debate brought the government to stalemate. Enterprising expansionists struck out on their own. In 1734 a group of Boston merchants formed a private bank that would issue notes redeemable in silver with interest in ten years. Their bills, however, proved to be so stable in value that they quickly vanished from circulation into the pockets of investors. Three years later another proposal was made to establish a private bank that would issue its notes based on land since silver had become so scarce. The proposals multiplied.

In 1740 one Bostonian lamented that "We have of late had so many Money Schemes upon the Anvil."[53] John Colman had revived his old land bank with expectations to issue £600,000 in notes. In retaliation a group of Boston merchants met to establish a bank that would issue notes based on silver.

Critics of the Merchants Bank warned that it posed a threat to the authority of government, exposed the people to the oppression of private individuals, and thereby rent the bonds of community and turned public virtue into a mockery. Their arguments derived from traditional beliefs. It was the purpose of government to restrain men who "would prey upon one another like Fish in the Sea." To allow such a project would be to break down "the Hedge or Wall" protecting the people from predators and profiteers.[54] Not so, countered the bank's defenders. The government had fallen victim to the influence of debtors who sought to escape their obligations and to cheat their creditors with worthless money. The bank's notes would provide the public with a stable and honest currency necessary for the people to realize their prosperity.

Proposals for reform multiplied and opinions grew more divisive. Clergymen spoke in alarm as they witnessed the twin evils of the marketplace, selfishness and factiousness, overcome the sentiments of public-mindedness. In the election sermon of 1734, John Barnard summoned the people to the spirit of public virtue that had guided their fathers. Massachusetts's rulers must root out "mercantile Craftiness" and deceit in "Barter and Exchange." They must take steps to fix the value of paper money. Four years later, John Webb of Boston's New North Church called upon Governor Belcher and the lawmakers to "prevent the cruel Oppression and Injustice that has, for a long time, been reigning among us, on the account of the uncertain and fluctuating State of our Medium of Trade." Yet factious spirits seemed to run rampant. They infected the House of Representatives, charged its critics, and were turning the democracy into a beast. Creditors lay naked and exposed before their debtors. In reply, others accused the rich and powerful of betraying their patriarchal duties and turning themselves into oppressors of the poor. But all agreed that the traditional ideals of public order were in jeopardy.[55]

New Englanders instinctively resorted to the conventions of the jeremiad to make sense of change. For many the vocabulary of declension provided the means for grappling with new issues—often of their own making—and to make them manageable. But what they called a crisis of spirit was, in fact, a significant cultural shift. While exploring new subjects—the operations of the marketplace, the impact of the Atlantic economy on their lives, the imperial relationship, and constitutional arrangements—they were trying out new vocabularies to explain money, value, and rates of exchange. Their discussions, which often turned to quibbling over definitions of terms; their exchanges, which degenerated into logic chopping; and their debates, which often turned to arguments *ad hominem,* all reflected the confusions.

New Englanders were not only in disagreement over specific issues, they were coming to their conclusions by different methods or styles of thought. These differences in style did not always appear to be diametrically opposed. Instead, new ways of thinking were emerging—from or alongside, but rarely in confrontation with—the traditional moral perspective. The differences were contained within what seemed to be a defense of the same moral order. Some, however, were not moved by the same sense of moral urgency. The world, especially the marketplace, was not so infected by human depravity. Self-interest did not rouse the traditional sense of horror. Some were coming to examine economic issues such as money without feeling the need to place their discussion within the traditional moral categories. Money could be treated as an issue separate from religion. They continued to discuss the moral sentiments that bound society, sometimes in very conventional terms. But they were more inclined to think of institutional systems, constitutions, and legal orders as the foundations for stability and order. They were beginning to search for numbers that seemed to promise greater clarity and precision than could be achieved by relying on a biblical injunction. These men were not challenging directly, but they were revising the traditional moral universe.

These revisionists were giving new significance to numbers. They were seeking to determine the wealth of a people, the volume of a nation's trade, rates of exchange, and fluctuations in the value of commodities and money. By counting they expected to gain greater understanding than could be achieved with the traditional moral categories. At the same time, they expected to achieve greater control over the marketplace. They were attending to the health of the body politic by compiling actuarial tables. For example, William Douglass proposed that the effectiveness of inoculation against smallpox could be assessed by assembling data. Soon after, he was gathering quantifiable data to advance his understanding of currency. Numbers meant knowledge that could be used for preserving the health of the body politic. These revisionists did not necessarily reject divine providence. But they were less inclined to explain hard times as a sign of God's ineffable will. Thus, they often wrote and spoke as if they supported the traditional moral order. But in their growing reliance on numbers as a tool, their inclination to expand the realm of human agency, their acceptance of self-interest, and their predisposition to separate the secular from the religious, they were, in fact, working a significant revision.

These men yearned to impose order on a society that seemed barely removed from the wilderness condition. They looked to the cosmopolitan center for inspiration and guidance and became conscious of their provincial-ness. They sought to establish order and to clarify status rankings by nurtur-ing standards of gentility that made social distinctions more visible. They looked to human institutions with growing reliance to maintain their positions and authority.

As they saw the divisions between rich and poor grow greater, they re-alized that human sentiments were too weak to hold the social order. Clergymen who preached deference and subordination also knew that the tactics of moral suasion were not enough. They turned to ministerial associ-ations and legal forms by which their positions would be protected from Congregationalism's democratic tendencies. Some may have looked to the episcopalian system. But most stayed within the church tradition to work their revision. Their wealthy counterparts moved with the same deliberation toward political reform. In Boston they proposed an aldermanic form of gov-ernment to check the democratic excesses of the town meeting. For the same reason they came to respect the royal prerogative in provincial government and looked to invigorate the Council as an aristocratic balance against the democratic House of Representatives. So too they turned to legal systems and the courts as bastions of order. What set these men apart was their growing inclination to rely more on institutions and less upon public senti-ments to preserve stability. Thus, they sought to impose order on the econ-omy by establishing government-regulated markets in Boston. For the same reason they looked with jaundiced eye upon schemes devised by private entrepreneurs to create banks separate from government supervision.[56]

The young Thomas Hutchinson represented this revisionism.[57] He en-tered the public scene during the Belcher administration with a deep sense of his roots in Massachusetts's history. His ancestors were among the Bay Colony's first planters. Except for his great-great-grandmother Anne, they had lived quiet lives in the pursuit of trade and had prospered steadily. Two had served on the governor's Council alongside Andrew Belcher; and Thomas's father sat on Governor Belcher's Council. The Hutchinsons were Congregationalists, and Thomas joined Boston's New Brick Church at twenty-four. Although he came to loath the Puritan ancestors for their big-otry, he did not make a public break with that church. By temperament, he felt closer to the Episcopalians and sometimes worshiped with them. Significantly, he entered the public scene in 1737 with his election to the legislature and a proposal for currency reform. He had calculated a method by which the existing bills of credit would be replaced with a new issue of paper money based on a fixed rate in silver. His arguments moved the legis-lature to issue a series of "new tenor" bills. Throughout his life he continued to contribute to the public debates on currency. Hutchinson had grown up in the company of men who struggled to reform Boston's town meeting, and in later decades he sought after methods for restraining the democracy by invigorating government's institutions such as the courts and the governor's Council. By temperament he was an avid student of constitutional arrangements. Thus, as a Massachusetts delegate to the Albany Congress in 1754, he made significant contributions to the drafting of the plan of union. Experience confirmed him in his conviction that without institutional reform appeals to the public would not be sufficient for maintaining social hierarchy and order.

Jonathan Belcher and the Hutchinsons moved in the same social circles. They sat with each other in government and often joined in common cause. Belcher thought well of the young Hutchinson. He was impressed by the youth's contribution to the currency debates. Hutchinson, in turn, became a strong supporter of the governor's administration. The two men often agreed on the issues. Yet they thought about them in very different ways. Belcher was by disposition uninterested in exploring constitutional matters. Even when governor and his position pressed him to grapple with relationships between the branches of government and between the provincial and imperial authority, he refrained from exploring fundamental political principles. His messages advocated a position without elaboration. Usually the argument was one of expediency.

So, too, Belcher never seemed inclined to explore the intricacies of money. Though he thrived in trade, he never contributed to the discussion of money. Friends gave him pamphlets they had written, but he did not comment on them. Money for him was a commodity, not unlike other commodities that were traded. Some went bad and some did not. By inclination he favored hard money and distrusted private banks. But he relaxed his judgment if he respected and trusted the men who supported a private venture. Character made the difference in his evaluation, not the scheme itself. He acted by the same principles that applied in trade: the value of a promissory note and the worth of a commodity to be shipped turned on his estimation of the merchant involved. His principles were simple and by his lights essentially moral. The Bible provided sufficient authority for his convictions. Thus, he concluded the debate on currency with the legislature on the same level that he had begun it. The injunction from Proverbs was enough: "Divers Weights and divers Measures, both of them are alike Abominations to the Lord, but a just Weight is his Delight."[58]

Yet men like Belcher and Hutchinson were working together toward revising the political culture. With others like them in government office and in the pulpit they were altering the meanings of words. The public prints and sermons still addressed the sufferings of the oppressed. The public still heard the voices of compassion expressed for the widow and the orphan. Ministers lamented the condition of fellow clergymen and of officeholders who lived on fixed incomes and were losing ground against the ravages of inflation. The declining value of paper money was attacked as an assault on the rights of the creditor. But the growing number of Boston's laborers whose wages were rapidly falling behind the cost of living was given less attention. When the poor were noticed, they were often dismissed for their slothful and improvident ways. The poor were falling from sight. These same leaders, both clerical and lay, were also forgetting traditional antimarket beliefs. Though they had not yet raised up the virtues of marketplace liberalism, they were speaking softly and indulgently of the impulses toward self-interest or what was once know as predatory greed. Moreover, they were working a significant revision simply by focusing anxieties upon the currency. By asking what was money and by probing into the natural workings of the marketplace, they were shifting attention from human responsibility. They were fixing on oppressive currencies and less upon oppressors. The vocabulary of sin and the concomitant attention paid to questions of personal accountability began to dissolve. As Massachusetts attended to its oppressions, its oppressors seemed to be vanishing.

Indeed, the debates over money were symptomatic of broad change in the political culture. Belcher and his cohorts were grappling with an inherited political terminology that defined their relationship with the public. They had learned that maintaining clearly defined distinctions between rich and poor, between rulers and ruled, was essential to the preservation of a well-ordered society. For them the relationships between leaders and followers were like those between fathers and sons. For the clergy and their congregations the relationship was like that between the shepherd and his flock. Leaders, both lay and clerical, exercised authority but always to nurture their charges. The relationship between the elite and the people turned on a joining of aristocratical and democratical principles. The people were expected to defer to their leaders, and leaders were expected to be guided by obligations to the people. Hierarchical social orders were bound by the principles of reciprocity and obligation. Rulers who forgot their duties became tyrants. Deference was extended only to those who proved themselves worthy leaders. When extended to tyrants it became slavishness. Thus, legitimate authority depended on the public's ready affirmation.

Social distinctions were, in fact, growing; the differences between rich and poor were becoming sharper; and the distances between top and bottom, between the province's fathers and their children, were becoming greater. The gaps separating Boston's rich and poor, its landed and landless, were also splitting the province's rural communities. Residents of towns came to resent nonresident land owners and speculators. Town governments were also confronting an increase in the wandering poor. In Boston, social division turned to violence. In the winter of 1737, Governor Belcher awakened to the alarm that rioters had broken into warehouses in search of food. In the next few days, notices were nailed to public buildings warning the governor that any attempt to apprehend the rioters would provoke a "Civil War." Benjamin Colman trembled at the "Shameful and vile disorders" and at the "murmering against the Government & the rich people among us."[59] He and his fellow clergymen lamented that so many of their colleagues were incessantly bickering with their flocks over salaries and annual allotments of firewood. Social differences also became more apparent as leaders self-consciously cultivated cosmopolitan styles to set themselves above and apart from their inferiors. New England's leaders sensed the gulfs. They could not hear the voices from below affirming their right to rule. If the voices became audible, they heard a raucous and irreverent democracy.

Clergymen who saw themselves harassed by their flocks and councilors who charged the House of Representatives with fomenting disrespect for their authority warned that social hierarchy and the habits of deference were in danger. Convinced that social gradations needed shoring up, they gave special emphasis to the hierarchical and aristocratical side of the social synthesis. They sought to set themselves apart by cultivating the cosmopolitan standards of gentility. They cultivated a polished and elaborate style of address, punctuated their speech with quotations from Latin classics, and paid special attention to their carriages, their powdered wigs and velvet waistcoats. Some like Belcher and later Thomas Hutchinson moved to the countryside in pursuit of the Horatian ideal. Many came to see the necessity for establishing institutions that might serve as barriers against democratic and leveling forces. Clergymen created associations to defend themselves and their privileges against the congregational majorities. Their civil counterparts turned to royal government as a necessary balance against the majority.

But when the Council was accused of separating itself from the people, it responded that its members held their positions by election not by appointment as in other colonies, and therefore were "no less bound up in the public Weal than that of the House of Representatives."[60] Massachusetts's leaders, both officeholders and clergymen, defined their authority in terms of their relationship to the people. The House of Representatives gained the strength to assert itself against the prerogative by claiming a special fiduciary bond with the people. It printed its journals and ordered them distributed to its constituent towns. When engaged in prolonged confrontation with the governor, it appealed to the public for support. Elisha Cooke cultivated his role as tribune of the people. His ability to engage with the governor stemmed from a confidence that he spoke with an authority that was derived from the people's assent. This was the claim that was contested by the Council. Without this relationship with the people, the house's authority turned into oligarchic despotism.

Fathers and shepherds were also coming to interpret the social synthesis with different accents. Ministers were troubled by the silences in their congregations and by what appeared to be a growing indifference or deadness to religion. Urban representatives, claiming close bond with the public, appealed to the people to affirm their roles. But they often heard nothing. Thus, they interpreted the silences as affirmation. Some began to experiment with ways to encourage the people to speak. They became conscious of the press as a device to address the public. Elisha Cooke and his allies in Boston constructed political organizations to control town meetings. They were seen in taverns consorting with the people, drinking with common laborers, and talking politics with the meanest mechanics. At the same time, clergymen troubled by the quiet were couching their sermons in a plain style and were directing their words at the heart rather than the intellect.

These movements—one toward bolstering authority and the other toward nurturing democratic associations—were tendencies or inclinations contained within the same culture, class, and even individuals. Differences were not always as sharp as the antagonists sometimes described them. Cooke's opponents did not reject his role as democratic tribune. Indeed, they felt discomfort when confronted by his claim to speak for the people. Therefore, they sought to transform his role into something else—the dangerous demagogue. Making him into a leveler and destroyer of social hierarchy was a distortion. But Cooke responded in kind when he tried to turn his enemies' defense of authority into tyrannical conspiracy. So, too, many cosmopolitan divines were intrigued with some of their colleagues' experiments with an evangelical style of address. The first awakenings that were witnessed during the Belcher administration did not evoke fears for the social order and ministerial authority.

As governor, Belcher sought to render an interpretation of his role that embraced these differences. He cherished his association with royalty because it elevated him among his people, and he methodically gathered the symbols of royalty unto himself because they were so revered by the people. At the same time, he consciously played upon his reputation as a native son who understood and sought after the people's welfare. Sometimes, he resorted to the patriarchal metaphor: "it has pleas'd God in his Providence to set me in the Station of a Father to my Country." He expected the same obedience from the people that he exacted from his own children. He regretted when his opponents had become "Wicked Children [who] don't love & honour their good Father for all the Care he has taken and is still willing to take, of them." In return for his care and "fondness" he expected obedience and love. He governed as a loving father and a Nehemiah. He liked to boast that he held office not only by the king's authority but at the consent of the people. If his office were elected, he estimated that he would receive "19/20ths" of the votes.[61]

The evangelicals caught his eye. He watched Jonathan Edwards's work at Northampton and rejoiced at the "wonderful things wrought by the Spirit of God on the Hearts of our People in the County of Hampshire." In the autumn of 1740, he eagerly awaited the arrival of George Whitefield. He attended the evangelist's sermons and was moved to tears. He invited the itinerant to join him and several of the town's ministers for dinner. Whitefield, he wrote, "has been highly honour'd of God with being made the Instrument of begetting many a poor Creature anew in Christ Jesus." When the evangelist took his crusade into the interior, Belcher followed him to Marlborough and to Worcester. After tearfully bidding Whitefield farewell, he rejoiced to see the "generall Rousing from dreadful Lethargy" that was sweeping the land. He avidly read the reports of the "Heavenly" itinerant and the other evangelicals and encouraged them as they traveled throughout the colonies.[62] He made himself a champion of their cause. Even when others turned against the evangelicals as enemies of social hierarchy and the habits of deference, Belcher did not falter in his enthusiasm.

The people became a necessity for playing the Nehemiah. When Belcher thought of presenting himself before the people, however, he recalled the insecurities and failures that accompanied democratic politics. Inevitably he heard the mocking voices in his imagination. Thus, he attended carefully to the public and its moods. He gave special attention to the public prints and to Boston's printers. In preparation for his triumphal return to Boston, he persuaded the English poet and dissenter Isaac Watts to compose a poem celebrating his arrival. It was to be printed in a Boston newspaper to set the mood for his return. When he encountered anything condemning the government in the Boston prints, he broke into a fury. He came to see the press as a tool to influence opinions. He prepared announcements to be printed in the newspapers with an eye on the public's response. "A good advertisement in the several News Papers," he thought, would work like a "Sword" upon the opposition. He courted the city's printers. Ellis Huske of the *Boston Post-Boy* received extensive patronage. In general, the press was not critical. Some believed that the printers were cowed. At the end of the Belcher administration, one opponent charged that most of Boston's printers refused to print opposition opinion "for fear of incurring the Governor's displeasure, which might prejudice them in their Business."[63]

Belcher was also moving toward speaking to the public directly. On occasion, when he dissolved a legislature, he anticipated a welling up of public support. Sometimes, especially in New Hampshire, he took steps toward devising election strategies, recruiting candidates, and appealing to allies to exert themselves in his behalf. He also instructed his allies to circulate among the people petitions that demonstrated his popularity. Once, when he thought the voters of New Hampshire would finally open their eyes and repudiate his opponents, he made plans to participate directly in the campaign. He would make a special trip to Stratham, the home town of one of his leading opponents, confront his adversary, and rally the voters in support of his own candidate.[64]

He did not foray into Stratham, however. The trip was a pleasant adventure to be enjoyed vicariously. Some of Belcher's contemporaries, such as Cooke, had the confidence to experiment with a democratic style, but others, such as Belcher himself, felt unsure of themselves in this unfamiliar and perilous world of popular politics. They had spent so much time in pursuit of the ideals of gentility that they were not sure how to couch their appeal to the people. Thus, Belcher consorted with Cooke but always remained ambivalent about the "Hero of the Mob." In his mind's eye he risked exposure, ridicule, and shame.[65] Thus, he could imagine no greater injury to inflict upon an adversary than punishment before the public.

But because the democracy remained essential to realizing the role of the good ruler, Belcher paid special attention to the staging of public appearances. While the public roused fears, it remained a necessity for fulfilling the role of governor. The staging of public appearances required careful planning. Ceremony set an official apart, inspired awe, and framed the moment so that it protected him from unexpected and raucous intrusions. Belcher fretted over his public performances. He purchased a special carriage for his trips to New Hampshire. He ordered that he be accompanied from the border to Portsmouth by a retinue of councilors, representatives, judges, militia officers, and several troops of militia. He refused to make the trip unless adequate preparations were made. "As I told you," he wrote to Richard Waldron, his chief New Hampshire ally, "it won't do for Govrs to make Sudden Excursions thro' their Governments. . . . They can't avoid the Ceremonies that will attend them. No!" Even though Waldron thought the trip imperative, Belcher could not be budged. It was not consistent with "the Govrs Honour to make the Trip." "Gentmn in publick Station" could not act so impetuously. "Every motion & Syllable, even the Gestures of their Bodies, must pass the Censure of the Staring Crowd." No matter the urgency, he would not expose himself to that "Sneer & ridicule."[66]

On another occasion, Waldron had time to make suitable preparations. A "cavalcade" of troops and a grand retinue of the province's civil and military officers were to assemble at the border and accompany the governor to Portsmouth. Belcher looked forward to the trip. "Perhaps," he replied to Waldron, "it may strike Terrour" in the ranks of his opponents. He was pleased when he arrived at the border. Waldron had assembled a "vast train of Attendants." Troops from the local militia marched at the head of the procession followed by the "under sheriffs, [and] after them the two High Sheriffs." The governor followed in his coach with officers and councilors riding in attendance. Another militia unit made up the rear. In Portsmouth, Waldron had prepared a grand banquet at the Green Dragon Inn, where the governor entertained the members of the Council and House of Representatives.[67]

Belcher found the security he craved elsewhere, in the act of writing letters. He wrote nearly every day with the dedication that others gave to their diaries. Indeed, his letterbooks acquired a personal significance comparable to that achieved by the diarist. While he wrote letters for practical purposes, he also wrote for self-expression. Letter writing, like the writing of his European journal, became a performance before an audience of his choosing and in a setting of his creation.

It was in the letterbooks that he indulged in religious ecstasy. Though he listened with rapture to the evangelicals, he usually kept his feelings hidden. His emotional outburst at church after his father's death was extraordinary. Whitefield noted his stiffness and chided him for his cold demeanor. But in his letterbooks he found the safety to express himself. Usually he felt most comfortable before clergymen and the women of his family. Only rarely did he reveal his religious feelings before men of affairs. Characteristically, he expressed himself through conventions, platitudes, commonplace expressions, and paraphrasings. He prayed with one correspondent: "God of his infinite Mercy Grant that the many Warnings we have of the certain Destruction of this vain perishing World may rouse us to True Repentence." He resolved to struggle against his frailties, to humble himself before God, and to "endeavour by Faith & Repentence to become acceptable in the Eyes of a jealous, holy God." Thus he wrote in rapture of "our Almighty Saviour." "All will be steady & safe if in duty & faith we can rest . . . on the shoulder of the wonderfull Counsellour, the mighty God, the Prince of Peace. . . . And he that trusteth in the Lord shall be as Mount Sion, which cannot be removed, but abideth forever."[68]

He sought out the champions of "vital religion" on both sides of the ocean. Isaac Watts and Samuel Holden were his favorite English correspondents. He invited Holden to join with him in reflecting on life's fleeting moments. "Our Life here is but a Vapour. . . . Oh then that we may obtain Grace wisely to employ the Talents God has committed to us, that at the great & general Audit . . . we may then hear the great Judge of Quick & Dead Say to us, you have been faithful unto Death, I will give you a Crown of Life." Perhaps he also wrote because Holden wielded great influence in English politics. He wrote to Daniel Neal because he had written a history of New

England. Belcher also cultivated a broad correspondence with New England's divines. When a minister wrote from Cape Cod on impending war with Spain, Belcher responded with pious reflections on the frailties of life and vowed "to promote the glory of the great Govr of Heaven & Earth to whom I know I must render an Account of all the Talents and Advantages he has put into my hands."[69]

His letters echoed New England's Jeremiahs. He regularly reflected on the fallen state of the people. "We seem (in this Generation)," he lamented, "to have lost our first Love." The "noble vine" planted by New England's fathers seemed to turn into a "degenerate Plant." By lamenting society's decline, he made himself a caretaker of the covenanted society. He wrote in that vein to men of affairs. After a disappointing session with the legislature, he wrote to John Chandler of Worcester County that the province stood at a "Critical dangerous Juncture." The last session "seems to me a presage of Judgement God is bringing upon this poor Country." These were not "new things under the Sun," however. "God's prophets of old tell us" that similar trials were visited upon the "Chosen people." He counseled Chandler not to despair and closed with the assurance that he would do his utmost for the "Welfare & happiness of my dear, dear Country."[70]

Belcher loved these moments when he could discuss the duties of his office. "We must not think we are born wholly for ourselves," he reflected with an associate. "Our Country has a Claim to us & to our Service." By joining New England's Jeremiahs in their lament for public morality, he was playing the Nehemiah. "My prayer to God," he wrote, "is that Rulers & Ruled may more & more devote themselves to seek the Publick good and more especially by promoting Vertue & true Religion. In this way we may hope to wrestle down a blessing for the present & future Generations." Fulfillment came in the routines and rituals of office. He relished the opportunity to sit at center stage during the commencement ceremonies at Harvard College. He attended carefully to the occasions when he issued a proclamation summoning God's people to gather in their churches for a day of fasting or thanksgiving. He attended to God's providences. After an earthquake he prayed: "God of his infinite Mercy Grant that the many Warnings we have of the certain Destruction of this vain perishing World may rouse us to a True Repentence and to a holy life and Conversion."[71]

Jonathan Belcher relished the commonplace. He took the cliches and platitudes of his society and constructed a worldview from them. The synthesis he created was not coherent in the sense that the parts fit into a congruent whole. Indeed, his worldview enabled him to absorb contradiction and tension. While he spoke as a conservator of the founders' legacy, he worked effectively toward incorporating fundamental revisions into that inheritance. What he achieved was an interpretation of his culture that was supple and resilient.

His worldview was flexible enough to embrace both Thomas Hutchinson and Jonathan Edwards, even though both men represented a fundamental contradiction. While Hutchinson viewed Puritanism as a burden to be cast aside if New England were to progress, Edwards dedicated himself to restoring and revitalizing that inheritance. Hutchinson celebrated the English connection as a necessary civilizing influence on this primitive society. Edwards was coming to see the cosmopolitan center as a corruption contaminating New England's soul. Hutchinson thrived in Boston's merchant community, while Edwards spent his days in pastoral Northampton. While the young merchant probed the mysteries of commerce and money, the minister began to grumble about the oppressions and injustices that came with trade. Both proposed reforms: one of New England's political institutions and the other of New England's soul.

Belcher took note of Hutchinson as a "Gentleman adorn'd with a great number of amiable qualities." He was impressed by the young man's understanding of the intricacies of trade and currency. He soon took a liking for Hutchinson and promised to do whatever was possible to advance his public career. In turn, when Hutchinson went to London, he worked to support the governor against his opponents. At the same time, Belcher was drawn to Jonathan Edwards. When he read the minister's first account of his efforts to awaken his congregation, he rejoiced at the "wonderful things wrought by the spirit of God in the County of Hampshire." He recommended Edwards's writings to friends of evangelical religion on both sides of the Atlantic. He soon entered into a correspondence with Edwards that would last a lifetime.[72]

Hutchinson and Edwards—both men fit into Belcher's world. They became complements to the governor's efforts for promoting the social welfare. He seemed oblivious to the contradiction in part because neither man confronted the other. Hutchinson lived in a world of courts and legislatures, constitutions and charters, banks and counting houses. When he wrote his history of Massachusetts-Bay, he organized his materials from that perspective. He did not confront the cannons of Puritan historiography directly, although he had cut himself free from that tradition. His was not a history of the covenant but of imperial expansion and whiggish principles. When he came to writing the history of his own time, he organized his story around the administrations of governors and made no mention of the evangelicals and their crusades. Jonathan Edwards did not appear in the story except by a single indirect reference in a footnote. In sum, he had written Edwards out of Massachusetts's history.[73]

Edwards, in turn, seemed to be oblivious to Hutchinson and his world. He did not write a history comparable to Hutchinson's, though he understood his times from a historical perspective, a perspective fixed on the progress of Christianity and the Protestant Reformation in America. Hutchinson's whiggery was simply irrelevant. Sometimes, when Edwards spoke of moral declension, he fulminated against the "grandees" of this world who forsook the faith of their fathers for worldly gain. At times, he condemned the sins of the marketplace and the selfishness that came with power and wealth. He may have thought of men like Hutchinson and even Belcher. But these worldly matters were peripheral to his concern for religious revival.[74]

By bringing Edwards and Hutchinson together, this pedestrian thinker was assisting in making a smooth transition in social experience and belief. He could do so because the role he played was conservative in tone. New England's first Nehemiahs came with the lust for land, profit, and empire. They spoke the vocabulary of parliaments and gospelized the Indians for profit. Belcher and Christopher Toppan continued in that tradition but with a different accent. While Belcher and his cohorts were refashioning this society and creating new arrangements and distributions of wealth and power, they presented themselves as protectors of a traditional social ethic. In the process they drained the vocabulary of concepts such as equity and a just price and thereby changed the meaning of community and social responsibility.

Belcher participated in these changes. Indeed, by making common cause with men like Thomas Hutchinson he promoted them. He did so unconsciously. At heart he thought of himself as a Puritan Nehemiah. Though an ally of institutional reformers such as Hutchinson, he was by temperament with the evangelicals who called for spiritual reformation. He cherished those moments when he listened to the province's leading clergymen praise him as a modern-day Nehemiah. Finally, it was Edwards who moved him. After Belcher left office, he did not correspond with Hutchinson, but he continued to write to the Northampton minister. It was this link to evangelical reformation that quickened his imagination and brought him fulfillment.

4

The Art of Politics

In 1730, when Governor Belcher took office, Massachusetts seemed to be teetering on the brink of grave crisis. The salary controversy, interrupted temporarily by the death of Governor Burnet, remained unresolved. Memories of the recent charter crisis haunted speculation about the new administration. In his first message to the General Court, Belcher explained the gravity of the moment by drawing analogy to the last days of the Roman Republic, when Cato stood at the walls of Utica defiantly awaiting Caesar's triumphant entry. Cato's "Stand for the Liberties of his Country" had become a model of heroic virtue for later generations. It provided "some Illustration of the Dispute lately subsisting between his Majesty and his People of this Province." But Cato's decision to kill himself rather than surrender to Caesar illustrated the folly of overzealous principle. "His murdering himself rather than submit to a Power he could no longer rationally resist, has left a lasting Brand of Infamy on the Memory of that Great Patriot."[1]

Lest anyone extend his argument into dangerous territory, Belcher hastened to assure his audience that he did not consider King George a latter-day Caesar. Massachusetts was fortunate to be ruled by the "best of KINGS" who "defends and protects the Liberties of his People with a most tender paternal Care." Belcher approached the salary question cautiously with an eye on the sensibilities of his audience. Before raising the constitutional issue, he had invoked the traditional symbols of the Nehemiah. His recent experience in London had taught him that the heroic adherence to principle could become vanity and histrionics. As agent, he had struggled to do everything possible "for preserving and lengthening out the Peace and Welfare of this Province." Cato's suicide seemed an appropriate illustration of his position. When faced with defeat, the province would do well to compromise, to give up some points, for the sake of the charter.[2] The lesson he drew was startling. Anglo-Americans had raised up Cato as the model of political virtue, not as an example of the vanity of principle. Belcher seemed to sense the awkwardness of his position. Indeed, he had played the resolute patriot willing to risk defeat rather than bend to the counsels of pragmatism when he was agent in London.

Governor Belcher found himself where other Nehemiahs had stood. Increase Mather—who had slipped the clutches of Sir Edmund Andros, sailed for London determined to restore the old charter, and returned with a new charter—had learned the necessity of making concessions. A generation later, Elisha Cooke, Jr., had embarked on a similar mission in defense of provincial rights but also learned the necessity of bending before imperial authority. While both men defended their concessions as necessary, both returned with their reputations tarnished by charges of political apostasy.

While the images of the Cato and the Nehemiah standing resolute against the outsider dominated political imaginations, New Englanders were also reinterpreting those roles to fit the times. New England's defenders needed "Practical and Political Wisdom and Prudence" and an understanding of the political process.[3] They must have the ability to manipulate men and factions on both sides of the Atlantic. They needed the talents of the dissembler, flatterer, and courtier. They must have the wisdom to compromise. In sum John Winthrop's heirs were coming to embrace the courtier side of the Nehemiah.

Belcher believed that he possessed the abilities to reconcile the people of Massachusetts with the authorities in London. The recent squabbles had been fired by Burnet's abrasive personality and his obsessive dedication to constitutional principle. Belcher's task was twofold: to convince his superiors in London, such as Martin Bladen and the Duke of Newcastle, that their suspicions were unfounded and to assure the people of Massachusetts that he had not betrayed their trust. He needed, in other words, to cultivate appearances of the faithful servant of the crown before the imperial authorities without provoking deep animosities in New England.

Appearances were important. In this political culture compromise and expediency seemed to turn into depravity and apostasy. The words to justify Belcher's undertaking did not come easily. Thus, Belcher stumbled in his reference to Cato. Although the idea of the Nehemiah seemed appropriate, it also opened dangerous tensions contained within the imperial relationship.

Belcher's political survival depended on a speedy resolution of the salary issue. For the moment the situation was fluid. Antagonists speculated whether the governor would abandon his recent association with Cooke or continue a vendetta against the Dudleians. No one seemed certain what position the governor would take on the salary question. Antagonists joined in pledging their support for the new governor and refrained from bickering. But few expected the calm to last.[4]

Belcher exploited these uncertainties. Shortly after his arrival he announced that with a change in governors the commissions of all officers on the provincial civil list were in suspension and that he would review all positions from justice of the peace to judge on the Superior Court. The announcement was unprecedented. The Council protested vigorously but in vain. Rumors flew that the governor was preparing a thorough purge. The next year Belcher removed William Dudley and Edward Hutchinson from the Suffolk County Court to make room for Elisha Cooke and Nathaniel Byfield. The changes sent a shock through the province, but they did not presage additional expulsions. Indeed, Hutchinson and Dudley kept their posts as justices of the peace.[5] Rather than purge the civil list of his enemies, Belcher chose to keep officials of all factions and persuasions in suspense and to avoid partisan association. Thus, he expected that politicians throughout the province would promise their support for the administration.

The tactic was not only a prudent one but it also brought personal satisfaction to have the province's leading personages come to court his favor, especially when Paul Dudley came to call. Belcher relished that moment. Clearly Dudley came in hopes of keeping his seat on the Superior Court. Years later Belcher recalled the scene as the judge made "so many professions of friendship & of his sincere Wishes for my Prosperity in the Government & of his great attachment to my Interest & honour." As he listened, he knew that Dudley "don't love me. & perhaps I mayn't continue him a Judge."[6]

Belcher toyed with "doing Justice" to his "Enemies." In his imagination he savored the thought of striking "terrour" in their hearts. He lacked the emotional resources, however, to act on these fantasies, especially against Dudley. The deep-seated sense of vulnerability that first inspired him to focus his resentments on Dudley also prevented him from confronting his adversary openly or turning him into a public enemy. He kept the judge dangling but in the meantime approved his reelection to the Council. Eventually he reconfirmed the judge's place on the Superior Court.[7]

Belcher's restraint also sprang from prudence and an ingrained understanding of provincial politics. The office of governor provided him limited powers to move the local and independent oligarchs sitting in the legislature. The Stoddards and Williamses of Hampshire County, who had come to dominate local government and were accustomed to sitting in the legislature, received Governor Belcher's appointments to the civil list in recognition of the positions they enjoyed in their own right. When the legislature created Worcester Country in 1733, Belcher extended appointments to the Chandlers and the Dwights. Since these families enjoyed prominence and security in their communities and regularly went to represent their neighbors in the legislature, the governor was confirming their natural places in the social order. To defy the wishes of these local oligarchs risked political disaster. Indeed, Belcher could count only a handful of appointments as his own. There were a few customs collectors in the ports. Sometimes he split offices between two individuals. There was never enough to create a following in the legislature.[8]

There were other ways for a governor to cultivate support. Governor Belcher worked systematically to deflect and subvert the enforcement of London's economic policies. English acts to regulate trade and control timber cutting were enforced laxly and selectively but always with the intent to protect and extend political alliances. When Boston's merchants learned that London was considering new legislation designed to discourage their trade with foreign sugar colonies, the governor attended to their concerns. Privately he confessed that he had "some doubt" that the bill "wou'd be any real Damage to New England." He also sensed the intensity of feelings in the merchant community. Thus, while he publicly refrained from joining the attack on the bill, he invited the house leadership to his home to confer on tactics. He assured the lawmakers that he had instructed his allies in London to prevent the bill's passage and regularly relayed the reports of their progress to the legislature.[9]

David Dunbar, the surveyor general of the king's woods, provided Belcher with the opportunity to prove his worth to provincial economic interests. The surveyor general quickly earned a reputation for his uncommonly zealous prosecution of illegal lumbering and in turn quickly learned that the governor simultaneously worked to prevent the execution of the law. In addition, Dunbar was acting as advance agent for a group of London adventurers who proposed to settle a colony in the Kennebec River region. Not only did the scheme intrude upon Massachusetts's territorial claims but it threatened to invalidate the titles of several prominent land speculators, including Elisha Cooke, Nathaniel Byfield, and Samuel Waldo. Again Belcher wielded his authority to block Dunbar from establishing the colony.[10]

Belcher had learned that for the good ruler to survive and to protect his people, he must become a master at the courtly arts of deception and duplicity. Just as he pretended to be a friend and benefactor of the Church of England, so too he cultivated impressions with his superiors that he was a faithful royal servant devoted to the execution of the trade laws. When his superiors in London had instructed him in his dual capacity as governor of Massachusetts and New Hampshire to sponsor and oversee a settlement of the long-standing border dispute between the two provinces, Belcher acted as if he were the neutral arbitrator. Yet he used his powers of adjournment to prevent the New Hampshire legislature from preparing its case and cooperated with the Massachusetts legislature in granting lands in the disputed area to improve its claims.[11]

The governor's tenure, however, depended on the outcome of the salary question and his ability to maneuver two irreconcilable positions toward a settlement. He did not agree with his instruction to secure a permanent salary, and he also knew that it could not be imposed upon the legislature. Failure to press the instruction, however, would only undermine his reputation in London. For Belcher the issue was not principle but practical politics. He also saw that the situation was fluid on both sides of the ocean. In London he had encountered officials like Lords Wilmington and Townsend, who were uncomfortable with the reformers' assault on local rights and charters and who yearned for a compromise, perhaps a salary that extended for more than one year but was not permanent. In Massachusetts there were many lawmakers who had grown weary of the turmoil and were disposed to support a salary that was less than permanent but more than an annual grant.[12]

At heart the issue was the character of the governor and his independence from legislative control. Belcher was confident that as a native son he could move the legislature to grant his salary for a period longer than a year. But he could not expect the lawmakers to provide for whomever succeeded him. He did not address the issue in terms of constitutional principle. What he sought was a solution to an unnatural rift between king and people that had been provoked by zealous imperial reformers. He would cultivate impressions in London that he supported his instructions and at the same time he would seek the first opportunity to abandon them. He would press and cajole the provincial lawmakers. He would keep them dangling in suspense. He would make alliances and then break them. Above all he would remove the salary from the public agenda.

During the fall session, majorities in both houses of the General Court seemed eager to wrestle differences on the salary instruction toward resolution. The House of Representatives under Elisha Cooke's lead offered to increase the governor's salary and to guarantee it for the duration of his term. The bill seemed to satisfy most of the councilors. Belcher read nothing objectionable in the offer, but he pressed the Council to reject it. For the sake of appearances in London he thought it too early to make concessions. At the same time he was determined not to press the issue so hard that it would undermine his relationship with the lawmakers. At the end of the month, he gently chided them for falling short of "his Majesty's just Expectation" but congratulated them for moving significantly toward expressing the "Duty and Respect" they owed the king.[13]

The chances for reaching a settlement were rapidly slipping from the governor's grasp. Elisha Cooke, still scarred by the crisis over the explanatory charter, became increasingly embarrassed by his association with the governor. By the end of the year, he refused to offer anything more than an annual salary grant. Opposition opinion was revived. A Boston press reprinted an article from the English periodical, *The Political State of Great Britain*, which reviewed recent exchanges on the salary question. The author concluded that the governor's behavior was "more proper for a French Monarch, or a Turkish Basaw than for an English governor." Belcher was livid when he complained to his superiors in London that the article had been re-printed "to poison" the minds of the people and to make the legislators "more obstinate in their refusal of complying with H.M. Instruction." Belcher did not exaggerate by much. When he dissolved the legislature and called for new elections in the hope of nudging the lawmakers toward a settlement, his action only seemed to invigorate the opposition.[14]

At the same time, the disputes over the power of the public purse and over paper money were forcing themselves into the political agenda. In the winter term, the House balked at the governor's instructions that limited the annual issuance of paper money to £30,000 to cover the government's annual expenses and that required the government to expedite the withdrawal of outstanding currency issues. When it proposed to petition the king for relax-ing these instructions, however, the Council declined. Moreover, long-standing disputes over the control of the treasury erupted with the Council pressing to regain control of public funds and the house accusing the Council of misapplying the people's money. For a moment the Council seemed to regain the initiative when the House passed a bill for supplying the treasury that relinquished its control over appropriations. But the House leadership vowed to resume the struggle for control of the treasury.[15]

Clearly several volatile issues were converging, and public discussions were being raised to a high moral plane. The country patriot scenario was being revived. In May the people of Boston returned Cooke and his patriot associates to the legislature and gave them strict instructions to "use your utmost Endeavour That the Great Priviledges we enjoy by the English Constitution & the Royal Charter, May be preserved from all Encroach-ments, And so handed Down to Succeeding Assemblys." The provincial gov-ernment was at stalemate, Belcher reported to the Duke of Newcastle. He accused the House of Representatives of "daily endeavoring to incroach upon the little power reserv'd to the Crown in the Royal Charter," and he vowed to "part with none without my royal Master's orders."[16]

His letter was written to deceive. The time had come for him to change tack, and he wished to be rid of the salary instruction. He also knew that he must distance himself from the House of Representatives. He wrote to his superiors condemning the legislature's petition for its disrespect for royal au-thority. At the same time he explained that despite all his efforts, he could not move the House to grant anything more than an annual salary. And so he served the king obediently but without compensation. He was sinking into poverty and was hard pressed to maintain himself in the manner befitting a royal servant. Lest he disgrace his station and the king, he prayed for permis-sion to accept the most recent offer of an annual salary.

The course he had set for himself required the skill of dissembling and the art of courtly intrigue. "I must," he confided to Partridge, "walk very Circumspectly, lest the King's Ministers shou'd imagine I am not Zealous enough for the Honour of the Crown, and lest the House of Commons shou'd think I bear too hard upon the Privileges of the People. I'll endeavour to steer as nicely as I can between both." Appearances were not always what they seemed. In the halls of government, Belcher's allies tilted against the House of Representatives and its agent Francis Wilks. But even while the governor and the agent seemed to disagree on the House petition, the two former colleagues worked together, sometimes with the legislature's knowledge, to circumvent the salary instruction. Belcher warned his son Jonathan, who had arrived in London, not to insult the agent. "He is my intire Friend. . . . And I know he's very capable & full of Inclination to serve me."[17]

"A Governor can't have too many Friends at Court," observed Belcher. Although his patron, Lord Townsend, had left office, Belcher was able to cultivate a "good Interest" among the government officials, including the prime minister and members of the cabinet, privy councilors, the speaker of the House of Commons, and members of parliament. He made Richard Partridge his principal agent. He valued his brother-in-law for his "great Freedom of Access to the King's ministers, and all the Publick offices" and for his standing in the Society of Friends, "which Body of men have at this Day a great interest at Court."[18] During the fall of 1731, Belcher watched his friends and allies move the government toward relaxing salary instruction. Knowing the Board of Trade's opinion of the governor, they went directly to the Privy Council and its presiding officer, Lord Wilmington. The Council was eager to discover a means by which it could balance respect for charter rights with the royal prerogative. It could not countenance the House's petition lest it appear to capitulate. But it did grant the governor permission to accept the last offer of an annual grant on condition that it be "for this time only."[19]

When Belcher signed the salary bill, he wrote to Wilks that the grant was but a "skinning over the Wound." "Disputes and Difficulties" were sure to break out again as long as the salary issue remained unresolved. But Wilks had also sent encouraging news in his last letter. Lord Wilmington had given the agent his private assurance that if the Massachusetts House were to revive the bill establishing a salary for the duration of Belcher's term, he would lend "his assistance in obtaining His Majestys leave for the Governour to Pass it." Belcher leaped at the idea. When he broached the subject with the House leadership, however, he sensed that Cooke was afraid to jeopardize his reputation with the public. Perhaps he hoped to win Cooke over by appointing him a judge and his son the clerk of the Suffolk Court of Common Pleas. At the same time, Belcher sought to apply another form of pressure.

He enlisted Wilks to convince the House of Representatives that its devotion to principle risked the king's displeasure.[20]

The tactic proved an immediate and dismal failure. Cooke saw no reason to risk his reputation. London's recent concession demonstrated a lack of resolve that discredited Wilks's counsels for prudence. Moreover, opinion in Boston was shifting against accommodation with the executive. Exchanges between the legislature and governor were growing more testy as attentions turned to the treasury. The House leadership was determined to regain control of appropriations. And it was listening to public support for paper money. On both counts its bills to supply the treasury were contradicted by the governor's instructions. Although the treasury was empty, Belcher had been obliged to veto the bills. There seemed little prospect for resolution. At the same time, the governor was losing control of the Council. In February 1732 the Council joined with the House to pass a bill for printing £50,000. When the governor vetoed the bill, it called upon him to reconsider his decision. Four months later Belcher rejected a similar supply bill passed by both houses. In addition, the Council was moving to join with the House in devising a strategy for petitioning the king for relaxation of the governor's instructions.[21]

Belcher tried to make light of the Council's defections. Councilors who worried over their reelection, he explained, were wont to bend to the House's opinions. But his administration was approaching a crisis of competence. He had failed to wring a concession from the House on the salary. In the summer of 1732, he confessed to his superiors in London that he was unable to gain more than an annual grant and asked for permission to accept the offer. There was nothing in the treasury, and there seemed little prospect for resolution of the issues while the House waited for its appeal. In the autumn session, the House voted fifty-six to one that compliance with the instructions would "tend to destroy the Powers and Priviledges granted to the General Court in and by the Royal CHARTER." In the spring session, the House explicitly focused its attention on the governor himself. It reminded Belcher of his recent service as provincial agent. Then, he had defended the House's rights to control the treasury. What had changed? Not the principles. "The Cause and Interest of the People is the same now as then." The explanation seemed obvious: "your Excellency's State and Condition is much altered."[22]

Belcher was desperate and furious. In June 1733 he was railing against Cooke: "The Ingratitude of the Hero of the Mob is what the whole World allows to be without a parallel." After a brief discussion, the newly elected House had voted to pass another supply bill "agreeable to the Bill passed for that purpose in June last." The House leadership had simply decided to wait for London's response to its petitions. Belcher declared: "I have much chang'd my political Views & Schemes. Nor will I support any one in Power Profit & honour that makes it his Business to keep the Government in perpetual Contention & Confusion." Resolving to make his administration "all of a Peice," he removed Cooke from the Suffolk County Court. The next day he disapproved the House's election of Edward Shove, one of Cooke's cohorts, as excise collector. In December, he ordered the Suffolk County Court to dismiss its clerk, Middlecot Cooke, and to appoint his own son-in-law, Byfield Lyde, to the post.[23]

On June 25 the *Weekly Rehearsal* published the governor's appointments. The list was long, including the justices of the peace in Suffolk, Essex, Bristol, and Middlesex Counties and the justices of the provincial Superior Court. Belcher issued the commissions with the intent to make a dramatic statement. Not only had he removed Cooke, but he had reappointed William Dudley to his former position on the bench. He had also confirmed Paul Dudley's seat on the Superior Court. Belcher expected that by favoring the Dudleys he had doubled the shock of Cooke's fall. Cooke's "Adherents" in the legislature were struck dumb with "Mortification & Terrour" and awaited additional punishments to be inflicted.[24] The remainder of the list, however, confirmed the incumbents whose commissions had been held in suspension for three years. With his dalliance with Cooke behind him, Belcher was embarking on a new legislative strategy.

He approached the House of Representatives by way of the rural lawmakers—those independent, indifferent, often absent, usually silent, backbenchers who made up the majority of the membership. Belcher knew few of them, since many did not stay for the full duration of a session, nearly half served only a single term, and more than that were gone in two. But he knew those who made a difference. There was John Stoddard of Hampshire County. The Stoddards with their relatives the Williamses dominated the towns of the Connecticut River Valley.[25] They and their ever-expanding network of relations presided over town meetings, preached from the towns' pulpits, commanded the militia, served as justices of the peace and judges of the county court, and represented their neighbors in the House of Representatives. At the head of this family stood John Stoddard, known to the world as the "squire" of Hampshire County. When he came to Boston, his presence was felt immediately. In the legislature his influence with the county's other representatives could make the difference on a critical vote. He was one of a handful of rural lawmakers to participate prominently in committees. But the "squire" often preferred to remain at home in Northampton. He came irregularly, usually when moved by issues related to the defense of the western frontiers.

Belcher watched the Chandlers and Dwights extend their influence in Worcester County.[26] When he signed the legislation creating the county in

1731, he had appointed John Chandler to the county court. Perhaps Chandler was an exception, for, unlike Stoddard, he seemed to thrive on legislative politics. From the moment he entered the legislature he served actively and regularly as a prominent committeeman shaping the House's agenda. Joseph Dwight of Brookfield did not attract as much attention as Chandler and was named to fewer committees. But as a descendant of Hampshire County's founding magnates, Dwight exerted considerable influence in the Worcester County delegation. Belcher named him a justice of the peace and later appointed him to the county court. These local oligarchs became crucial for Belcher's strategy. His task was not so much to convince them of his position as it was to beg and cajole them to make the trip to Boston.

Belcher had set for himself the task of moving an inchoate body of indifferent, independent, and unorganized lawmakers, nearly a hundred in number, to his side. When the lawmakers gathered in Boston, he watched their proceedings carefully, assessed their opinions, and counted votes to estimate the strength of his support. No lawmaker, no matter how insignificant, escaped his notice. Thomas Westbrook came to the House for the first time in 1733. The representative from Falmouth did not sit on a single committee, he stayed for only a few weeks and was fined for his absence, and he did not return the next year. But he caught the governor's eye. Belcher believed that Westbrook was listening to Cooke and had become "one of the Cat's Paws Tools, & f——ls, of the Party." He let it be known that he was considering the lawmaker for appointment to officer's rank in the militia. The tactic seemed to work. Belcher learned from friends in the legislature that "the Falmouth Gent begins to be more Cautious." In turn he let it be known that he held the lawmaker in "good Respect." But Westbrook was an unsteady ally and finally chose to follow Cooke. "I know he can't well avoid holding a Candle to the Devil," concluded Belcher. The governor's efforts were making differences, however. Even one of his critics conceded that he "has been very active in endeavouring to persuade many Members of the Court" to support him on the treasury "and not without success."[27]

Cooke's strength depended on his ability to play the country patriot version of the Nehemiah. But if his defiance of London's authority provoked dangerous consequences, if his heroism appeared to be an irresponsible posture, or his self-proclaimed virtue turned into demagoguery—if he failed to play the role convincingly, his following evaporated. From the moment of his accession, Belcher had been struggling to impose an alternative scenario on the political debates. In his first address to the legislature he had struggled, albeit clumsily, to recast the script. A majority of lawmakers still heeded Cooke's arguments that conceding control of the public purse was premature as long as their petitions remained unanswered. If the government in London would only give a "conclusive Answer" to these petitions, Belcher appealed to Newcastle in June 1733, then "these Affairs may have Dispatch, and thereby the King's Government & People be deliver'd from the Dangers & Difficulties they now lye expos'd to." Within weeks he received the news he had expected. The king had expressed "his high Displeasure" at the petitions, and the House of Commons had in the same vein branded them as "an high insult upon his Majesty's government . . . tending to shake off the dependence of the said colony upon the Kingdom." Belcher rejoiced. The news had "so qualm'd our petit House of Representatives That there is a rational Prospect of their Supplying the Treasury when they meet."[28]

Lest the initiative be lost, Belcher wrote to John Chandler thanking him for his support in the last session and urging him to attend in the fall. He also appealed to Stoddard. He accepted the "squire's" excuse for not attending the last session. But "I shall by no means be so (easy), if you fail of Coming (with all your County members) at the Adjournment of 3: October next. And it will be best that you all be here the first Day of the Court For the Affair of the Treasury must no longer be trifl'd with to the Ruin of the Province & the Government." Belcher had reason for concern. He had communicated London's opinions to the House during the August session. Although the king's rebuke dampened opposition spirits, Cooke was still undeterred. With Stoddard and the western representatives absent, the opposition leadership convinced a majority that a day should be set aside for "publick Prayer and Humiliation" and that in the meanwhile no concessions be made.[29]

In October Stoddard arrived with his cohorts. While the lawmakers deliberated over the treasury issue, Belcher sensed the outcome was uncertain. Each day the lawmakers spent "considerable time in debating." Both Cooke and the governor's friends appealed to a wavering core of undecided voters, and neither side could muster a steady majority. On the afternoon of October 25, after three weeks of debate, Stoddard reported from committee a final version of a bill for supplying the treasury. After deliberating on the bill for the remainder of the day and part of the next, a majority rejected it by a vote of fifty-one to twenty-seven. In the afternoon, however, several members called for a reconsideration of the vote. According to the record the motion provoked "considerable" debate. Several amendments were made, and the bill was passed by a margin of fifty to twenty-five. The governor's friends had prevailed upon the House to pass a bill without provision for House supervision of public funds. They had done so by also allowing the opposition to attach a statement of principle that affirmed "the Right of the Court to Supply the Treasury in the manner lately insisted on."[30]

Soon after the legislature's adjournment, Governor Belcher wrote to London announcing that "the great Dispute respecting the Supply of the

Treasury" had been won. He reminded Charles Delafaye, Newcastle's under-secretary, that when he had first applied for his commissions, he had promised that he could succeed where his predecessors had failed largely because he was a native New Englander. No one else could have "manag'd So Stiffe a People as these are. But I am so well knowing of their Humours and Circumstances, that they have not been able to impose upon me, or to make those Evasions, they might have done with a Stranger." He wrote letter after letter to disprove his critics. "I don't Suppose His Majesty cou'd have committed His Royal Commission to any Gentleman" so well deserving of that trust.[31]

In fact, Belcher was moving the province toward a political settlement. Although Cooke had declared his intention to renew the struggle over the treasury, he could no longer muster an audience. At the same time, Belcher's allies in London were successfully arguing for permission to accept another yearly salary grant. Their applications were becoming routine with the passage of each year. Belcher requested that he be relieved from repeating the process and that he be given a general leave for accepting the annual grant. In 1735 the Privy Council agreed. Thereafter, Belcher's salary would be passed each year by the legislature.[32]

Thus, within three years the governor had manipulated the political systems in London and New England. He had deceived and dissembled; he had switched allies when necessary; he had blustered and threatened; he had made compromises and concessions. He had proved himself a master at simultaneously maneuvering through the anterooms of power in London and manipulating the sensibilities and prejudices of the provincial legislature.

The administration's success also depended on avoiding confrontation over the paper-money question. While Belcher believed that the government's bills of credit had become a "publick Fraud," he also considered London's policy excessive. The colony's economy depended on paper money, and more than what his superiors allowed. Moreover, to press his instructions on a legislature that resisted currency contraction and the concomitant increase in taxes was foolhardy. Thus, Belcher prodded the lawmakers to attend to the issue. On occasion he chided them for failure to act. But he refrained from provoking controversy.[33]

His task was to steer a middle course between what were becoming increasingly irreconcilable positions. In 1733 the House leadership proposed a bill for the emission of £50,000 to be redeemed in bullion. Satisfied that the notes would not fall in value but mindful of his reputation in London, Belcher promised to ask his superiors for permission to approve the measure. A few months later, a group of merchants proposed to issue £110,000 in notes redeemable in silver. Usually Belcher distrusted private banks, but he knew and respected the men behind this project. While afraid to endorse the project, he did nothing that would endanger its success. The merchant notes, however, proved so sound an investment that hoarders quickly withdrew them from circulation. Meanwhile, London had rejected Belcher's arguments in favor of a government emission based on bullion. No solution to the money question seemed within reach. Belcher kept the peace by occasionally allowing a public emission in excess of his instructions and usually by avoiding the thorny issue of redemption.[34]

Belcher proved more adept at the simpler forms of calculating political interests. In 1735, when Boston's merchants and the legislature complained that the port's new naval officer, Benjamin Pemberton, was "extorting" "exorbitant and extorsive fees," Belcher proved himself again to be a sympathetic audience. When they demanded that Pemberton be removed, he explained that the office was no longer in his appointment. The Duke of Newcastle had imposed Pemberton on him, but he assured his visitors that he was working with his agents in London to regain control of the office. While he thought it imprudent to associate himself publicly with the merchants, he assured them that he was determined to protect their interest.[35]

The issue that proved most effective in creating support for the administration was the border dispute with New Hampshire. Diverse interests joined to support Massachusetts's claims. Several towns such as Salisbury, Amesbury, and Haverhill had extended their claims into the disputed areas; and the General Court had awarded large tracts in the contested region to the descendants of veterans of King Philip's War. Belcher's instructions required him as governor of both provinces to bring the two legislatures to negotiations. While he deliberately cultivated the impression of neutrality before his superiors in London, no New Englander doubted where his sympathies lay. As the negotiations proceeded, he worked with the Massachusetts legislature to bolster its claims in the disputed territory and simultaneously used his authority over the New Hampshire legislature to frustrate its preparations. Later Thomas Hutchinson recalled that as long as the border dispute continued "every party" cooperated "in defense of the right of the province." And so "we hear little of a party in opposition to the governor for several years together."[36]

The voices of opposition were becoming weaker. Elisha Cooke had lost control of the public agenda and the ability to impose the country's dramatics on political discussion. His self-proclaimed patriotism had turned to irresponsible demagoguery. Allies in Boston abandoned him. He became desperate and acted rashly. While the treasury dispute hung in the balance, he joined with David Dunbar. The surveyor general openly consorted with the governor's enemies in New Hampshire, had been recently appointed the province's lieutenant governor, and was therefore the most influential of Belcher's enemies. Cooke tried to keep his new association secret. Although Massachusetts had defeated Dunbar's challenge to its Maine lands, the surveyor general remained generally despised in Boston. Belcher, however, knew that the "two wretches" were "plotting & Caballing." Friends had intercepted their correspondence and had passed it on to him. Soon the Cooke-Dunbar alliance was common knowledge in the streets of Boston. Old allies abandoned Cooke. A coalition of merchants, many of whom were Belcher's friends, mounted the first effective challenge to his political organization in Boston. Although Cooke retained his seat in the legislature, his influence with his colleagues was on the wane. Belcher gloated: "The sot & his Adherents look like Fellows doom'd for Destruction." "Cooke is shrunk into an old Indian squaw." The administration, which Belcher likened to the "House of David," was triumphant.[37]

Hyperbole came easily to the governor. Belcher had prevailed in the legislature in part by playing a credible Nehemiah and thereby appealing to deep-seated conservative sympathies among the backbenchers. By framing the debates in his terms, he had denied Cooke his persuasive powers. But the old parliamentarian had not disappeared. The House majorities still allowed him great influence in the shaping of the agenda. His participation on committees had not declined appreciably. Moreover, Belcher's success rested on fragile foundations. His adherents were not dependable. His powers of patronage had limited effect on the leadership. Thus, Cooke continued to wield significant influence during the routine course of the legislature's business.

Belcher's dependence on "Squire" Stoddard served to remind him regularly how fragile his influence with the legislature was. As each session of the legislature approached, Belcher wrote to his "particular Friend" in Hampshire County urging him to attend. "I desire you wou'd not fail to be here with all your Friends." He assured Stoddard that the sessions would be short. Once he hinted that war was sure to break out in hopes of pricking the "squire's" concern for the frontier's defense. Belcher regularly listened to Stoddard's advice on appointments to the Hampshire County civil list and wrote to assure him that "the Officers of your County are settled as you have desired." Sometimes he withdrew a candidate of his own preference in deference to Stoddard's opinion. Stoddard's attendance, however, remained unreliable. Belcher offered his ally a seat on the Superior Court, but the "squire" did not wish to be kept in Boston and declined the offer.[38]

Thus, the governor's influence with the legislature remained evanescent. Although Elisha Cooke had lost the initiative, he still played a leading role in the House's proceedings. The backbencher majorities still allowed him to sit prominently on the important committees that set the legislature's agenda. Cooke continued to demonstrate his skills at parliamentary maneuver to the detriment of the governor. Convinced that agent Wilks worked for the governor, Cooke and his cohorts moved for his dismissal. When discovering that the opposition was discussing "Secret Attempts" against the agent, Belcher warned the House that he would dismiss the legislature for even considering such a move. His threat was heavy-handed, but he could not muster enough lawmakers in defense of the agent. Belcher often awakened to Cooke's abilities to manipulate the legislature. Once, during the fall session of 1736, Belcher helplessly watched a friendly majority evaporate. At the opening of the session, he concluded that the legislature was "one of the best . . . since my Arrival." The chances were good that the lawmakers would increase his salary to compensate for inflation. But soon he realized that Cooke was prolonging the proceedings. Each day the backbencher members were leaving for home. "The Enemy lay close in their lines . . . 'till my Friends were most of 'em tired and drew into home Quarters." Then the House voted not to increase the salary and to cut spending for defense. Belcher prevailed only by threatening the veto the entire salary bill. Again, without influence, Belcher had no choice but to employ the paper powers of office.[39]

Jonathan Belcher cultivated an image of himself as a master of political intrigue. It was a self-portrait that he dared to disclose for fleeting moments and always before a select circle, but it was an essential complement to his public image as the keeper of the covenant. He disclosed this other side of himself when he wrote to his son Jonathan. While dispensing advice, the father posed as model for emulation. Belcher presented himself as a man who knew the inner workings of English court society and who understood the rules for success. Often he couched his knowledge in aphorisms: "Secrecy is the Soul of Business"; "Prudens Qui Patiens." Success depended on cultivating impressions, sometimes even dissembling. It required the careful cultivation of "interests"; one "can't have too many Friends at Court." Political survival sometimes required "steering" between opposing camps, cultivating an image with one group and the opposite with another. It required the ability to keep interests dangling in suspense, to shift alliances and positions.[40] And while these skills were, no doubt, a necessity for political survival, Belcher also liked to consider himself a master of political manipulation and calculation.

When Belcher's critics branded him an apostate, they spied that part of him that was attracted to the art of courtly politics. Indeed, he did not hesitate to write the most fawning and sycophantic letters to his superiors in London. But others who raised Jonathan Belcher up as a keeper of the covenant also understood him. Though the roles of courtier and Puritan were not compatible, he never seemed troubled by the contrast, in part because he played each role separately before different audiences. Though he felt the seductions of the courtier, he kept that part of himself private, segregated, always secondary to the public role of covenant keeper. Like the cup bearer of the king of Babylon, he had mastered the art of political intrigue so that he might become the "Intercessor" between king and people and thereby the protector of the Puritan heritage.[41]

5

The Soul of Politics

In contrast to his leadership in Massachusetts, as governor of New Hampshire Jonathan Belcher revealed himself to be vindictive, petty, domineering, and factious. He forgot the virtues of "prudence and patience" and acted on impulses that he dared not display in Boston. Impulsive in his relationships with the province's political leaders, he repaid every slight, imagined or real, without calculating the consequences. If support was offered, it was scorned. Allies were not courted but provoked. Enemies, once made, were bullied, humiliated, taunted, and punished. Belcher's friends were appalled and warned that his behavior would work his downfall. But he ignored their warnings. Often he pursued an adversary simply to humiliate him. He entered a dark world in Portsmouth, one in which he felt himself surrounded by "vile" and "despicable" conspirators. He thought of his administration as the "House of David" and in his mind's eye he saw himself beset by the consorts of "Beelzebub the Prince of Devils."[1] Thus, at the same time that he pursued a political settlement in Boston, he was creating an opposition steeled in its determination to unseat him.

Yet Governor Belcher began his administration in New Hampshire on a happy note. Both Lieutenant Governor John Wentworth and his bitter rival Richard Waldron had pledged their support to the administration. When Belcher paid his first official visit in August 1730, he presented the legislature with his instruction for a permanent salary. The lawmakers saw no "inconstancy" between the prerogative and the liberties of the people and established an annual salary of £200 guaranteed for the duration of Belcher's term. In turn, the governor approved a bill for the emission of £1,300 in bills of credit. He objected that the House exceeded the limits set by his instructions when it voted to issue another £6,000 for the repair and erection of frontier defenses and courthouses. He did agree, however, that the lawmakers were acting "for the Interest of the Province" and promised to recommend the bill to his superiors in London. The legislature concluded the session by approving an address to the king thanking him for appointing this "kind father to this Province."[2]

But Belcher was already taking steps to foul the scene. Shortly after arriving in Portsmouth, he was informed that he was not the first to receive the lieutenant governor's support. On Burnet's death, Wentworth had made his offer first to Samuel Shute. No doubt he, like many others, expected the former governor to be the most likely candidate. He did not know of Belcher's bid for the office, but when he did, he immediately promised his cooperation. Belcher read the act as a sign of duplicity and disloyalty and summarily severed all relations with his lieutenant. According to custom, the governors, who resided in Boston and occasionally visited New Hampshire, allowed their lieutenants one-third of their salary. Belcher, however, refused to share the allowance. Although John Wentworth died before the end of the year, Belcher was already laying plans to drive all the Wentworths and their allies from government.[3]

Governor Belcher had blundered. He compounded the error by casting his lot with Richard Waldron. For three generations the Waldrons had figured prominently in New Hampshire politics.[4] Richard Waldron's grandfather had settled at Dover in the mid-seventeenth century, when it was part of Massachusetts; his trade in furs, timber, and lands turned a quick profit; and he was soon elected to the Massachusetts legislature, where in turn he was chosen its speaker. When New Hampshire became a separate province in 1679, he was appointed to the governor's Council. Meanwhile, his son, Richard's father, was elected to the House of Representatives, then selected its presiding officer, and later was appointed to the Council. While Richard Waldron grew to maturity, he heard stories recounting his father's part in deposing a lieutenant governor, and he saw his father acquire such appointments as colonel in the militia, provincial secretary, and judge of common pleas. Richard had gone to Harvard to prepare to take his father's place. When he returned in 1715, his uncle George Vaughan was appointed lieutenant governor. Vaughan, however, lasted only two years and was replaced by John Wentworth, who in turn saw to it that Waldron's father was removed from the Council.

Waldron had watched in dismay as the Wentworth family gained the ascendant. The Waldrons had made bitter enemies, but John Wentworth, a relative newcomer to provincial politics, quickly proved the most formidable adversary. During the 1720s, while Governors Shute and Burnet were preoccupied with Massachusetts politics, the lieutenant governor enjoyed a free hand in the distribution of favors. Two of his favorites were the wealthy Portsmouth merchants, Theodore Atkinson and George Jaffrey. Atkinson was appointed collector and naval officer at Portsmouth, sheriff, and clerk of courts; Jaffrey, already a councilor, was named treasurer, receiver general, and chief justice. Both would marry Wentworth's daughters. Wentworth also built his following by systematically granting lands on the frontier. In May 1727, for example, he created five new townships and issued grants in each to every member of the House of Representatives. Both because his government was small, with only eighteen representatives elected to the legislature, and because his family was large, with numerous opportunities for strategic marriages, Wentworth was able to secure an influence far greater than was possible in Massachusetts.[5] By 1730 he had built the foundations of a dynasty that would exercise unrivaled political dominance for two generations.

After his first visit to New Hampshire, Governor Belcher dismissed George Jaffrey from the Superior Court and then turned on Atkinson, stripping him of his sheriff's commission and the Portsmouth collectorship and naval office. He made these removals in part to strike "terrour" into potential adversaries. He also wrote Waldron asking for lists of the "Schemists" who wished the government ill and promised to "make thorro Work" of them. "And this I will do without respect to Persons, but the bigger they Are the more I shall be Inclined to Practice so Wholesome a Rule in Government." In December he dissolved the legislature and called upon Waldron to rally his friends to exert themselves against the "Grumbletonians" in the coming elections. Instead of routing the enemy, the "House of David" suffered its first defeat at the polls.[6] Indeed, the governor's behavior seemed to provoke opposition.

Belcher had miscalculated, but he had not acted from ignorance of New Hampshire's political scene. His wife was the daughter of the former lieutenant governor, William Partridge. He had done business with prominent Hampshiremen. He had even influenced appointments to the governor's Council during the Shute administration. Nor did he come to office with any great grudge to settle. John Wentworth had become lieutenant governor by deposing George Vaughan, who had married Belcher's sister Mary. But Mary had been dead for nearly twenty years. Moreover, Belcher had boasted that he had played an "important hand" in Wentworth's appointment. Twelve years later, when Belcher was in London applying for his own commissions, he had employed his influence successfully to remove Lieutenant Governor William Dummer from Massachusetts. He made no move against Wentworth and, instead, sent word ahead to assure the lieutenant governor of his favor.[7]

Belcher's change was largely due to Richard Waldron's influence. Waldron quickly insinuated himself into the governor's confidence. Skillfully, instinctively, he played upon the governor's sense of vulnerability and his craving for revenge and domination. Doubtless it was he who convinced Belcher that Wentworth preferred Shute and, therefore, was not to be trusted. He was such a master at speaking to the governor's heart that Belcher quickly made him his principal if not sole adviser and confidant on New Hampshire affairs. A remarkable and intense relationship developed.

For Waldron, who had grown desperate in his futile attempts to check the Wentworth "clan's" ascendancy, the governor proved essential. In turn, Belcher referred to Waldron as his "prime minister" and on occasion compared him to Sir Robert Walpole.[8]

The correspondence between Belcher and Waldron discloses a relationship remarkable and revealing, indeed one without compare in the governor's letterbooks. The two men began to write regularly shortly after their meeting at Portsmouth. There is no record of their correspondence before; suddenly they were writing weekly. What is most noteworthy is that their letters often contained little of substance. Waldron relayed every rumor of conspiracy, every whisper of insult, to his chief. His letters worked to prick Belcher's fears and his sense of vulnerability. They spoke to Belcher's heartfelt sense of society.

Through this correspondence the two men entered a dark and sinister world. They made their references to prominent "Grumbletonians" in code. There were "frogs paws," "Sancho," the "loon," the "ape," "guts." While the relationship enabled Waldron to repay long-standing resentments, it gave Belcher the opportunity both to express his sense of vulnerability and to pursue his enemies without restraint. He could bluster and vow revenge against the "male contents" and "Grumbletonians" in ways he dared not in Boston.[9]

For Belcher the relationship meant rare opportunity to give free rein to his most vengeful fantasies. He also found Waldron's dependence attractive. Waldron, in turn, played to Belcher's need to dominate. Belcher appointed Waldron provincial secretary on his father's death. Though others might be "obliged" to the governor, Waldron assured his chief that he had the greatest reason to be grateful. "How much more than the rest am I indebted in that regard who have been distinguished (perhaps) above all others who have had your Smiles in these parts." In response Belcher wrote that "when there is Opportunity to serve You, You'll be sure of my Friendship."[10]

Belcher governed by correspondence and by proxy. He rarely came to Portsmouth. Public business took little time, and he did not consider the province worth much attention. Not only was there little business to conduct, but he also had little respect for the leadership. The Wentworths were like himself, and unlike the Dudleys, newcomers. They were men of wealth but new wealth—not fixtures in New England's pantheon of greats. They did not inspire the awe that Paul Dudley did.[11] Moreover, Governor Belcher rarely had to confront his opponents. He had set a stage that enabled him to act on his impulses and without fear. Most important he had found the proxy to act for him.

With Waldron as his aide, Belcher plunged recklessly ahead. Defeat at the polls caused them to embrace stiffer measures, including a thorough purge of the civil list. Andrew Wiggin, the representative from Stratham and a Wentworth ally, had been chosen speaker again. Waldron reported that Wiggin valued his commission as justice of the peace "almost as his life" for it made him a "little God at Stratham." He promised that dismissal would prove an "unspeakable mortification" for Wiggin and would "Strike a dread on all that dare so much as to think dishonourably of your Excellency." The dismissal, however, should not be read in the usual manner before the Council. To be truly effective it should be announced in public before the "open Court" of general sessions. Belcher liked the advice. He also savored Waldron's report that the "Stroke upon Wiggin . . . has pall'd the party prodigiously" and that the "clan" was "dreading what will come next."[12]

If his friends were to "exert & bestir" themselves, Belcher expected that they would rout the opposition at the polls. As the elections of the summer of 1732 approached, he ordered Waldron to "struggle hard" and to call out the friends of the "House of David." When the votes were counted, however, Waldron reported that "The Discontented have Succeeded in their Choice almost to a Man." The lawmakers were governed by "Envy malice & hate and all the other Attributes of Satan."[13]

Few Hampshiremen seemed eager to associate themselves with the administration. In Portsmouth, Waldron found a handful of men, such as Henry Sherburne and Benjamin Gambling, who shared his resentments of the Wentworths. The governor's strongest supporters were in the interior towns of Exeter and Dover, which thrived on illegal timber cutting. Belcher had done business with the Gilmans of Exeter and the Gerrishes of Dover. As governor he made it clear that he would do nothing to enforce his instructions to prosecute illegal cutting and that he would do everything possible to check the surveyor general of the king's woods. The lumberers also knew that when they brought their contraband to Portsmouth, the customs officials were instructed to look the other way.[14]

Waldron and Belcher made out commissions for justice of the peace and militia officers for the Gilmans and Thyngs of Exeter and the Gerrishes and Millets of Dover. They agreed to appoint John Gilman to the Superior Court. When vacancies arose in the Council, they often turned to these families for nominations. But these allies were not enough. While Waldron had no difficulty compiling lists of Wentworth men to be purged, he could find few to take their place. No one in Stratham was willing to take Wiggin's post. The list of vacant positions grew. "What a Miserable Condition is this poor little Province in for want of Men of ability, & Integrity to fill ye vacant places in ye govern[ment]." From the justice of the peace to the Superior Court, the judicial system became virtually extinct. So, too, Waldron scoured the province in vain for candidates willing to challenge the "clan" at the polls.[15]

The Council seemed secure—at least for the moment. Of the four councilors who usually met with the governor, three—Shadrach Walton, Richard Wibird, and Henry Sherburne—were friendly. George Jaffrey, the only staunch Wentworth man, usually stayed away. With half of the dozen seats vacant, however, the balance might tip. Belcher nominated Waldron and Gambling and invited them to take their seats even before London had given its approval. Again he found it difficult to find others willing to accept. There were too few Hampshiremen qualified to sit on the Council, reported Waldron; and of those who were, most refused to lay out the money for the fees required to process the appointment.[16]

Being a Massachusetts man affected Governor Belcher's reputation significantly. New Hampshire, though separated from Massachusetts for nearly two generations, remained in the shadow of the parent colony. In time of war this little frontier colony looked southward for security. Since it had no newspaper of its own, Portsmouth relied on Boston's press. Its leaders—Richard Waldron, Benning Wentworth, Theodore Atkinson, George Jaffrey, Benjamin Gambling, Henry Sherburne—boasted Harvard educations. They often married into Massachusetts's leading families. As this little society grew, however, Hampshiremen in growing numbers were becoming impatient with their subordinate condition. Portsmouth's commercial community resented Boston's domination of its trade. The long-standing border dispute revealed Massachusetts's imperial ambitions to reduce New Hampshire. The Wentworths spoke to these resentments. Perhaps symptomatic of this mood, Atkinson, Jaffrey, and Wentworth had forsaken the church of their Puritan fathers and were organizing an Anglican church in Portsmouth. For the Wentworth men, the continuing union of the New Hampshire with the Massachusetts executive had become intolerable. Even while they consolidated their positions, they remained insecure and vulnerable as long as the governor in Boston could meddle in their affairs. Thus they sought not only to remove Belcher but to convince London to give the province its own separate governor.[17]

The first step toward complete political separation was a satisfactory resolution of the border dispute. Obviously, if Massachusetts were to uphold its claims, New Hampshire would be so reduced in size that separation would be a worthless prize. The province would be too small and poor to support its own governor. In addition, the separatists were land speculators who looked forward to realizing profits in the contested territory. They also expected Governor Belcher to act with extreme bias on the border issue and, thereby, to demonstrate their case for separation. They were disappointed, however, when Belcher transmitted his instructions to the two legislatures calling on them to appoint their negotiating teams. Governor Belcher was so confident

in the strength of Massachusetts's claims and in its resources to support a pro-
longed legal battle that he saw no reason to subvert the process. The
Massachusetts delegation, however, abruptly withdrew from the negotiations.
In the meantime, John Rindge, Portsmouth's representative, had set sail for
London with a petition signed by two Wentworths, Andrew Wiggin, Atkinson,
and Jaffrey, which argued for a separate governor.[18]

Waldron responded with his own petition and circulated it among the
Sherburnes, Gilmans, Gerrishes, and Thyngs. The governor's friends protested that they could not remain "Dumb" while "some Restless Persons"
contrived to "Disquiet the minds of the weaker sort amongst us" and to "sap
the very foundation of our Happiness." While Waldron resurrected familiar
arguments that New Hampshire was too poor to support a separate governor
and too weak to defend its frontiers alone, his arguments sprang from fears
that without the governor he and his friends would stand defenseless against
the "clan." Some of the governor's dependents were so desperate that they
advocated New Hampshire's complete and permanent annexation to
Massachusetts. Waldron pressed the idea upon his chief: "Oh, how happy
would our Union to ye Massachusetts be." In the meantime he worked
against the separatists by conferring with Massachusetts's representatives on
strategies for overturning New Hampshire's claims.[19]

Belcher did not share Waldron's sense of urgency and dismissed the call
for annexation. New Hampshire's affairs were a distraction from his more
immediate concerns with the Massachusetts legislature. Disappointed when
the border negotiations collapsed, he felt irritated with Cooke and the
Massachusetts leadership. But he did not worry about the separatists' challenge to his government. Confident that his friends and allies would easily
defeat Rindge's agency, he was not concerned by the weakness of his New
Hampshire alliances or by their association with annexation. The separatist
challenge only confirmed his opinion of the "clan's" depravity and its intolerable insubordination. "The Party . . . must not imagine that I will ever bear
any Slight or neglect" from those "who can't Submit to practice their Duty to
the Governor."[20]

Belcher was stunned, however, when within months of John Wentworth's death the king had named David Dunbar as lieutenant governor.
Dunbar's sponsors at the Board of Trade in particular were the same men
who were displeased by Belcher's appointment and were determined to
strengthen the surveyor general's powers. News of Dunbar's elevation
"amazed" Waldron. He reported that Dunbar was already consorting openly
with the governor's opponents in New Hampshire, that the "clan" was already
predicting the governor's fall, and that many Hampshiremen who were otherwise favorably disposed toward the administration had become faint of heart.
Dunbar's letters were intercepted and confirmed his association with the

"clan." The lieutenant governor corroborated accusations against the governor, supported the petition for separation, and nominated George Jaffrey to replace Belcher.[21]

Dunbar's presence, however, did not move Belcher to reconsider his course. He assured Waldron that his friends in London would prevent the "clan" from working further mischief. His immediate objective was to make the lieutenant governor powerless. In June 1731, just months after his appointment and while Belcher was in Boston, Dunbar approached the Council posing the question whether he had the right to sign legislation in the governor's absence. Waldron argued against the request, but while listening to Jaffrey press the point in the lieutenant governor's favor, he sensed that a majority was afraid. After strenuous argument the Council declined to take a stand. Belcher agreed with Waldron that Dunbar must be prevented from exercising any executive powers, even during the governor's absence. Dunbar was denied the right to convene the General Court, to sign legislation, and to command the military. He was not allowed a share of the salary, and he was denied use of the official seal of government, lest it be affixed to separatist petitions.[22]

Belcher acknowledged that the powers at question were sometimes "trifles," but he explained that his subordinate needed to be taught who was master. His object was to catch Dunbar "like a Bull in a Net." He was pleased with the thought of Dunbar grasping in vain for his official powers. Their "Denyal may serve for a little teazing." And Dunbar wrote home complaining that the governor had "maltreated" him: "I am of so little significancy that I am really ashamed."[23]

Dunbar's letter would have delighted Belcher. His friends in London, however, were appalled. Richard Partridge had no love for the Wentworths, but he found Belcher's lust for revenge excessive and his factiousness an embarrassment, impossible to defend. He warned that the Board of Trade's preference for Dunbar presaged future reversals, especially if Belcher continued to behave with such intemperance. Belcher dismissed his brother-in-law's letter as "taxing." He replied that he had "no need or desire to Create Enemies." He had acted in response to malicious provocations and only against those "who wou'd Affront & do me all the Ill Offices they Can." The punishments they received were "justly deserved."[24]

Partridge had reason to worry. In the winter of 1732, the king appointed Benning Wentworth, Atkinson, and Joshua Pierce, Sr.—all Dunbar's nominees—to the Council. Belcher was furious, even though Waldron and Gambling were also confirmed. "It's a new Thing under the Sun," Belcher protested to the Board of Trade, to give such preference to the recommendations made by a subordinate officer. To favor men "So obnoxious & opposite to the Govr" was "subversive of all Order & Government." His protest only earned him a stinging rebuke. The Board of Trade explained that he was wrong to "imagine" that because he was "directed" to make nominations to the Council, the government was obliged, in turn, to select from his list only. "We must inform you that you are very much mistaken."[25]

The reversals only seemed to steel Belcher in his determination to "trounce" his "vile" opponents. Before Wentworth, Atkinson, and Pierce received their papers of appointment, Belcher had resolved to "take the first fair Opportunity to Suspend them." Any evidence of defiance to his administration or disrespect for his office would suffice. In December 1732 Wentworth, Atkinson, and Pierce had received their appointment papers but agreed to postpone submitting them to the governor until the end of the next session of the legislature. All three held seats in the lower house and believed that they could do more damage to the governor there than in the Council. In response Belcher issued a proclamation demanding receipt of the papers "on Pain of His Majesty's Displeasure, and of such Penalties as may incur by Neglect and Disobedience." Pierce buckled. After he had humbled himself sufficiently before the governor, he was admitted to the Council chamber. Wentworth and Atkinson were unmoved, however, and led the House in opposition to the governor on the supply bill. Before dissolving the assembly, Belcher scolded the lawmakers for allowing "Sinister" men to influence their "insolent behavior" and for the "mischief" they had inflicted on the public. When Wentworth and Atkinson presented themselves to the Council, he then refused them admittance.[26]

"Doing Justice to my Enemies" became Jonathan Belcher's guiding principle in his government of New Hampshire. While instructing Ellis Huske, his naval officer at Portsmouth, to allow Exeter's illegal timber cutters free passage through the port, Belcher also encouraged him to seek out violations by the "clan" and to "lay his Paw" on illegal traders. He seemed especially happy when he heard that Huske was making ready to confiscate ships owned by either John Rindge or Benning Wentworth. Once, when Wentworth refused to pay the duties on one cargo, Belcher wrote to Huske encouraging him to proceed toward confiscation. "Notwithstanding the young Gentlm's pertness you may let him know I will be his master & Everybody's Else."[27]

Meanwhile Waldron was scouring government records and had discovered that Jaffrey and Atkinson were delinquent in their taxes. Prosecutions were initiated and Jaffrey went into hiding. Belcher gloated that he had driven "the Scotch loon" underground. Waldron also searched the records of land grants made during the Wentworth years. Large tracts that had been made out to the "clan" and its associates had been issued under the customary provision that the land be developed but, in fact, remained unimproved speculations against future sales. On discovery of such titles, Belcher and

Waldron denounced them as illegal and took stops to revoke the grants. Furthermore they denounced Lieutenant Governor Wentworth's behavior as an illustration of his flagrant and unjust use of privilege. Belcher found one grant of three hundred thousand acres that Wentworth had issued to himself and his family. In a proclamation of confiscation, he explained that such favoritism "by which some were to have all, while many not less deserving were excluded" from owning land could not be tolerated.[28]

While unrelenting in his determination to punish the "clan," Belcher seemed interested for a moment in improving his relationship with Dunbar. Rindge returned from London a complete failure; the "clan" seemed incapable of harming the governor. London, however, was attending sympathetically to Dunbar's claims for executive powers. Belcher pressed Partridge to "make a good stand in the Affair" and at the same time decided to assume a conciliatory manner with his lieutenant. He wrote to Dunbar in the summer of 1733 that he was ready to forget "all that has past between us. It will be a Pleasure to me to live with you for the future in a good understanding." He instructed his allies "to treat His Honour with . . . Respect & good manners" and ordered them to recognize the lieutenant governor's authority over Fort William and Mary. He sought out Dunbar's advice regarding patronage. He even attempted a casual familiarity with his one-time adversary. The day after a long evening of dining and drinking, he wrote confessing to Dunbar that "I am become so Silly a Piece of Clockwork."[29]

It was a clumsy gesture. Nor was he deceived when Dunbar expressed interest in a settlement. "Monsr," he confided to Waldron, "can turn into any shape to serve his turn." But the appearance of an accord might satisfy London. In the meantime Belcher made certain that all concessions extended to his lieutenant fell short of "substantive power." In December the lieutenant governor went before the Council demanding that he be invested with full executive powers in the governor's absence. After long and tense debate, Waldron prevailed upon a majority to deny the request. Belcher was triumphant upon receiving the report. During the next week he turned Dunbar's behavior into an unforgivable act of insubordination and depravity. "The more I dive into him the more I despise him as one abandon'd to Honesty & Honour, nor do I think any Work too dirty for his frog paws." No longer able to contain his feelings, he summarily broke off all communications with his lieutenant.[30]

The following spring Dunbar gave added cause for provocation. The surveyor general had sallied forth from Portsmouth at the head of a party of followers to arrest illegal timber cutters. When he arrived at Exeter, a band of men dressed as Indians descended upon him and drove him from town. When he appealed to three justices of the peace, John and Nicholas Gilman and Bartholemew Thyng, for assistance, they pretended ignorance of the deed and advised him to leave lest the "Indians" return. Dunbar wrote to the governor accusing the three justices of being accomplices to the rioters and demanding that the governor assist in the apprehension of the lawbreakers.[31]

Three days later Dunbar went before the Council demanding its support against the "Indians." The meeting had taxed Waldron sorely. Before the Council convened, two of the governor's allies had fled town. When the lieutenant governor demanded that the Council allow him to issue a proclamation posting a reward for the apprehension of the rioters, a majority seemed inclined to accede to his demands. Only after strenuous argument was Waldron able to convince the Council to vote that it was not capable of determining whether Dunbar had the right to issue a proclamation. Waldron understood that he had won a hollow victory and warned "Two or three Councils more will at last do something" for the opposition.[32]

Governor Belcher was not inclined to bend to Dunbar's demands, especially at the expense of his friends at Exeter. To refuse his lieutenant's request however, only gave his enemies the evidence they needed to remove him from office. The situation required the art of dissembling.

A week after the Council meeting, Belcher issued a proclamation ordering New Hampshire's officialdom to join the surveyor general in ferreting out the rioters. "And I do hereby also declare that who soever shall detect the Offenders . . . shall receive all proper Marks of the countenance & favour of this Government." Dunbar was furious: "Favorable Marks of countenance" alone would have little effect. If he had been governor, he would have ordered the sheriffs to raise posses to "Assist and Protect the Kings Officers." As matters stood, the rioters were free and the surveyor general dared not venture into the interior. When he called upon Ellis Huske to stop the export of contraband timber, the governor's ally paid him no attention. Dunbar saw himself powerless and alone, beset by the "Governour's Friends" who were joined in a "General Conspiracy." In rage he wrote to Belcher: "Well may ye People call your Administration calm, when they go unpunish'd for such Outrage."[33]

Belcher gloated at the thought of Dunbar thrashing helplessly in his "net," but he worried when he considered London's response. "Its certainly wise," he wrote Waldron, "to prevent Monsr from having the least Pretence of making a true & just Complaint against the Govr & Council." Thus, he issued another and stronger proclamation directing the justices of the peace to confiscate all illegally cut timbers. His orders came in autumn, after the lumbermen had time to rid themselves of their contraband. One justice, George Jaffrey, leaped at the opportunity to incriminate the governor's friends but quickly discovered what Belcher already knew. "Your Excellencys Warrant to us," he wrote, "Came too Late." "If it had been seasonable We should have Exerted our Selves for his Majestys Service in Obedience to your

Excellency." When the next snows fell, signaling a new cutting season, the lumbermen commenced their operations unimpeded by the surveyor general.[34]

The riot not only confirmed Governor Belcher in his opinion of Dunbar but also convinced him that it had finally revealed his lieutenant's "vile," "insolent," and violent character to the world. He explained to the Duke of Newcastle and the Board of Trade that the issue was not the enforcement of royal forest policy but Dunbar's violent and tyrannical deeds that "wou'd better suit to the government of France or Turkey than what is marked by the constitution of Great Britain." Belcher was dissimulating when he presented himself as a friend of England's forest policy. He also wrote from solid conviction that the surveyor general's behavior was reprehensible. He expected the riot would awaken the people and spark a rekindling of public virtue throughout the province of New Hampshire. "Methinks these Violences must open the Eyes of the whole Province." The people would no longer allow themselves to be "bamboozl'd" by a small band of "Male contents." The next elections would bring final victory to the "House of David." In the meantime he laid plans to circulate a petition in support of his government throughout the province.[35]

Waldron was skeptical. He had been witness to the failed attempts to rally the people at the polls against the "clan." After one such rout in which the "WiseAcres" and the "Discontented" had succeded "in their Choice almost to a man," he advised his chief that "frequent Dissolutions" may be a "necessity . . . till the People's eyes are enough open to discern their own interest." A year later he despaired at seeing a change in the electorate and concluded that it made no difference whether the governor kept or dissolved the present House of Representatives.[36] Waldron already understood that the Exeter riot had not altered public opinion. Few were willing to sign his petition in support of the governor. "It is [a] difficult task to engage People in a Controversy . . . between a Governour & Lieutenant Governour especially on ye side yt [that] they apprehend is Sinking. 3/4 of Portsmouth & all Stratham with most of Newington & Many in other Towns believe at this Instant that Don Quixoite [Dunbar] will be the Chief in a month."[37]

More than the Wentworths' popularity or superior organization plagued the governor. Belcher's manner of governing contributed to his own undoing as well. His reputation as a Massachusetts man, his preference to govern from Boston and by proxy, and his habit of visiting Portsmouth only occasionally caused Hampshiremen to listen with skepticism when he professed concern for their welfare. They had little cause to trust his offer to act as impartial mediator of the border dispute, especially when his closest associates were advocating annexation to Massachusetts. Indeed, his response to the province's economic hardships bespoke an indifference, even a callousness, toward the public welfare. Both friends and enemies of the governor believed that the province was too poor to raise the taxes necessary for redeeming paper money. When London refused to heed the province's request for permission to emit more than what was allowed by the governor's instructions, Belcher pressed the legislature to withdraw the currency in circulation. The house responded that the governor's policy would put "the People whom we represent, under the most distressing circumstances imaginable." The government's expenses could only be met by paper money. "An additional tax . . . would have a greatr tendency to fill the Publick Goals than supply the Treasury." Belcher would not compromise. He rejected the house's measures to supply the treasury. By 1734 the government had been without funds for over two years and the exchanges between the governor and legislature were becoming more rancorous.[38]

The governor's allies disagreed with him. Waldron urged his chief to relent: "calling in ye Debts of ye Province . . . must inevitably ruin a Considerable number of Persons & family[s]." Redemption was universally obnoxious. If the lawmakers were to follow the governor's lead, "they would be basely slur'd as Conspirators against ye Common interest of ye people." Belcher did not heed this advice, however. When the legislature declined to take steps for withdrawing paper issued at loan, he issued executive orders for the prosecution of delinquent borrowers and if need be the confiscation of their lands given in surety.[39]

In contrast to his behavior in Massachusetts, he acted ruthlessly, even against the opinion of his allies. In 1735 the governor's supporters Sherburne and Wibird joined with leading members of the "clan" to create a private bank, which would issue £25,000 in notes. Belcher was appalled. It was a "Bank of Wind"; its notes were "fit for bottoms of pyes (or fouler uses)." Unlike his response to the Merchants Bank in Boston, he responded viciously and without restraint, even though Waldron counseled moderation. He discovered that Wibird was "a very mean narrow spirited Creature" and revoked his appointment as sheriff. Alarmed by Sherburne's "unsteadiness," he wrote reminding him that he had appointed Sherburne treasurer and his son clerk of the inferior court. It was a thinly veiled threat. When he called on the New Hampshire legislature to take action against the bank, Representatives Rindge and Gerrish put aside their animosities to defend the project and to blame the governor for undermining the economy.[40]

Even Waldron's spirits seemed to flag. In early 1735 he wrote to his chief confessing that he had been meeting with the opposition. He thought that a settlement could be achieved if his chief appointed Wentworth and his leading allies to the government. Belcher was disgusted when he read the letter. He conceded that appointing his opponents to "Places of Profit and Power" would have a "healing Vertue." But Waldron's proposal was a "Delirium." The

"Grumbletonians" deserved the gallows and "Neckcloths . . . of the intended Manufacture." He would not rest until he had made Dunbar, that "finisht Villain," into a "complete Victim."[41] He left Waldron little choice but to forget a settlement and stand fast against the "clan."

The "House of David" stood in ruins, its allies dispirited and ineffective. Even the Council was becoming unreliable. In the spring of 1734, eight councilors had signed a petition to the government in London defending the governor and calling for Dunbar's dismissal, but Waldron had seen allies lose their nerve and absent themselves from critical meetings. A quorum stood at three, and with "one or 2 of ye right side being absent" the opposition could steal control of the Council like a "thief." Thus, he wrote to Boston that he "always thot it best to have no Councils but in case absolute need."[42]

As the governor's influence dwindled, he was left with only the paper powers of his office. Even his power to make appointments did not translate into effective influence. He jealously guarded his powers to convene, adjourn, and dissolve the General Court and to sign or veto its legislation. In desperation Waldron and Belcher sought to stretch the powers of the executive. After watching the "clan" take its campaign from one town to the next during the several days that the polls were open, Waldron recommended that the elections be held on a single day so that "there wont be so good an opportunity for ye Clan here to ride from Town to Town." His researches suggested that if the governor had the right to reject a speaker of the house and to dismiss a councilor for bad behavior, he also had the authority to annul the election of representatives he deemed obnoxious. Waldron promised that by doing so the governor would "keep the enemy in awe & in the greatest dread." Belcher was intrigued, and in the spring of 1735 he ventured to deny the oath of office to two opposition lawmakers. He must have felt discomfort, for when the House insisted that it alone had the right to "judge of the due or undue Elections," he swiftly backed down.[43]

He showed no inclination, however, to alter his approach to government in New Hampshire, largely because he did not believe the Wentworth alliance capable of doing him serious harm. Although his superiors in London had on occasion reprimanded him and even forced him to admit Wentworth and Atkinson to the Council, he was confident that his agents and allies wielded more influence than the "clan." Although the Board of Trade had found in favor of Dunbar's right to wield executive powers, Partridge had used his influence so that the report lay "stale & dead" in the government's back offices. Although Dunbar's friends at the board were pressing their investigation of the Exeter riot, Belcher's friend Sir Charles Wager from the Admiralty managed to move the file to his office, where it was buried. Dunbar grew impatient and by 1735 was writing home that he was thinking of resigning his commissions. His letters were intercepted, and Belcher gloated when he read them. He also dismissed the "clan" and its campaign for separation. Rindge returned home in defeat. Even though the separatists had found a more able agent in John Thomlinson, a London merchant, Belcher remained confident that he was safe in Partridge's hands. Moreover, he was sure that Massachusetts's superior wealth and the influence of its agent Francis Wilks would eventually wear down the separatists in their campaign for a favorable border settlement. [44]

Belcher and Massachusetts's lawmakers had grown arrogant in their belief that by clever maneuver and procrastination and with more money they could overcome the separatists' petitions for the appointment of a royal border commission. In January 1736 Thomlinson convinced the Privy Council to appoint a royal commission. Wilks had been completely outmaneuvered. When he tried to influence the selection of the commission members, Thomlinson easily persuaded the Privy Council to reject his nominations. The Board of Trade quickly drafted the final orders for convening the commission on August 1, 1737, in the disputed territory at Hampton. Massachusetts was amazed. Belcher scolded Wilks: "it has been more than once flurted that Captain Thomlinson was too cunning and out-witted you." [45]

The separatists celebrated. But they had come to know their opponent well and had learned to anticipate that he would somehow devise a scheme to "distress this Province." Thomlinson understood that the initiative must not be lost. While the Board of Trade was preparing its instructions to Governor Belcher and to Lieutenant Governor Dunbar outlining the procedures to be followed during the border negotiations, the agent called on Martin Bladen requesting that he be given both copies for delivery to America. If Dunbar alone received the instructions, he could summon the General Court into session during the governor's absence and thereby give the lawmakers the opportunity to prepare their arguments free from Belcher's interference. Furthermore, if the governor were kept in the dark, he might stumble and upset the proceedings. And if his behavior could be construed as prejudiced, it would provide corroborating evidence for separation. Bladen agreed. [46]

The instructions arrived in Portsmouth during the winter of 1737. Waldron reported that they "are now and then Traveling thro ye Province, to be read in Every Chimney corner." Belcher fumed with rage as he reflected on the "insult." When he opened the intercepted letters between his opponents, he saw that they were preparing not only to prevail on the border but to use his behavior as evidence in support of separation. The situation required all his skills at deception. "I am determined," he confided to Waldron, "not to act one thing that shall [appear to be] the Face a Block to their way."

He cultivated the appearances of impartiality. Yet he assured Waldron that the separatists would encounter "many Obstacles."[47]

Belcher enjoyed two advantages. First, Dunbar was eager to leave New England in the spring. After six years of futile sparring with his chief, he promised himself that he would not postpone his departure even to convene the General Court in the governor's absence. Second, with Dunbar gone, Belcher could turn the separatists' tactics against them. He could claim that he had not received a copy of his instructions and that if he by chance acted incorrectly, he had been made the dupe of his enemies. Even after he had in fact received a copy of his instructions in late April, he continued to feign ignorance.

In March 1737 Belcher went to Portsmouth to meet with the New Hampshire House of Representatives. He announced to the lawmakers that recent reports from London caused him to believe that the government had made a decision on the border. While claiming that he had not learned anything substantial, he recommended that the legislature begin preparing its case. On April 1 the House proposed a joint committee to gather evidence and chose four of Belcher's opponents to serve on the committee. The proceedings went smoothly. After three weeks Belcher adjourned the house until July 6. Although the house had not yet named its delegation, it would have nearly a month before the royal commission began its proceedings.[48]

At the end of June, Belcher moved the date for reconvening the New Hampshire House to August 4, three days after the commission was scheduled to begin its hearings. When the commission convened, it first heard a petition from the joint committee of the New Hampshire legislature, arguing that it be recognized since the House had not been allowed to appoint an official delegation. The petition was accepted and the commissioners began to hear New Hampshire's arguments. But Massachusetts was not present. Belcher had kept the Massachusetts legislature in session from the end of May to the first week of July—ample time to prepare its case. Then, still feigning ignorance, he adjourned the legislature until August 10—more than a week after he knew the royal commission would meet. A week passed filled with confusion and delays before both official delegations appeared. Belcher knew that the proceedings were already fraught with enough errors to "vitiate all present Proceedings of the Commissioners." He assured Waldron that they "may have their business to do over again."[49]

On September 2 the commission reported its conclusion. If, as Massachusetts argued, the charter of 1691 did give the Bay Colony "all the lands granted by the Charter of King Charles the First," its claims were valid. If not, New Hampshire's claims should stand. Since the commission could not decide, the question should be referred back to the Privy Council. The commissioners then adjourned to October 14 to give each province time to prepare its response.[50]

Belcher kept the Massachusetts legislature in continuous session from August 10 to October 20. As he and the lawmakers prepared their case, he assured Waldron that Massachusetts would prevail. New Hampshire's claims were "vile," unworthy of consideration, and indefensible. At the end of the session the lawmakers granted the governor £300 for his "extraordinary Trouble and Expence in the Service of the Province." By contrast Belcher kept the New Hampshire lawmakers in adjournment from the moment the commission had delivered its ruling until October 13. New Hampshire had a single day to prepare its response. The House of Representatives under Wentworth leadership hastily drafted its reply but on sending it up to the Council learned that the upper house had already resolved not to make an appeal and had adjourned for the day. Belcher was so confident of his majority at the Council table that he did not bother to attend until the next day. Thus, the House was forced to submit its appeal without the Council's approval. [51]

By 1735 it was clear that the "House of David" stood in ruins. The separatists were making their points against the governor in London. The governor's friends were an isolated and ineffective minority in New Hampshire. Belcher's dreams for a moral awakening had not come about. His enemies had joined with "Beelzebub the Prince of Devils" to seduce the people. "It has always appeared odd to me," Belcher reflected, "that our Friends, who hold all the Places of Power & Profit have not been able to carry greater Sway among the Multitude." He had lost the House of Representatives where the "Devil" had forged "so many Links to his Chain." The Council, his last redoubt, seemed to be slipping from his grasp. [52]

Belcher might have steered his administration in another direction. He owned that he might have made peace with the "clan" and made himself "perfectly easy." He also denied that his troubles were the result of his "irreconcileable Temper"; to the contrary, he reflected to Waldron, "you shan't find me more backward to live in peace with all mankind." The price of peace with the "clan" was too high; it was not consistent with "the King's Honour & my own." It required him to abandon "all my Friends." "It is not in my Nature to be guilty of any Thing so mean, so villanous & so dishonourable; no, I had rather be entirely quit" of the government than stoop so low.[53]

He had not acted from political expediency or from an instinct for survival, as had Waldron. Indeed, at the outset of his administration he did not believe that the "clan" constituted a threat. His vengeful conduct in New Hampshire stood in marked contrast to the "prudence and patience" he exercised in Massachusetts. He never attempted to keep New Hampshire's political elite dangling in suspense. The opposition that he encountered at Portsmouth represented an insufferable test of his authority and power. The challenge became a matter of honor. Thus, with Waldron at his side, Jonathan Belcher entered a dark and foreboding world filled with conspirators. In turn he allowed his vengeful impulses free rein. In Portsmouth he wielded his authority in an overbearing manner that he dared not reveal in Massachusetts, except in the privacy of his home and in his relations with his sons.

In time he came to recognize that his powers of office had little influence. Isolated, he saw no end to "Plagues and Fluctuations." "You are," he wrote to Waldron in righteous resignation, "certainly in a sad Condition both in Church & State." He could do no more. He prayed that "unless Heaven is kinder, than those that rebel against it deserve, & deliver you, I see no End of Confusion." His lust for vengeance turned to pious reflection. Unwilling to alter his course and incapable of striking "terrour" into his foes, he preferred not to confront the situation in New Hampshire. After the border negotiations, Belcher did not venture into New Hampshire again for more than a year. Recognizing that the House of Representatives was "always a dead weight against me," he called only four sessions during the next four years.[54]

Meanwhile, he knew that the "clan" was sending petitions demonstrating his prejudices against the province's welfare. His agents in London were harried by the complaints regarding his conduct of the border negotiations. "Every ship," he wrote to Waldron, "will plague us with new Complaints." He urged his stalwart to prepare his own petitions. The weakness of Belcher's position seemed to become more evident. Allies defected. A few die-hards, such as Waldron, pinned their political survival on annexation to Massachusetts. Belcher put aside his initial reservations and supported New Hampshire's reincorporation with the Bay Colony. Waldron, in turn, could find few Hampshiremen to sign his petitions, and he reported to his chief that several town meetings passed resolutions condemning annexation. Belcher concluded that the governor's allies were "so intimidated that they dare not pursue the honest sentiments of their Hearts for the happiness of their Country."[55]

The reports from London were discouraging. John Thomlinson was busily constructing a formidable alliance and directing a several-pronged assault on the administration. He mustered fresh evidence regarding illegal lumbering and the Exeter riot. Ralph Gulston, a London merchant and mast contractor to the royal navy, was convinced that the king's timber reserves would be secured only with a different governor. In addition Thomlinson was convincing imperial officials that the governor's behavior was "opprobrious," a sufficient cause for dismissal, and reason to consider complete separation of the two governments. Thomlinson was also meeting with Massachusetts's discontented to coordinate a joint assault on both governments. With Dunbar out of the way, he turned to Benning Wentworth as his prime candidate.[56] Belcher read the reports from London with growing concern. "I beg of you," he wrote Partridge, "to go on to use all the Interest you can make to prevent" the loss of the New Hampshire government. The post was a "mean" one, but its loss would be a "leading Card" to removal from Massachusetts.[57]

Slowly Belcher began to prepare himself for defeat by playing the victim of factious malcontents. Instead of the avenger, he began to play the martyr beset by wicked predators. He prayed for the people: "the vulgar, ignorant People of New Hampshire (which may in every place always be computed at 19-20ths) have been deluded & misled. Yet I really pity 'Em." He resolved to continue the fight for the "House of David." "I must fight upon my own Stumps, & make the best Defense I can for myself & for [the] poor deluded People."[58]

6

Servant to the King and People

During the autumn of 1739, Governor Belcher congratulated himself: "How happy is it . . . That my administration is Extending itself to ten years."[1] He loved to boast of his achievement, and he seized every opportunity to explain that his endurance rested on the justice and righteousness of his government. He had fulfilled the promises he had made when taking office: as a native son he could restore peace among his people and reconcile them to the king. These were the twin pillars of his government—king and people. He liked to pose as the faithful servant of both king and people and to claim that he had, in turn, won the approval of both. Another and less visible part of him, however, played at the imperial manipulator and courtier, the calculator of interests, and dissembling tactician. These, too, were talents necessary for a Nehemiah to succeed in this whiggish age.

Belcher grew steadily confident in his abilities, especially after he had maneuvered Massachusetts's constitutional disputes to resolution. By 1736 he felt sure enough of himself to challenge Paul Dudley. On the eve of the councilor elections, he and his friends privately pressed the lawmakers not to cast their votes for Dudley. When Dudley was returned with 117 of 124 votes, Belcher tolerated his "insufferable Insolence" for another year; the following May he rejected Dudley's reelection. Two years later, however, he was dismayed, first, to see that the people of Roxbury had sent his adversary to the lower house and then to learn that the lawmakers had chosen him speaker. Belcher rejected the selection. On the next day he disapproved Dudley's election to the Council. Convinced for some time that Dudley was conspiring with Jeremiah Dummer to undermine his standing with the government in London and that his old nemesis was the chief instigator of the opposition in the General Court, Belcher could no longer contain his rage. Soon reports of the feud were rippling through the anterooms of the powerful in London. Belcher's friends wrote to warn him that Dudley had influential friends who were expressing concern and displeasure with the governor's behavior.[2]

The Dudley-Belcher feud illustrated the nature of the governor's relationship with the people and the king. Although Belcher demonstrated a talent for political survival, his relationship with the public and with his superiors always rested on fragile foundations. His own experience and successes in London had taught him to understand the vicissitudes of imperial politics. A single individual with a few well-placed connections and a talent for courtly intrigue could work significant and damaging effect on an administration. So, too, Dudley's standing with Massachusetts's lawmakers repeatedly demonstrated the limits of the governor's influence. The people's approval, like the king's, was a fabrication necessary for Belcher to fulfill the ideals of his role. In both cases approval dissolved into indifference. Indeed, his success and endurance rested on a public that did not bother with his government and an imperial authority that was irregular, even fickle, in its attendance to his affairs.

Belcher was always fretting over London's intrigues. Each year he watched the discontented set sail to air their grievances before his superiors. In addition to the New Hampshire separatists, there was a handful of dissatisfied Massachusetts men who sought to do him harm. Though the causes for complaint were often petty and personal, Belcher knew the ways of London politics well enough not to discount any of his critics. Thus, he felt compelled to defend his treatment of Dudley. Whenever an opponent set sail, he dispatched letters to friends and agents warning them of his malevolent intentions. He waited impatiently for letters from his allies and gleaned their reports for every scrap of information and hint of intrigue.

Perhaps it was inevitable that some of Boston's merchants would break with the administration. Samuel Waldo, who had joined with Elisha Cooke in speculating in lands in the Maine region, had good cause to support the governor against David Dunbar. With the settlement of the dispute with Dunbar, however, Waldo moved in another direction. As an agent for the powerful English mast contractors of Ralph Gulston and Company, he collided with illegal timber cutters who were protected by the governor. Waldo began to work with the New Hampshire separatists and Dunbar. Belcher responded by challenging Waldo's claims to the Maine lands. In the name of fair play, he encouraged the local Indians to accuse Waldo of cheating them of their lands. Waldo took his case to the Massachusetts Council, but to no avail. Desperate and embittered, he left for England to work for the governor's dismissal.[3]

The Allens also turned on the governor. In the summer of 1736, Belcher disapproved the reelection of Jeremiah Allen as provincial treasurer after twenty years of service. Although Belcher justified his decision on the grounds that the old man was "render'd incapable by a numb Palsey," Allen's sons, James and Jeremiah, were furious and openly joined Elisha Cooke and his cohorts. When the younger Jeremiah sailed for England in quest of revenge, Belcher wrote warning Partridge to keep a lookout for the "young Spark." Partridge reported that Allen was consorting with the New Hampshire separatists and that he was encouraging an ambitious and well-connected young Englishman, James Glen, to apply for the Massachusetts government. Though disappointed when Glen became governor of South Carolina, Allen persisted in his campaign. When he learned that Belcher was delinquent in his debts owed to the Lloyds, he pressed them to support his efforts to remove the governor. Belcher tried to dismiss Allen's assault as "ridiculous," but he was soon preparing the sale of lands in order to satisfy his creditors.[4]

Though the Allens were no great threat in America, Jeremiah Allen might discredit the governor with an important London official. He might defeat the governor on a minor issue, but a small point gained in London could be blown up into a major defeat for the administration in Boston and Portsmouth. Belcher knew that his New Hampshire allies listened to the rumors of his imminent dismissal, and he sensed their timidity. He was constantly seeking to counter impressions of his weakness.[5]

Belcher felt the insecurities that came from the distance separating him from the seat of power. He became especially dependent on Richard Partridge, and he waited often impatiently for his letters. Often he was vexed with his brother-in-law for not writing as regularly as he expected or for failing to include as much information as he required. In times of crisis, Belcher relied on his son Jonathan to assist Partridge. Though they were on opposite sides officially, Belcher also turned to his former associate Francis Wilks. He noted that Wilks was close to Wilmington and had spent an evening dining with the privy councilor. Whenever possible, Wilks used his influence in London and with the House of Representatives on behalf of the governor.[6]

Belcher felt exposed to his enemies from the moment he left London. Lord Townsend, who had been instrumental in gaining Belcher's appointment, had resigned shortly after Belcher had returned to Boston. Yet Newcastle remained in charge of colonial affairs; Martin Bladen continued to sit at the Board of Trade, where he frankly expressed his contempt for the governor; and Prime Minister Robert Walpole was indifferent to Massachusetts politics. Belcher's chief advocate in the government was Sir Charles Wager, who took an active interest in colonial affairs, was a close associate of the prime minister, and was appointed first lord of the Admiralty in 1733. Lord Wilmington, the president of the Privy Council, and Arthur Onslow, the speaker of the House of Commons, also seemed friendly to the governor.[7]

Belcher sent gifts to Walpole, Wilmington, and Newcastle. He regularly wrote to his son prodding him to cultivate an interest with the government. He advised Jonathan to overlook the opinion of his critics and to ingratiate himself with them whenever possible, to avoid making insults or treading on the interests of the powerful, and to be constant in currying the favor of friends and patrons. He penned fawning letters to the Duke of Newcastle and proposed that his son write and publish a poem in honor of the duke. When besieged by enemies, he appealed to Queen Caroline, whom he knew was a close friend to Walpole and the prime minister's faithful advocate to the king. After reminding the queen of his first audience with her at Hanover, he pled for "a Share in your Justice & Favour, that I may still enjoy the Royal Grace."[8]

The courtier's arts of pleasing and flattery were not enough to survive, however. Belcher understood the inner workings of government—especially the necessity for subterfuge, dissimulation, and backroom intrigue. He became assiduous in his attention to London politics, the shifting relations within the government, and the jostlings for power among cabinet ministers and imperial administrators. He was constantly dispensing advice to his allies. He reminded his brother-in-law that Bladen could be expected to oppose him on anything "as he wou'd 'a' done My being Govr if the Board of Trade had known it." Since he had "no Dependance" on the board, he proposed that Partridge work secretly, "privately," "without [its] Knowledge." When the board began to review Dunbar's account of the Exeter riot, Belcher's allies seemed unable to check the governor's opponents until Sir Charles Wager maneuvered the case to his department, where it was safely lost.[9]

Belcher's most reliable support came from outside the government. Organized Protestant dissent had impressed Robert Wapole and his allies. In return for votes, the prime minister lifted civil disabilities from dissenting Protestants and extended patronage to their leaders. In the 1730s Congregationalists, Presbyterians, and Baptists came together in the Protestant Dissenting Deputies to act as a lobby with the government. Among its leading members were Samuel Holden, Benjamin Avery, and Isaac Watts—all of whom were Belcher's frequent correspondents. Perhaps Robert Walpole did not pay much attention to the governor of Massachusetts, but he did listen to these dissenters and did not forget their efforts on his behalf during the elections of 1734. Belcher was quick to recognize that "Mr. Holden's great Interest with Sir Robert" was crucial to his survival. He actively courted the Dissenting Deputies and often relied on Benjamin Colman to write on his behalf.[10]

So, too, Belcher understood the weight of Quaker influence. When confronted by possible defeat at the Norwich elections, Walpole had called upon the Quakers, in particular his friend John Guerney, for support. Similarly, the Duke of Newcastle actively courted Quaker votes in his bailiwick of Sussex. And Belcher, in turn, counted on Partridge's standing in the Society of Friends. He was quick to remind the English Quakers of his service on behalf of their coreligionists in Massachusetts. Partridge had no difficulty in mustering support for his brother-in-law. In 1737 the London Friends appointed a committee "to write Letters up and down the Kingdom in behalf of the Governor and to engage all their good offices for his Service." Partridge wrote to the Quakers of Coventry and Sussex urging them to write a "Suitable letter to your Members of Parliament" and advising them to "meet with ye proper Persons in Authority in behalf of Governor Belcher." The English Quakers came quickly to the governor's support. Belcher regularly wrote to "My Good & Worthy Friends" and sometimes separately to Guerney to thank them for "the great Respect & friendship you have manifested to me upon the many Efforts my Enemies have been making to have the Commissions I have the Honour to hold superseded."[11]

Belcher thought of himself as a master of political intrigue and manipulation, and those who struggled so long to unseat him agreed. His political fortunes also rested on the indifference of English officialdom, on the inefficiencies within the imperial administration, and on rivalries within the government. The Walpole government was a coalition of political rivals. Townsend, Wilmington, and Newcastle sparred with each other and tested each other's influence by meddling in colonial appointments. Townsend advanced Belcher to humble Newcastle. And Wilmington used Belcher to test Newcastle's influence. What was at stake was not London's government of the colonies; it was control of England's domestic affairs. And Belcher was a token in these gambits. If he became important to the prime minister, it was because English domestic interests worked in his favor. Belcher also survived because he took advantage of government floundering, in particular the propensity for agencies to work at cross purposes. Thus, he could evade the influence of both the Board of Trade and the secretary of state for southern affairs. It was these inefficiencies and rivalries that stymied imperial reform. In sum Belcher survived by exploiting these contradictions. He endured by playing the pawn. But he kept office without the strong support of a patron.

Belcher was not ignored entirely. Sometimes London attended to his government in a manner that was intrusive and, indeed, subversive to his administration. Young men from England regularly descended on him with letters of recommendation or papers of appointment. In 1731, a letter arrived from Lord Barrington, Shute's brother-in-law, proposing that a place be found for a family friend, John Boydell. Belcher complied by splitting the Boston naval office in half and later by moving Boydell on to the port's postmaster.[12] Later, he received William Fairfax, a relative of a commissioner of customs and of Martin Bladen. After scouring the province for a suitable position, he installed Fairfax as a naval officer at Salem. When he advanced the young man to a collectorship at Boston, he wrote to Bladen that the appointment was "one of the best in the King's Gift, in this Government."[13]

Political survival dictated that the governor accommodate London's patronage mongers. In turn, by relinquishing important powers of appointment, he deprived himself of the means to build support for his governments in New England. There were too few offices at his disposal, he complained. The few plums at his disposal were gobbled up by English placemen. The situation was the same in New Hampshire. In the autumn of 1731, Anthony Reynolds arrived with letters of introduction from his father, the Bishop of Lincoln, and from Martin Bladen suggesting that he be appointed customs collector and naval officer at Portsmouth. Again Belcher complied by dismissing two of his allies.[14]

Accommodating the strangers was the price to be paid for staying in office, but Benjamin Pemberton was too much for Belcher to endure. In 1733 Pemberton, an English merchant down on his luck but with good connections, arrived with the king's warrant directing the governor to appoint him to the Boston naval office. Belcher read the order as tantamount to theft. The appointment was by custom his to make. It was the "best Perquisite . . . , the only thing of Profit absolutely in my Gift." He had appointed his son-in-law, Byfield Lyde to the post. But "Where there is the Word of a King there is Power, and When my Master Commands my Duty is to obey, altho' it be to take Bread from my own Family." He obeyed, while protesting vigorously to his superiors that the order was unconstitutional, "hard & Severe," even "cruel." Appointing this "obscure Creature" was an insult that he could not forget, a price too high for him to accept. A year later he wrote to Walpole and Newcastle requesting that the injustice be corrected and to Partridge instructing him to seize the first opportunity to regain control of the office. At the end of the decade he was still pressing for the office.[15]

Of all the strangers imposed on him, Belcher came to recognize one as "Dangerous." In the fall of 1731, he received William Shirley. Clearly the young attorney had come to New England because he was down on his luck. Like others he came with only one asset—a letter, in this case from the Duke of Newcastle. At first, Belcher was not moved to take special notice of the adventurer. He wrote the duke that he would recommend the attorney to the county courts and promised to consider him if a vacancy should open. He soon came to realize that he had underestimated Shirley's relationship to Newcastle. Several letters from the duke reminding the governor of his promises prompted Belcher to appoint Shirley to the Admiralty Court. Soon after, Shirley had promoted himself to the court's advocate general. His legal business flourished. But Belcher sensed that the young man was still not content, and he grew anxious as the duke continued to write prodding him to promote his protégé. Moreover, Shirley began prosecuting timber cutters and Boston merchants who were the governor's allies. Belcher chided him for being "too Busy" in the service of the king. He worried over reports that Shirley was consorting with Waldo, Dunbar, and the Wentworth "clan" but still felt it prudent not to force a confrontation.[16]

Although Shirley moved cautiously to avoid challenging Belcher directly, he was becoming impatient. In 1736 he sent his wife, Frances, to England to take his case to Newcastle. The governor's anxieties rose. Soon he was receiving reports from his allies that Frances Shirley was frequently seen in the duke's attendance. The Shirleys grasped for positions in New York and in Virginia. When they reached for the Boston naval office, Belcher rebuked Shirley sharply and instructed his agents to block Frances Shirley's application in behalf of her husband. Belcher succeeded in checking the Shirleys, but in doing so he made them more desperate. After consulting with the governor's opponents in New Hampshire and Massachusetts, Shirley became convinced that with their aid and his patron's influence he could become the next governor of Massachusetts. Still wary of the governor's influence, he allowed his new allies to initiate the campaign.

London always seemed to be undermining Belcher's ability to govern. His boast that he enjoyed the king's confidence was not convincing, even to himself. Too often London elevated his enemies to key positions in his administration. In addition the imperial government reprimanded the governor for his conduct regarding naval stores and currency policy, and it ruled against him on the authority of the New Hampshire lieutenant governor and on the border dispute. When London agreed with his position, it failed to support him. For example, when he explained to his superiors that a speedy ruling against the Massachusetts House of Representatives on the treasury issue would help to break the deadlock in Boston, they acted with characteristic lethargy. Together these acts impressed New Englanders with the weakness of the governor's position. His opponents created the impression that Belcher would soon be dismissed and that alliance with the administration was foolhardy.

That Belcher kept office for more than a decade, twice the average tenure of a royal governor, was testament to his political talents. That he could not claim powerful personal attachments or patrons in the inner circle of government—he had no one comparable to Shirley's Newcastle—only made his endurance more remarkable. His position always rested on fragile foundations: interest groups in England who demonstrated to a largely indifferent prime minister that it was to his advantage to retain the governor and agents who had the ability to maneuver around hostile officials and to manipulate political rivalries. At the same time, he remained vulnerable to the interferences and impositions of this inefficient and indifferent government. Finally, his tenure lasted as long as the balance of power in London remained unaltered.

Separated by distance and time from the seat of empire, Belcher anxiously studied every report from London to estimate his political stock. He understood the nature of courtly politics well enough to know that a

dinner invitation, a smile at court, a hard stare were as important as committee reports and official instructions to assess the scene. He knew from his
own success that even an obscure provincial could surprise the world. He
anxiously awaited letters from his friends and constantly prodded them to
write more frequently. He fretted when he suspected that Lord Wilmington
or Holden had grown cold to his welfare. He was always urging his agents to
work harder in his behalf. The situation excited his innate sense of vulnerability.[17]

By 1738, however, the dangers were real and unmistakable. Shirley and
the separatists were assembling a powerful network of interests against the
governor. The campaign focused on New Hampshire where, as Belcher
owned, the border policy and timber issue made him most vulnerable. In
London Thomlinson was using both controversies to achieve separation and
was promoting Benning Wentworth for governor. He was forging important
alliances with English mast contractors, such as Ralph Gulston, who agreed
to support Wentworth's appointment in return for assurances that his interests would be protected by the new administration. At the same time, Shirley
endorsed the separatist cause as a preliminary to deposing Belcher in
Massachusetts.[18]

Belcher did not know the details, but he gleaned enough from his
agents' reports and from intercepted correspondence. His attempts to ingratiate himself with Newcastle were fruitless. Frances Shirley, Waldo, and
Dunbar were meeting regularly with the duke. Survival depended on the dissenters and their relationship with the prime minister. But Belcher could not
fully appreciate that the Walpole government was growing weaker. The prime
minister was losing the ability to keep his coalition of rival factions and personalities together. Newcastle, who had been chafing at Walpole's meddling
in colonial appointments for some time, was growing increasingly impatient
with his chief's reluctance to risk war with Spain and was beginning to
speak for the merchant and patriot factions in opposition. At the Privy Council, Lord Wilmington also aired old resentments toward Walpole. For the
moment neither man was willing to risk breaking with the prime minister.
Newcastle, especially sensitive to the dissenting interest in Belcher's favor,
encouraged the governor's opponents while advising them not to press their
cause too forcefully.[19]

Shirley and the separatists realized that their fortunes depended on a
shift in English politics, which they expected to see in the aftermath of the
imminent English elections. In the meantime, they worked to discredit the
governor by advancing their petitions documenting his behavior regarding
the border and the king's woods. In hopes of dislodging Wager from the
governor's coalition, a forged letter allegedly composed by four of Belcher's
New Hampshire allies was delivered to the Admiralty. The letter accused the

governor of misleading them, of consorting with illegal lumberers, and of betraying the king's interest.[20] Shirley concluded that the dissenting community must be separated from the Belcher alliance. Soon after, his friends in London delivered a letter to Samuel Holden from Benjamin Colman and several other prominent New England clergymen. It was a forgery in which the ministers charged Belcher with secretly conspiring with the Anglican clergy. The same accusations were circulated among other prominent English dissenters. At the same time Shirley's aides assured leading Congregationalists and Quakers that they would be as comfortable with Governor Shirley as they "possibly can have been with the present Governor."[21]

Partridge easily demonstrated that the Colman letter was a forgery and quickly mustered the dissenters to the governor's aid. After meeting with the prime minister, he felt assured that Belcher's position was secure. But as he attended to the opposition's petitions lodged at the Board of Trade and Privy Council, he discovered that he could not command the audience he once had. When complaints were lodged at government offices, he was denied copies to prepare his response. His petitions and appeals were summarily dismissed. By late 1739 Partridge was in despair. The Privy Council had ruled in favor of New Hampshire on the border dispute, condemned Belcher for his obstructionist behavior, found him guilty of violating English forest policy, reprimanded him for his high-handed treatment of the opposition, and was considering his replacement.[22]

Belcher was dismayed. Even Saint Paul had been given the privilege of appeal before Caesar. For a moment he abandoned his courtly manner and wrote to Wilmington expressing his bitterness. He simply wanted a fair hearing, a chance to defend himself, copies of the charges leveled against him, and a chance to respond. He could barely contain himself: "altho' I am at such vast distance in my order of Life from the Exalted Sphere in which your Lordship moves with so great Honour—yet let me beg of your Lordship to think how you might feel to be attackt in such an unfair & unjust a manner by those who might envy & hate you & every thing they should say should pass for exact truth (tho never so false) and your Lordship to have no opportunity to do yourself justice." The letter was not sent. In private and with his allies, however, he continued to rage about the injustices that he suffered.[23]

In late 1739 the government in London was changing noticeably. Newcastle gained the courage to challenge the prime minister. As the discontented gathered around him and as he pressed more vigorously for war against Spain, he acquired more power within the government. At the same time he consolidated his control over colonial patronage. At the end of the year he had pushed Walpole to accept war. Though the prime minister remained in office, he could no longer keep his subordinate in rein.

The war brought Belcher a momentary reprieve. London looked to its American colonies for military support in its projected expedition against Cartagena. The campaign depended on the cooperation of the provincial governments for recruiting troops and raising funds. This was not the moment, Newcastle informed Shirley, to change governors. In the meantime, he recommended patience and cooperation with the governor's military preparations. The war, known in America as King George's War, gave Belcher the opportunity to demonstrate his worth to London. He wrote in elation, "I still firmly believe We shall be crown'd with Victory."[24]

Governor Belcher liked to think that he ruled the people like a caring father who had the interest of his children always in mind and who, in turn, received their love. His imagination quickened as he listened to the clergy raise up the image of the good ruler who protected and preserved the traditional moral order. He savored those moments when a minister made him into a modern-day Nehemiah. With the dissolution of constitutional controversy, he congratulated himself that he had brought leaders and commons together in harmony. The church of the fathers remained intact and the moral order was preserved. By his estimate the vast majority—perhaps "19 in 20" or "9 in ten"—supported his administration. Only a few malcontents beset him. Slowly he came to accept that he had lost most Hampshiremen, but he blamed the loss on the scheming of miscreants and "Grumbletonians." Increasingly he preferred to stay in Boston, where he could not hear these dissonant voices.[25] But he could not block out the grumblings that could be heard in Boston. The townspeople rioted over the price of bread. The currency issue was provoking renewed debate.

For a time—after the resolution of the treasury issue—the voices of opposition had grown faint. Belcher gloated as Elisha Cooke's influence declined in both the Boston town meeting and in the legislature. But he had built a peace on fragile foundations. Neither he nor Cooke wielded much influence over the independent backbencher majority, and what influence they did enjoy came not from organization but by deft maneuver. As long as attentions remained focused on the border issue and as long as the governor could avoid confrontation over paper money, the government seemed to provoke little animosity.

Moreover, the Congregational clergy joined in publicly praising the governor. Each May, when the governor joined with the newly elected House of Representatives for the election sermon, a clergyman invoked familiar ideals of the good ruler. These clergymen gave more attention to Jonathan Belcher, for he was, unlike his predecessors, the quintessence of the good ruler. They reminded the people that this governor was truly a "Nursing Father" of "vital religion" and New England's churches; he was a caretaker of the hedges that kept the covenanted people secure; he was the protector of the people and their "intercessor" with the king. Repeatedly they told the story of when as a young man Belcher had been summoned by his father to go to London to protect the people and their charter from an evil governor. In the election sermon of 1734, John Barnard explained that God had "honoured" the young Belcher with the mission to "preserve our Liberties." He turned to the governor: "When we consider your Excellency, not only as one of the Sons of our People, but the Son of such a Father . . . , we may, doubtless, with safety repose our Confidence under your Shadow." Barnard drew directly from Benjamin Colman's sermon of 1718. By repeating the story within New England's rituals of commemoration, the clergy was writing the Belcher family into the history of the province. In 1740 William Cooper repeated the story of Belcher's youthful accomplishment. In 1741 William Williams turned to the governor. "Your own honoured Father," he recalled, had proved himself "also a Father to his Country . . . when our Charter . . . was threatened and in Danger."[26]

Cooper echoed Benjamin Colman's earlier sermon when he reminded his audience that Belcher was a Nehemiah. The ideal fit this administration. Echoing the governor's own first address to the General Court, the clergymen gave thanks for a ruler who was "flesh of our flesh." When they resorted to the conventions of the Nehemiah, they did so from the conviction that Belcher truly fit that ideal. In 1733 Samuel Wigglesworth directly addressed the governor: "Your Self shall have an honourable Name to all Futurity with Jehoiada, Nehemiah, and others, who have headed Reformations in most Corrupt and Degenerate Ages." And when Belcher's enemies began to converge in London, Benjamin Colman rallied the clergy of Boston and the surrounding towns in his defense. He drafted an address to be sent to the prime minister, Lord Wilmington, and the Duke of Newcastle. The reports circulating in London that Belcher had betrayed the king and violated the people's trust were "malicious" libels. He and his fellow ministers could not imagine a "greater Calumny and more injurious Falshood."[27]

Boston provided the right setting for Belcher to play his part. The audience seemed appreciative. The voices of dissent seemed scarcely audible or were not directed at him. The legislative sessions progressed smoothly with only occasional moments of disagreement. The clergy seemed to set the tone of public affairs when it called upon the people to give thanks that they were ruled by such a model governor. Samuel Fiske addressed the governor in the name of the people: "we thank God for the good Example, you long since gave, in your Person and Family, and in our Churches, of which, you are so happy, as to be a very Honourable Member, by Birth, Baptism and Choice."[28] Belcher, in turn, found fulfillment by enacting the rituals and conventions associated with the protection of this convenanted society. By issuing a proclamation setting aside a day for public fasting or thanksgiving he became a protector of the New England way. Perhaps more important, at those moments he stood at the head of the people summoning them in their separate churches throughout the province to join together. It was a powerful image of himself in relationship to the people. But it was also an illusion. If he had perused the church records in the towns of the interior he would have been as likely to find the town that heeded his summons as he would have one that ignored him.[29] The voices he heard were largely from Boston's lawmakers and clergymen. The shepherds of the backcountry congregations paid little heed to Boston—at least no more than did the representatives from these same towns.

The quiet that he took for approval was indifference and apathy.[30] Belcher's government was distant, removed, indeed inconsequential to the rural and isolated backcountry towns. The provincial government was in itself small. Besides the governor and his lieutenant, the administration consisted of a few poorly paid clerks, a handful of councilors, most of whom lived in Boston, a few customs officials, and a small military. The annual budget amounted to less than £30,000. A few officers and soldiers stood quiet vigil on the frontiers. There was the boat at Castle William to repair. Fort Frederick to the north, Fort George to the west, and Boston's Castle William needed improvements. Many isolated towns in the interior saw little reason to send representatives to Boston.

Despite his efforts, the governor had limited influence over these lawmakers. By midpoint in his term, he had given civil or military commissions to over half of the lawmakers. He understood, however, that appointing these men did not make them his followers. Instead, good relations with the House required that he attend to the wishes and recommendations of the province's local oligarchs. In addition, Belcher was always fretting that he had too few offices at his disposal to reward his followers. He struggled to extend his appointive powers by naming two men to a single post, by threatening to purge his enemies, and by holding all appointments in suspension—but to little avail. The few offices in his control were usually customs collectors or naval officers in the province ports. London's patronage mongers, however, continued to gobble up these positions. Belcher was constantly complaining "how few . . . places" there were at his disposal "& of what trifling Value they are." He wrote to Richard Waldron summarizing his position: "As it is here, so it is with you, not a Place of £5: a year, but there are ten Suitors for it."[31]

Other, less practical, considerations influenced the governor's patronage policy. Belcher was by temperament disinclined to defy New England's established families, especially in his own Massachusetts. In part, he refrained from using his powers of appointment to their fullest for fear of confrontation with men he respected. He also failed to act because he only

partially understood his powers in the modern sense. Although he sometimes counted his appointments as a tool to construct a loyal following, he
often saw them as the means to maintain the traditional moral order. It was
his task to single out and reward men of social standing and education, virtue
and religion. By recognizing the fathers of the towns and the county oligarchs with appointments to the courts, he preserved the established and
venerable families in their positions. By doing so he made himself the preserver of this traditional order. By dispensing appointments to the virtuous,
he placed himself at the head of this hierarchy. To do otherwise—to pander
to selfish ambition and to build a coalition on private ambition—would be to
deny himself the fulfillment of playing the Nehemiah and to reveal himself
as the artful courtier.

Belcher's achievement rested on his ability to strike a balance between
the indigenous moral order and royal authority. He did so by compromise,
dissembling, guile—in short, by making himself master of the courtly arts.
But throughout his term he played to the sensibilities of his fellow New
Englanders. It was his ability to gather the symbols of good government and
legitimate authority unto himself that enabled him to preside over this political system. As he was reminded when he sought to purge Dudley from the
government, his influence did not translate into effective power.

Even during times of tranquillity, the economy continued to nag at the
governor and to defy resolution. Boston's trade languished and its shipyards
remained quiet throughout his administration. Prices for food and firewood
doubled, and wages did not keep apace. The lists of the poor grew longer, and
the voices of discontent grew louder. In the early spring of 1737, desperate
Bostonians disguised as clergymen destroyed three market buildings in futile
protest against rising prices. Belcher ordered an investigation; local officials
ignored him. Notices appeared in public places warning him that he risked
provoking a civil war if he were to call out the militia. Belcher did nothing.[32]
But he could not ignore the voices from other quarters. Each May's election
sermon seemed to give greater attention to the depression, especially the unstable value of currency. Unless the government fixed the medium of exchange securely, deceit and "merchantile Craftiness" would continue to
flourish and the people would continue to suffer "cruel Oppression and
Injustice." The clergymen addressed the governor and the legislature from a
growing sense of urgency.[33] While they refrained from advocating solutions,
other Bostonians were publishing their proposals for the currency crisis.

The currency question touched the political community more broadly
and more deeply than had the recent constitutional debates. First, redemption of the outstanding notes turned on the question of taxation. Representatives from the interior, even those on the outer periphery of the market
economy, could be moved to oppose increased tax levies. Second, paper

money touched a broad spectrum of representatives whose lives intersected with the marketplace from its periphery to the core. Many came to see paper currency as a necessity. They may have been ready for fixing its value against inflation but not at the expense of both increased taxes and a shortage of currency. Then there were a variety of positions expressed: those proposing to issue money at loan were answered by the defenders of public emissions; the advocates of private emissions again debated those who supported government control. Though disagreements raged, a broad spectrum of opinion supported paper money in one form or another and converged with growing opposition to increased taxation and the governor's instructions.

Belcher had tried to pursue a flexible and pragmatic response to the money question by balancing political considerations against vague economic beliefs and prejudices. Like most New Englanders, he believed that the conditions of the colonial economy made paper money indispensable.[34] The question was how much could be tolerated. Belcher was inclined to listen to men like the Hutchinsons, who advocated a tight paper-money policy. While disposed to believe that the government emissions were more secure than private, Belcher was not rigid on this matter. He was flexible and unwilling to press a monetary principle to the point of wrecking his administration. As 1741 approached, however, pressures on both sides of the ocean gave him little room for maneuver.

For a moment in 1737, however, Belcher's policy of "prudence and patience" seemed to be working. First, the legislature endorsed the Hutchinson program to issue a new series of notes backed by gold and silver and to withdraw £45,000 in "old tenor" notes by raising taxes. Although more than £200,000 in "old tenor" notes remained outstanding, Belcher was elated. Each "new tenor" note was worth three times the value of the old emissions. "I think our Paper Currency is growing better," and, he observed, the legislature "seems inclin'd to go on to make the money better & better."[35] The next year, Representative Hutchinson devised another scheme. The government would issue £60,000 in "new tenor" notes as loans at no interest to investors. Sound currency and no-interest loans appealed to conservatives; another emission of paper appealed to their liberal counterparts. The bill passed the legislature and Belcher would have approved it if it were not for his instructions. Instead, he offered to send the proposal to London with his strong recommendation for permission to sign it.

The governor was losing the ability to act on his own. He already sensed that conditions in London prevented him from sidestepping his instructions as easily as he once had. His superiors were listening to London's merchants, who were pressing for tighter controls on colonial currency. Shirley's supporters were also using Belcher's record to discredit him. Within months Belcher learned that the Board of Trade had rejected the £60,000 emission. At the same time, opinion was moving in the opposite direction in Massachusetts. Hutchinson and his allies were defeated in the May elections. The House was clearly not ready to accept withdrawal of paper money by 1741. The governor and House could not agree on a supply bill, and the treasury was empty. That fall Belcher hoped that the threat of war would break the deadlock but was disappointed. He despaired. He could not accept the House's method for supplying the treasury. Meanwhile, the House declared that it would do "nothing" until it had heard from the public. It dismissed Wilks as agent and appointed Christopher Kilby, a known opponent of the governor, in his stead. "I am really sorry," Belcher reflected, that the House was "running Wild at such a Critical dangerous Juncture. It seems to me a pressage of Judgement God is bringing upon this poor Countrey."[36]

Governor Belcher welcomed the news of war with Spain. He expected to rally patriotic sentiments to the support of his administration. For years he had been nagging the Massachusetts House of Representatives to vote funds for the repair of frontier defenses but had been told that the appropriations were too burdensome as long as he disallowed additional emissions of paper money. He expected the exigencies of war would force the legislature to accept currency reform. At the same time he predicted that by redeeming the value of Massachusetts's currency and by demonstrating his effectiveness in support of the war, he would redeem his reputation in London. "I doubt not," he wrote, "but my upright endeavours in both Provinces to support the King's honour & Interest, with the true welfare of his people, will go a great way in the sight of God . . . and I have strong faith that I shall soon see my Enemies Gnash their teeth and melt away."[37]

When he received instructions to raise troops in both provinces to join an Anglo-American campaign against Spanish Cartagena, he leaped at the opportunity to demonstrate his usefulness. The several colonial governments were expected to raise thirty-five hundred troops. Belcher was given no specific quota. At most he was expected to raise four regiments or four hundred troops. As Newcastle explained, the king "has not thought proper to confine you to any particular number" but expects "that you will procure as many as you possibly can." On receipt of his instructions and four blank captain's commissions for him to fill out, Belcher replied that he would raise one thousand recruits from Massachusetts and another one hundred from New Hampshire. He asked for additional blank captain's commissions. "I hope," he wrote the duke, "my raising a Third part of that number in this Province will find a gracious Acceptance with His Majesty."[38]

Wartime patriotism was not enough to compensate for the administration's ineffectiveness. Recruitment proceeded slowly, especially for the six additional and uncommissioned regiments. Belcher blamed his superiors.

They were negligent in responding to his requests for the officers' commissions, and prospective recruits were hesitant to enlist until they were sure who their officers would be. He also reminded the English command that because it had not delivered the arms that had been promised, New Englanders were loath to risk a trip to West Indies in a defenseless condition. By the end of the summer, it was clear that enlistments came principally from the ranks of Boston's poor and not from the interior. All six of the governor's additional regiments failed to be filled and were merged into a fifth unit. In addition, New Hampshire could not raise a single regiment.[39]

The war had done little to alter the behavior of the political elite. Local leaders squabbled over commissions to command the regiments.[40] The two legislatures had not forgotten old grievances. In New Hampshire the legislature voted support for the war but also used the session to air its dissatisfactions and to charge the governor with obstructing its efforts to recruit troops. In Boston the legislature voted the repair of Castle William on condition that it superintend the spending of military funds. Belcher rejected the House's proposal, and the controversy soon provoked a heated series of exchanges with each message more caustic than the last. The House accused the governor of seeking to "divest the Assembly of this Privilege, so consistent to [the] CHARTER." Belcher had brought the "People of this Province" to a "deplorable Dilemma": either to "part with their ancient Liberty and Usage" or to "lie in their exposed [and defenseless] Condition. This is truly Shocking!" In addition, the House reminded Belcher that it could not support the Cartagena expedition as much as it would like as long as he continued to stick so closely to his currency instructions.[41]

Not only had the governor promised more than he could deliver, he had in the process exposed himself to partisan attacks. When he received a copy of an intercepted letter from London to a Massachusetts lawmaker urging him to do everything possible to discourage preparations for the Cartagena campaign, his suspicions were confirmed. Even though Shirley offered to aid in recruiting troops, Belcher correctly read the situation that the opposition was simply using the war to discredit him. He also watched Paul Dudley, the newly elected representative from Roxbury. When the House of Representatives refused to support the additional uncommissioned regiments and voted to send those troops home, Belcher blamed his old adversary. Until the last session, he recounted, the House had done "everything well," but it had "Pist Backwards, about the Expedition" largely due to Dudley's influence. "Mr. Dudley was more fierce, than anyone Member besides." His "violent manner, in his Debating and Votings" was a disgrace to the province and an insult to the "King's Honour and Authority."[42]

Nor had the war altered opinions on the money issue. The House had no intention to withdraw the £250,000 in outstanding bills of credit. When

Belcher reminded it that money was the "Sinews of War" and that military preparedness required speedy redemption of the currency, it replied by passing a bill for emitting another £100,000. When he vetoed the bill, the House saw no reason to respond. The government was at deadlock. The House instructed agent Kilby to seek relaxation of the instructions restricting colonial currency. Belcher knew that negotiating with the lawmakers was futile. They were oblivious to "all reason, Justice & a sense of their duty." Instead they were appealing to the public for support and for alternative solutions to the currency crisis.[43]

Two proposals were submitted.[44] First, John Colman resurrected his idea of 1714 to create a private bank. It would issue £150,000 to be loaned to its subscribers. The notes would be secured by land mortgages and would be repaid in local manufacturers or agricultural products. The Land Bank gained broad support across the political community. Petty traders and prominent merchants, artisans and shopkeepers, even entrepreneurs from the interior county of Worcester were eager to invest. In January 1740, 395 subscribers had come forward. The number had doubled by June, and by the fall it stood at 920. Many conservatives watched this groundswell with alarm. They did not trust the bank's stability and also feared private institutions that were free of government control. One hundred and forty-five Boston businessmen, convinced that the bank would trigger another round of inflation, signed an agreement not to accept its notes. Soon after a rival proposal appeared. Several of Boston's wealthiest merchants joined to create what was called the Silver Bank. It would issue £120,000 in notes based on silver and redeemed in fifteen years. The subscribers also agreed not to accept Land Bank notes.

First impressions of the debate were that opinion divided along familiar lines, with the most prominent merchants engaged in the transatlantic economy opposing and the lesser merchants and entrepreneurs supporting the Land Bank. But the controversy was unsettling and provoked new divisions. Many did not distinguish between the two banks. Some opposed both and others supported both. Opinion on the Land Bank cut across earlier divisions on paper money. Legislators who opposed quick redemption of the government's paper money were as likely to support as they were to oppose the Land Bank. As the controversy raged, it inspired new and strange opinion. Advocates of the Land Bank were extolling a free market and experimenting with the vocabulary of what would become economic liberalism. Also the issue was moving more people from the backcountry and from the lower social orders into the public forum.

In the spring of 1740, the legislature began its investigation into the two bank proposals. While the Council was more inclined than the House to take action against the Land Bank, the two houses came to agreement that both banks should suspend operations. When the new House of Representatives met after the May elections, however, it decided by a vote of fifty-nine to thirty-seven not to take action. Popular sentiment seemed to be shifting in favor of the Land Bank. The bank's opponents in the House repeatedly tried to reverse the vote but to no avail. When their cohorts in the Council proposed a joint committee to consider the issue, the representatives refused the invitation.

Belcher was caught in crisis. For some time he had sensed that he was powerless to move the legislature toward currency redemption. He had written to his superiors that resolution of the stalemate depended on Parliament's action. At first, he seemed uncertain how to respond to the two private banks. Both schemes roused deep conservative prejudices against paper money, especially the kind issued by unregulated private individuals. Slowly, however, he came to discern a difference. In mid-summer of 1740, he issued a proclamation warning that the Land Bank notes tended to "defraud Men of their Substance, and to disturb the Peace and good Order of the People." He had singled out the Land Bank for stern measures. While he had not embraced the Silver Bank, he held its principal supporters in high regard and attended to their advice on fiscal affairs. During his talks with the Silver Bankers, he slowly moved them to make additional assurances of their notes' value. He concluded that the bank's notes were "not only an honour to the government, but of service to the people as a medium in commerce, for they are truly & really equal to gold and silver to the possessors, according to the value exprest in the bills."[45]

At the same time, he pressed the Land Bankers. After summoning his Council to a special session in early November, he issued a proclamation prohibiting everyone holding civil and military commissions from transacting any business with the bank. At the end of the month, he notified the legislature that the Land Bank was already printing its notes, which had "no honest or solid Foundation." It became a moral imperative for the government to protect "unwary People from the Injuries they might otherwise suffer" and to "stop any further Proceedings of those Projectors." Convinced that the bank was an "Iniquitous institution" and a "vile fraud," he vowed "to do all in my power, to put a Stop to the vile projection now on foot, for deceiving and cheating all mankind."[46]

The House refused to join him. Belcher's position was rapidly deteriorating as irreconcilable forces in England and America pressed against him. London's merchants were mounting their own campaign to reform American paper money. While their agents petitioned the legislature in Boston to stop the Land Bank, they were applying to the Board of Trade, Privy Council, and Parliament for protection against the bank. The governor's enemies were manipulating the issue to their favor. John Thomlinson was most conspicuous in his efforts to turn merchant opinion against the governor. As political expediency required Belcher to take a stronger stand against the Land Bank, his behavior seemed to push legislative opinion in the opposite direction.[47]

Isolated and ineffective, Governor Belcher wielded his powers in an increasingly arbitrary and vengeful manner. Letters were dispatched to the commanders of the county militias ordering them to search out their subordinates for those who held Land Bank notes. The governor and the Council began to scour the civil list. Justices of the peace and judges of the county courts who were suspected of harboring sympathies for the bank were summoned to the Council chamber. In early December Belcher began to issue proclamations announcing the dismissal of Land Bankers from the civil lists. George Leonard, a judge on Bristol County's court; Joseph Blanchard, a justice of the peace in Middlesex County; Andrew Burleigh, justice of the peace in Essex County; John Darrell, coroner in Suffolk County—all were removed from office. No distinction was made between investors in the bank and those who accepted its notes. The governor and Council ordered the registers of property deeds in the counties to compile lists of bank subscribers. Warnings were issued to the keepers of shops and taverns that their licenses would be revoked for taking the notes. And the Council resolved that no one connected with the bank would be allowed admission to its chamber.[48]

Messengers from the Council interrupted the proceedings of the House of Representatives to summon one lawmaker after another to answer accusations brought against him. Some buckled before the governor's threats. John Chandler did. But Samuel Watts of Chelsea, Joseph Blanchard of Dunstable, and Robert Hale of Beverly resisted the governor's threats and lost their offices. Nine officers in Worcester County's militia signed a public letter to the *Boston News-Letter*, explaining that though they had not invested in the bank, they believed it served "the true Interest of our native Country." They chose to resign their commissions rather than comply with the governor's orders. One dismissed justice of the peace declared that although he had acted from "conscience," he had become the victim of "civil persecution." The House of Representatives echoed these sentiments. After investigating Belcher's attempt to coerce the province's tavern keepers, the legislature condemned him for violating their "just Rights and Liberties as well as . . . Property."[49]

Benjamin Colman warned the governor that his purges played into the hands of his enemies. "Those that are not so friendly to you" are "crying out at 'arbitrary dismantling of ye whole Militia for a Party Cause.'" The minister conceded that the critics were "no doubt partial." But, he continued, even enemies of the Land Bank and "Men of great Knowledge & Moderation" thought the removals were "arbitrary." If the governor persisted, he would lose office. Colman's advice was not heeded, however. Belcher had forgotten the virtues of "prudence and patience."[50] Instead, he reverted to the vengeful instincts that had guided him in New Hampshire.

The signs were unmistakable that Belcher stood alone and powerless against a popular uprising. The House of Representatives was printing critical roll-call votes related to the banking controversy in its journals, clearly with an eye toward influencing public opinion. In March 1741 news arrived that Parliament had applied English legislation outlawing unincorporated joint stock companies like the Land Bank to America. The representatives responded by dismissing their longtime agent Francis Wilks. Belcher applauded Parliament's act but believed that it was an empty gesture. Stronger, more forceful measures were required to suppress the Land Bankers. In a letter to Thomas Hutchinson, who was then in England, he observed that Massachusetts was teetering on the brink of civil war. "The Common People here" are encouraged by their leaders "to believe, they are pretty much out of the reach of the Government" in London; they think the legislature is as "big as the Parliament of Great Britain"; and they have "grown so Brassy, & hardy, as to be now combining in a Body to raise a Rebellion."[51]

As he wrote, he was sitting with the Council attending to reports from the backcountry that five thousand, perhaps twenty thousand, friends of the Land Bank were preparing to descend on the government. Orders were sent out to justices of the peace to apprehend the conspirators. A notice had been nailed to the meetinghouse door at Braintree summoning the people to join the march on Boston; the Land Bankers in Bridgewater threatened to destroy Robert Brown's warehouse unless he accepted their notes; and William Royall of Stoughton had heard that the bankers would descend on Boston on May 19 to get "free corn for their families." The Council paid careful attention to Thomas Crosby of Braintree when he charged that Captain William Pierce of Milton was one of the principal leaders of the march. After interrogating Pierce, it ordered that he be held over for further investigation. As the proceedings continued, warrants of arrest were issued.[52]

Although nothing came of the reports, the governor and Council had reason to sense that they faced a popular uprising. The elections to the House clearly turned against the administration not only in Boston but elsewhere. In Salem Benjamin Lynde, whose family had traditionally controlled town affairs, watched helplessly as the Land Bank insurgency swept the elections. In Worcester John Chandler also lost his seat. "The coming Assembly," Belcher observed, "is generally thot will be *Malefactory*." Only two in five incumbents were returned. Three-fourths of those who had recorded their votes in opposition to the Land Bank were defeated, while half of those who voted in its favor were returned.[53]

The first act of the House of Representatives was to select its speaker. For the past decade, it had chosen Braintree's John Quincy, but Braintree had not returned Quincy and had selected a William Hunt instead. The House chose Samuel Watts, the representative from Chelsea and a prominent organizer of the Land Bank. Belcher, who had already revoked Watts's commission as justice of the peace, promptly rejected the choice. When the House proposed another Land Banker, William Fairfield of Wenham, Belcher recognized the futility of his position and accepted the selection. Later that day the legislature proceeded to elect the Council. At the end of the first ballot, only two councilors had been chosen. The selection was not completed until after six ballots—an unusually high number. Twelve incumbents were returned—an unusually low number. Belcher looked at the list and promptly rejected thirteen names. Later that afternoon he cut proceedings short and sent a message to the House. The Council elections "discover to me so much of the Inclination of your House to support the fraudulent, pernicious Scheme commonly called the Land-Bank . . . that I judge it derogatory to the King's Honour and Service, and inconsistent with the Peace and Welfare of this People, that you sit any longer." After two days the House was dissolved, and new elections were called.[54]

Belcher could see the foundations of his government collapsing. He did not expect the elections to bring an improved legislature. Although he had made "truth reason & Justice" the "Basis" of his government, the people had gone mad over paper money.[55] He stood alone against the people he had served. The reports from London were unmistakable; the king had also turned against him. In April the Wentworth "clan" had convinced the Privy Council to recommend that the king appoint a separate governor for New Hampshire. At the same time, the Duke of Newcastle had ordered the Board of Trade to prepare the papers appointing William Shirley governor of Massachusetts-Bay.

For the past year Belcher had watched his position in London deteriorate steadily. He raged helplessly as he read the reports from London. His allies were disappearing: Samuel Holden had died; Admiral Wager was too old to attend to political intrigue any longer. In the meantime London's merchants had become disenchanted by the governor's record on paper money, and many were turning to William Shirley. Charges that Richard Partridge supported the Land Bank undermined Belcher's reputation with the government.[56] Lord Wilmington, who had broken with Walpole and joined with Newcastle, was listening to the opposition. By the spring of 1741, he had thrown his support to William Shirley.

Belcher became a sacrificial pawn in the jostlings for position within the English government. As the elections of the spring of 1741 approached, the governor's allies struggled to muster the dissenting interests in his favor. This time Shirley's agents knew how to unhinge that connection. They manufactured evidence that Belcher was plotting with the Anglican leadership against the nonconformists and that New England's Congregationalists saw no threat from a Shirley government. They produced dissenters who endorsed Shirley's appointment. Deals were struck. Thomas Hutchinson recalled the elections at Coventry, where Lord Euston, a Newcastle man, worried that his influence was not sufficient to carry his candidates. Shirley's allies proposed to work in Euston's favor and in return were promised that their man would be appointed. Recognizing that the dissenting community was critical to the outcome and had in the past supported Belcher, they fabricated evidence that Belcher was working for the Anglican interest. One leading Congregationalist "swallowed the bait" and "used all his interest for lord Euston" and his candidate's victory. "A day or two after" the returns were counted, "Mr. Belcher was removed." In Sussex, Newcastle's bailiwick, Thomas Western represented Shirley's interest. First, he assured the duke that notwithstanding earlier nonconformist support for Belcher, "the Quakers & dissenters will be as well-pleased" with Shirley's conduct as they were with Belcher's. Western also suggested that he might stand for election against Newcastle's men, unless he received assurances that Shirley would be appointed. The duke agreed. Orders were given to prepare Shirley's commission. In return Western withdrew and threw his support to the duke's candidates, who received "the greatest victory that ever was known."[57]

Meanwhile Belcher waited and fretted over his helpless position. He dwelt on the persecutions and injustices he suffered. "It is strange, the Ministry will be so teaz'd and plagu'd with Every ill natur'd Fellow, that conceives a Prejudice at the Governour. Why won't they see thro' their Spight & Malice & bid 'em be quiet." His superiors were indifferent to his services; allies proved themselves unreliable, even unfaithful; the people had turned their backs on righteousness to follow false leaders. As he had during earlier trials, he sought refuge by playing the martyr. Even Saint Paul had been treated better. He hoped that the "Heavenly Whitefield" and his evangelical cohorts would stir an awakening among the people. He quickly realized that just as "many People take great pains, in natural Life, to destroy their Constitutions, by whoring, drinking &ca," the political community of Massachusetts was destroying itself with "other Sorts of Vices, as Pride Obstinacy, [and the] wanton use of Liberty."[58]

Some supported his view. When William Williams delivered the election sermon of 1741, he elaborated at length on the virtues of the present governor and the looming economic and political crisis. The people would weather the crisis only if they continued to be led by a Nehemiah like Belcher.[59] The prospect of a new governor who was not a native son and who was indifferent to the New England way caused Jeremiah Allen to reconsider his politics. Still in London seeking his revenge against the governor, Allen was also working with the Protestant Dissenting Deputies and New England's leading ministers, including Benjamin Colman, to defend the Congregational establishment against the continuing Anglican assault. He soon realized the necessity of retaining Belcher, especially when he considered that Shirley was an Anglican. The entire structure of the New England Way would collapse. He foresaw the day when Massachusetts would lose control of its "darling" college to Cutler and the Episcopalians would become the establishment. In a letter to Benjamin Colman, he reviewed the crisis. The Privy Council was listening to the complaints of Massachusetts Anglicans against the Congregational establishment. Allen had not changed his opinion of Belcher, but he did not question the governor's loyalty to the New England Way. "I must think, (As do our Staunch Friends Here, Who are far from being the Governour's Personal Friends, yet on Account of his Attachment to the Dissenting Interest, are prevailed on to be His Advocates) That whenever He is removed and succeded by an Episcopalian, you may conclude ye College lost, & the Dissenting Interest in a declining way."[60]

Although gratified by Allen's change in heart, Belcher could read the signs of his imminent collapse. As he had before, he protected himself by assuming resignation and humility. "I am in the hands of a wise & good God, and pray for his Grace, that I may be inabled at all times to submit cheerfully to his will." When the news arrived at the end of June that he had lost his commissions, he could not disguise his rage. For a few moments he could not restrain his thoughts regarding his superiors. He recalled that the prime minister had given his "Solemn & sacred Assurances of Friendship and of my continuance." Other reports confirmed that his record on fiscal matters had not been cause for his dismissal. He was the victim of courtly intrigue, of Robert Walpole's "treachery, falseness, perfidy and hypocrisy." Belcher shed his courtly manners: "I plainly see truth and justice must never stand in the way of the Ease & Conveniency of Great men." His sufferings confirmed his view of the world: "There is no Faith in man, whose heart is deceitfull above all things, & desperately wicked." He submitted himself to "God's holy will."[61]

Throughout July Belcher waited for the arrival of William Shirley's commissions. When the newly elected legislature convened, it chose a friend of the Land Bank as its speaker once again. Again Belcher rejected the choice. When the lawmakers responded with a similar choice, however, he bowed to their will. The session's principal purpose, however, was to make preparations for the inauguration of the new governor. On August 14, 1741, after serving the king and people for eleven years, Jonathan Belcher watched the town of Boston turn out for the transfer of power. An escort of councilors, representatives, and leading members of the provincial judiciary proceeded with William Shirley to the governor's home, where a smaller and less impressive delegation of "several gentlemen" had assembled to accompany Belcher. The rivals exchanged pleasantries and proceeded through the streets to the Council chamber. Belcher presented himself with the dignity befitting his station. For the last time he took the governor's seat and listened while the oaths of office were administered. Then he shook his successor's hand in congratulations, yielded his official chair, and wished the new administration prosperity and success.[62]

Privately, however, he prayed for the people whom he had protected and nurtured for so long. The rejected Nehemiah feared for the future and prayed that God "in whom we ought to trust, can bring light out of darkness, and Ease, even in distress. May it be so, to the People of the two Provinces, for his son Christ Jesus Sake, amen."[63]

7

Exile and Fulfillment

Belcher assured his friends that he was "abundantly satisfy'd in Retirement." No longer hounded by his malignant enemies, he had found peace in the solitude of "Milton cottage," where he spent his days cultivating his garden, reading the works of evangelicals, and improving his soul. In a letter to Isaac Watts requesting a collection of the English minister's sermons, he reflected on his removal "from the tip top of honour, & power, in this part of the world, from crowding Courtships, and from every Gay Scene of Life." He had endured a "great & sudden transition," but he had resigned himself to God's will. Belcher prayed that his enemies would be forgiven for their "lying & Forgeries" and that the people of his beloved Massachusetts would continue to enjoy heaven's blessings.[1]

His professions of resignation and contentment were poor disguises for his restless ambitions. By the middle of his first winter at Milton, even before he had completed furnishing his "cottage" and stocking its wine cellar, Belcher was writing to his allies in London, probing them on the possibility of a return to court. The bucolic world did not suit him, and he grew impatient with its solitude. When he visited Boston, he felt ignored and inconsequential, and he returned home each time more embittered by his fall. His prayers of forgiveness could not hide the resentments he held toward the "Miscreants" who had done him wrong.[2]

Life at Milton turned into a lonely exile. With the exception of a few household servants, Belcher lived alone. Mary Belcher had died in October 1736. During his remaining years as governor he made no mention of her to his correspondents. Suddenly he began to toy with the idea that he might "commit Matrimony" again.[3] He had expected to find compensation for his disappointments in his children's achievements. Instead of playing the patriarch, esteemed and revered for his labors, he felt forsaken, unappreciated, and betrayed. Andrew seemed ill fitted for the countinghouse. When Belcher asked him for an accounting of his affairs, Andrew procrastinated. When Andrew finally delivered his records, they only served to confirm his father's low opinion of his character. Meanwhile, Jonathan, Jr., was also proving to be a disappointment. After ten unimpressive years in London, he had removed to Dublin in hopes of making a living. Neither son seemed able to support himself. The father scolded them incessantly for their "Ingratitude" in the hope of rousing them from their "Sloth." Neither could be moved. He expounded relentlessly on their filial duties but to no avail. Andrew would not visit. Jonathan would not write.[4]

Belcher's son-in-law Byfield Lyde had proved an even greater disappointment. When Belcher reviewed his accounts, he could see that Lyde was incapable of supporting himself and his family. Not only was Belcher taxed by children who could not live by their own means, but he was dunned by creditors for debts that stood outstanding after twenty years. He saw no recourse but to sell property. He had turned sixty in 1742. "And what says the Royal Psalmist? The Days of our Years are threescore years & ten." He grumbled that although he had labored long to plant a "vineyard" for his family's welfare, he could not expect to enjoy the fruits of his labors.[5]

The loss of office remained at the heart of his discontents. He could not lay aside his feelings of humiliation, and he longed to return to public office. When he considered seeking an appointment, however, the old fears of failure and "ridicule" welled up in his imagination. He took his first steps cautiously. He portrayed himself as the patriarch who, betrayed by his enemies and hounded by his children, was denied the opportunity to rest. He needed the money that came with office for his children's sake. What he dared not admit was that he craved that moment when he might once again stand at center stage.

When Belcher first suggested that he might return to London, he aired the idea as if it were a casual aside. Sometimes he advanced it as if it were a proposal made by others. When his allies in London wrote to discourage him, he promptly disclaimed any serious intention of returning to office.[6] But he continued to test the idea on his friends. Clearly he was also uncertain what to expect if he were to make another trip. Revenge, the renewed fulfillment of holding office, financial necessity—all these considerations tumbled through his mind. Though unsure what appointment he might expect, he convinced himself that somehow the trip would redound to his success as had his earlier ventures. After several false starts, he informed his friends in London that he was coming. In the fall of 1743 he booked passage on the *Polly*.[7]

This crossing was his fifth and in his estimation the most perilous. His ship was "very Leaky," and it caught fire once. Four times the watch sighted enemy vessels. After seventeen weeks at sea, Belcher disembarked at Kinsale. Instead of taking passage for England, he set off north to Dublin, where his son Jonathan was waiting. After thirteen years of separation, the reunion went well. Belcher laid aside his criticisms of his son, at least for the moment, and preferred to dwell on Jonathan's success in Dublin society and the "good reputation" he had earned "in his profession." He was especially gratified when he realized that Lord Hardwicke, an important figure in the new English government, had taken a liking to his son.[8]

Belcher lingered in Dublin for three weeks. Perhaps, he prolonged his visit for fear of the reception that awaited him in London. When he arrived in the capital, however, he was received hospitably by Richard Partridge. The Quaker community and the city's Congregationalists welcomed him and promised their assistance. The dissenters, however, seemed to have little influence on the new government. With the Duke of Newcastle in control of colonial affairs, Belcher could claim little support in the government. With his old allies Wager and Wilmington dead, he realized that his son's patron, Lord Hardwicke, was his most likely spokesman. In a long letter to Hardwicke, Belcher recounted the injustices he had suffered and explained that he had come to London to redeem his honor and to undo the wrongs he had endured. He seemed to receive a polite hearing. Hardwicke assured him that his dismissal should not be taken as a reflection on his character and promised that when the "proper Opportunity" arose, he would not be forgotten. In the meantime, Hardwicke advised the former governor to wait in patience on the "King's pleasure."[9]

Hardwicke's promises were hollow. The Duke of Newcastle would not abide Belcher's return to office, especially in Massachusetts. Belcher became desperate as his expenses mounted and his prospects dwindled. When he applied for a pension, the duke quickly dismissed the idea. After a year in London, Belcher wrote the duke disowning any desire for William Shirley's post. Six months later he applied to unseat the governor of South Carolina, James Glen. After charging that Glen was a man of "little merit," he suggested to Newcastle that England's Quaker voters would be grateful for his appointment. Again the government proved indifferent to Belcher's application.[10]

Three years after leaving Boston, Belcher was still "dancing attendance" at court and waiting in the anterooms of government ministers. As he endured daily condescension and indifference, he recalled the past injustices he had suffered. He grew weary of the polite society he had once sought out. He regretted his trip to London, but he could not return to Milton cottage without admitting defeat and facing further public humiliation. To stay, however, meant incurring greater debt. He had put himself in a "Purgotory."[11] The dissenting community became a haven. Belcher faithfully attended the church of Thomas Bradbury and sought out the companionship of like-minded dissenters. The Quakers also proved friendly. At Partridge's home he met Louisa Teale, a widow. His thoughts turned to marriage. She seemed the proper woman, "agreeable in Years, Person, Temper & Fortune." He had doubts about her children but laid these considerations aside when he considered her wealth. He was not willing to commit himself or disclose his intentions, however, until he had found an appointment.[12]

Suddenly, in June 1746, his prospects improved with the news that Lewis Morris, the governor of New Jersey, lay dying. The post was no prize, but Belcher was desperate. New Jersey, a minor colony formed at the beginning of the century from the two stumbling proprietaries of East and West Jersey, had been governed by New York's executive until Morris's appointment in 1738. The governor's salary was meager. Moreover, proprietors had been quarreling with farmers over land titles, and riots had broken out in the eastern counties. The government was at deadlock with the governor and his Council pressing the Assembly to protect the proprietary interest and the representatives resisting recommendations to suppress the riots. A handful of candidates—George Clarke, the lieutenant governor of New York; Sir Peter Warren from the Admiralty; and Christopher Kilby, the Massachusetts agent—expressed interest in the office. Belcher's most serious opponent was Ferdinand John Paris. Paris did not want the office himself. He acted as agent for Morris and the proprietors, and he was determined to name a friendly replacement, possibly the governor's son, Robert Hunter Morris.[13]

To everyone's surprise, especially Paris's, Belcher quickly gained the initiative. No doubt, he owed much to Hardwicke's influence, but Paris concluded that the Quakers made the critical difference. The English Friends had not forgotten Belcher but were not disposed to exert themselves on his behalf until they learned of the New Jersey vacancy. New Jersey Quakers, situated principally in the western section, resented Morris for his intolerance and for his favoritism toward eastern and Anglican interests. Led by the Smiths, a prominent merchant family from the port of Burlington, the Friends appealed to the London Meeting for Sufferings to embrace their cause and to secure a favorable appointment. Partridge easily convinced his fellows at the meeting house to move their organization and influence behind his brother-in-law. Thus, before Paris had received instructions from America, Belcher's appointment had been confirmed. Paris was furious. He had represented Belcher's opponents in New Hampshire and warned his employers their new governor was not to be trusted. Noting that antiproprietary riots sprang from communities of transplanted New Englanders, Paris predicted that since Belcher was a New Englander, he could be counted on to embrace his fellow Calvinists.[14]

Belcher understood what everyone knew—that he was a pawn in the quarrels raging in an "Obscure Corner of the World." His appointment was a Quaker victory. Once they had named the governor, London's Quakers set out to remove the most prominent Morrisites from the governor's Council. Meanwhile, they made arrangements so that the new governor would reside at Burlington, a Quaker stronghold, and that his new neighbors, the Smiths, would prepare for his reception. For Belcher, success was bittersweet. Though the Quakers congratulated him, he could not forget that he had risen as their dependent. The thought of spending his declining years in this minor position caused him to cringe, and he applied for permission to visit his beloved New England as often and as long as the duties of office would permit. His appointment papers, however, remained unprocessed until the requisite fees were paid. Belcher lacked the funds. He was heavily in debt, and his credit was stretched too thin. The delay gave Paris the opportunity to protect the Morrisites' seats on the Council. In desperation Belcher appealed to his brother-in-law. Once again Partridge responded and called upon Quakers throughout the nation to contribute to the governor's cause. Belcher finally appeared before the offices of the Board of Trade in early 1747 with the money in his pockets.[15]

While his papers of appointment were being prepared, Belcher booked passage for New York aboard the *Scarborough* and left London in early summer. The crossing was uneventful and left him with the time to brood upon his recent trials, the three years of "killing attendance" at court, his waiting on the pleasure of indifferent officials, his debts, which had grown by another £1000, and his poor health. He concluded that not even appointment as "Vice Roy of English America" would have been compensation for his tribulations. Instead, he was going to an obscure wilderness colony, known to some as Nova Caesarea. The emoluments were small. A turbulent political crisis awaited him. In addition, Belcher's application for permission to visit New England had been denied. As he reflected on his condition, his thoughts turned to Ovid who, when banished from Caesar's court to the Black Sea, wrote the *Tristia*. As he read the Roman poet, Belcher also saw himself as an exile, not to the Pontius but to the "wilds of Nova Caesarea."[16]

By the time he had disembarked at New York, Belcher had fully absorbed his new role as exile. He lingered a few days in the city, where he was entertained by that colony's governor, chief justice, and other local dignitaries. He was pleased to discover that Ebenezer Pemberton, the son of his minister in Boston, held a pulpit at the city's Presbyterian church; and he rejoiced when George Whitefield, that "seraphick Creature," came to preach before the congregation. In mid-August, he bade his hosts and friends farewell and crossed over to Perth Amboy. Before taking the post road south to Burlington, he tarried in Essex County at Newark and Elizabethtown. These communities of transplanted New Englanders celebrated his appointment. Newark's minister, Aaron Burr, the son-in-law of Jonathan Edwards, and Elizabethtown's Jonathan Dickinson were both champions of the evangelical cause; and Belcher quickly warmed to their company.[17]

As he listened to ministers, mayors and aldermen, and representatives to the Assembly describe conditions in the colony, the discussions inevitably turned to the recent land riots. Everyone joined in condemning the violence, but many prominent leaders in Essex County also drew attention to the provocations that had driven many deluded people to extremes. They charged that Governor Morris had conspired with a pack of favorites in the Council to bend the government to their selfish interest and had sought unconstitutional control over the treasury, the civil list, and the militia. The Essex County representatives recounted Morris's confrontations with the Assembly and the studied contempt he displayed for the lawmakers and for their constituents' rights and liberties. Thus, when the former governor called for increased military powers, even Jerseymen who were appalled by the riots joined the opposition.[18]

As Belcher progressed westward, he encountered a world that seemed by his lights devoid of social order. New Jersey was a hodgepodge of immigrants from England, Scotland, Ireland, New England, Holland, Germany, and Sweden. If a religious census had been taken, it would have indicated a variety of denominations, including Presbyterian, Baptist, Quaker, Anglican, Dutch Reform, and Lutheran. Many Jerseymen lived their lives without knowledge of the gospel. And rumor had it that the Roman Catholic Mass was performed in some remote areas. The contrast with New England was stark. Towns were few, and the people lived on scattered, isolated farms. There seemed to be no center to provincial life. The government convened alternately in East Jersey at Perth Amboy and in West Jersey at Burlington. There was no press, and the people relied on the newspapers of New York and Philadelphia. Belcher considered the inhabitants an uncivilized lot. Though they treated him with respect, he viewed them as ignorant and unpolished in their manners. There were no institutions of higher learning. The people were often seduced to follow ignorant ministers. Heresy abounded. Belcher's experience quickly confirmed him in his conviction that he had entered the "Wilds of Nova Caesarea."[19]

Belcher arrived at Burlington, where the Smiths had been making their preparations. They had found an elegant country estate befitting the governor's station. Belcher was pleased with his new home and was soon busy ordering furniture, carpets, paintings, and dinner wares. The Smiths welcomed him into their society, but Belcher felt lost and isolated. The town's places of worship were the Quaker meeting house and an Anglican church. The nearest Calvinist congregation was across the Delaware River in Philadelphia. He was appalled to find that so many of his neighbors were so casual in their observation of the Sabbath—at least by New England standards. Belcher longed to see Boston's church spires once again and urged friends and relatives to come and visit him at "World's End." He longed for Mrs. Teale's companionship.[20]

The self-styled exile, nonetheless, pretended contentment to his friends. He turned to William Livingston's "Philosophic Solitude" and delighted in the young New York poet's evocation of the Horatian ideal.

Far from th' eternal hurries of the great,
The din of cities and the farce of state:
There let me pass the golden hours away,
While books and walks prolong the silent day

Belcher played at the bucolic role before his correspondents. Each day he awakened at dawn "so as to salute the first Ray of ye burning orb." After taking a light breakfast of two cups of tea, he spent the hours walking about his estate, laying plans for its improvement before his prospective bride arrived, and reading in his library. He professed contentment in his "Solitude." Yet, like the New York muse, who chose not to make his home a "real hermitage" or to make himself a "recluse," the gentleman farmer opened his home to the pleasant companionship of "perticular Friends."[21]

Although Belcher promised himself not to permit the burdens of office to intrude upon his life at "World's End," the bitter quarrels between the Council and Assembly that had brought the government to deadlock could not be ignored. An empty treasury, unpaid salaries, and continuing riots demanded his attention. During the last two years of his administration, Lewis Morris had by force of his personality as much as by the issues he raised driven the province's disparate elements into a united opposition. Longstanding divisions between the eastern and western sections, between rural and urban elites, and between religious denominations were laid aside. Burlington's urban Quakers, who in normal times were more inclined to vote with Perth Amboy's Anglicans than with their coreligionists from the country; the rural delegations, which were usually divided by section, religion, and economic interest; even western Quakers and eastern Presbyterians—all these lawmakers joined in common cause against the proprietors and Governor Morris.

Morris had made New Jersey's normally jumbled political alignments simple. The eastern proprietors stood alone. Except for Perth Amboy, they could no longer influence the elections to the Assembly. The Council remained their only secure bastion in the government. From their perspective the province stood on the brink of civil war. Their enemies were principally New England Calvinists, and they were Anglicans; the principles and issues that they confronted were the same that had driven England to civil war in 1641. Their opponents also saw the division in simple terms. The eastern proprietors employed their influence in the Council and with the governor to construct a "Court Party" that conspired to topple the "ancient principal Pillars of the Constitution" and trample on the people's "natural Rights" and liberties. Though many assemblymen were appalled by the riots, they were loath to support the governor's request for increased military powers to establish order. Self-styled country patriots were haunted by memories of Stuart tyrannies.[22]

Governor Belcher hoped to avoid partisan entanglements and, as he had in Massachusetts, to keep contending parties in suspense. The Smiths, however, had already defined his appointment as a factional coup. The Presbyterian evangelicals rejoiced when they received news from their English cohorts of the appointment, and many of their neighbors who opposed the proprietors by violent and nonviolent means received assurances that the new governor would listen to their petitions for relief. Even before Belcher's arrival, meetings were arranged with leading opponents of the proprietors. The Morrisites were troubled. While receiving the governor with professions of support, they could hardly hide their concerns. Some, especially Robert Hunter Morris, were already preparing for the worst.[23]

Even while Belcher was consulting with antiproprietary interests, he sought to avoid antagonizing the Morrisites, especially the former governor's son. He acted from political expediency. Robert Hunter Morris and his senior ally, James Alexander, clearly dominated Council proceedings and, in addition, enjoyed significant influence in London. Belcher's behavior also stemmed from deep fears of conflict. Robert Hunter Morris was a commanding personality. Educated, urbane, wealthy—he quickly assumed his father's place at the head of the eastern proprietary faction. Self-assured—indeed, arrogant—he expected to assume the governor's seat and resented Belcher's presence. Like his father, Morris loved to argue. His presence, especially the prospect of confrontation, roused in Belcher old feelings of vulnerability. Within months Morris began to spar with the governor, as if to test his mettle.[24] A pattern emerged, reminiscent of Belcher's relationship with Paul Dudley in Massachusetts. Belcher nursed his wounds but refrained from matching wills with Morris.

At first, the governor's restraint seemed to work a salutary effect upon the political scene. Jerseymen, except for the most extreme partisans, had grown weary of the recent disputes and were eager for their resolution. Lewis Morris had forced Jerseymen to extremes that caused them discomfort. Even the allies of Lewis Morris privately conceded that his abrasive personality had unnecessarily exaggerated political differences. Councilors like Alexander were willing to give the new governor the benefit of the doubt. At the same time, lawmakers from the western counties began to separate themselves from their die-hard antiproprietor colleagues from the east. As the anti-Morrisite majority dissolved, an agreement was reached with the Council. In exchange for a bill extending clemency to rioters, the lower house acceded to the Council's demands for a more stringent riot act. Only Morris in the Council and two eastern representatives opposed the compromise. Belcher boasted that the stalemate had been broken and that "Thro the good hand of God . . . Considerable harmony" had been restored to the land. "Not only the Body of the People but the general Assembly treat me with much Respect and have granted me as large a Support as they have ever given any of my Predecessors."[25]

Belcher boasted too soon. The violence continued. Rioters broke into jails to liberate their friends while sheriffs watched helplessly. Councilor Morris pressed the reports upon his colleagues. The pardon act had become an object of mockery: few rioters were disposed to apply for pardon and those who were so inclined were quickly dissuaded by their neighbors. Alexander conceded that the Council had erred on the side of mercy. In the meantime, Morris turned to the governor. Everyone knew that Belcher met with leading antiproprietors. What came of these meetings was becoming clear as the governor began to remove Morrisites from office.[26]

In December 1748, a delegation from the Council with Robert Hunter Morris in the lead confronted the governor. Belcher listened anxiously as the councilors reviewed the crisis. Since the Assembly had refused to consider more stringent legislation and had thereby lent encouragement to "Traitors and Rioters," the Council saw no alternative but to appeal to London and now asked the governor to join in its petition. Belcher had been forced to concede that the pardon had not brought peace, but rather than make a public declaration that might alienate either the proprietors or his friends in the Assembly, he continued to call upon both parties to settle the dispute amongst themselves. Morris, however, was determined to force the governor's hand. Later that day, when Belcher met with the Council to sign several bills into law, Morris insisted that he and his colleagues must "Advise" the governor on the crisis. Belcher was desperate to avoid a decision and reminded Morris that the Council had no right to express its opinion unless called upon. Morris would not be put off: it made no difference "whether his Excellency demands That advice or not"; it was, he said, the councilor's duty to the king and to the people to speak his conscience. Belcher was outraged and repeated: "When I want The advice of the Council I shall ask for it." Morris persisted: "I believe, Sir, the Council will hardly wait for that." Belcher sat stunned, speechless. Without a word he rose and strode angrily from the Council chamber.[27]

Belcher had been caught unprepared. Though leery of Morris's intentions, he preferred not to trouble himself with the political situation. Besides, he had been busy preparing for the arrival of Louisa Teale. He did not even inform his family of his intentions. He even hesitated to write to the widow.

At least, he left few copies of his correspondence with her in his letterbooks. Perhaps he was not certain of her intentions and feared rejection. Later he explained to his son Andrew in characteristic fashion that he was loath to "Amuse my Friends (or the World) with an Affair that might have been stifled in the Birth." But Mrs. Teale did arrive in the summer of 1748. In early September Belcher married his "Queen of Nova Caesarea." Within a fortnight, he succumbed to "several Attacks of a Fever." For a time friends feared for his life. He recovered slowly. Unable to travel, he postponed his meeting with the legislature at Perth Amboy until mid-November.[28]

No matter the state of his health, Belcher was inclined to spend as little time as possible on the duties of office. He remained an inveterate letter writer, even though he complained of a progressing paralysis in his hands. His letterbooks during these years contained fewer references to government matters than were found in the earlier volumes. Rarely did he write to discuss political affairs with other prominent leaders, even trusted allies. His communication with London officialdom also dropped off markedly. What did increase was his correspondence with religious leaders throughout the Atlantic world.

From the moment of his arrival, Belcher had been listening to the region's evangelicals as they laid out their plans to build a college in New Jersey.[29] Pemberton, Burr, Dickinson, Gilbert Tennent—all recounted their struggles to raise funds and to fend off an opposition led by Governor Morris. After a decade of disheartening struggle, they rejoiced to learn that a true friend of evangelical religion had been appointed governor. They easily awakened Belcher to their cause. Within months he was writing that the province desperately needed a "seminary of Learning." Such an institution would lift this people up from their wild ways. It would serve as a bastion of civilization just as Harvard had in New England. Moreover the project and the evangelicals' expectations of him awakened in his imagination those powerful images of himself as the good ruler and the Nehemiah.[30]

Belcher quickly realized that endorsing the college drew him into political controversy. In Burlington he could see that while a few Quakers supported the college in the belief that education would foster prosperity and civility, most agreed with the Smiths that the project was a pretense for converting their children into Presbyterians. The Morrisites were also divided with some, such as Andrew Johnston in the Council, endorsing the college but with most in opposition. Many recalled Governor Morris's warnings that the college's promoters were the same people who opposed the proprietary interest. The riots confirmed that these latter-day Puritans were, like their ancestors, fomenters of rebellion. Determined to quash these revived spirits of rebellion in whatever form they might take, Morris had summarily rejected the evangelicals' applications for a college charter. After his death, however, the interim executive had approved a charter.[31]

But the college's opponents persisted. When Governor Belcher arrived, they pressed him to withdraw official recognition. Their arguments tried his patience. When one delegation called for revoking the charter, he blurted out: "Pray Gentlemen, make yourselves easy, if their Charter is not good, I'll get them a better." Soon after he publicly declared his resolve to increase official support and to make the college his pet project. Thus, he proposed to reform the college government by increasing the size of the Board of Trustees and by including in its membership four councilors and the governor. Perhaps he expected that by expanding the board's size he could recruit broader public support for the college. No doubt, Harvard's example inspired him to link the provincial and college governments.[32]

Tennent was appalled by the governor's reforms. He did not object to Belcher's presence on the Board of Trustees. What concerned him was the provision to make the governor an *ex officio* member of the board. How, he asked, would the college fare with an unfriendly governor sitting on the board? When Tennent threatened to withdraw his support for the college, others seemed inclined to follow his example. Belcher listened but could not be moved. Tennent, he responded, had "dress[ed] up Spectres and Apparitions into Substances." The governor, Belcher assured Burr and Pemberton, could cast but one vote at board meetings. Harvard had not suffered by this practice. Finally, he warned that unless his terms were accepted, he would withdraw his support for the college. The threat convinced his critics to accept his reforms.[33]

The company of the evangelicals stirred images that had been lying dormant in the recesses of Belcher's imagination. While at home in Burlington, he found renewal by writing to Edwards, Whitefield, and Pemberton. Through the act of writing he discovered the means to express his beliefs and hopes for religious revival and to share vicariously in the evangelicals' crusades. By writing he also began to work his own transformation from self-styled exile to political missionary. Perhaps most revealing, but not exceptional, was a letter he addressed to John Sergeant, a missionary at Stockbridge and a native of New Jersey. Belcher devoted much of the letter to recounting the "uncouth" conditions he had encountered. The people, "not only the lower sort but those of a better distinction[,] seem to have very little Taste or Relish for the ways of Virtue and true Religion." His description was not unusual. Then he stopped to ask himself: "What is my Duty[?]" To which he answered: "Why to make it the Care and Business of my Life to be a Pattern of Christianity and so to Conduct my self that those under my Care may Join with me in Living as the onely true and Acceptable way of speaking for the praises of God." "These things constantly hang upon my mind." It seemed to be so. The image of the good ruler leading the people into righteousness by virtue of his example appeared with increasing frequency in Belcher's letters. Weeks later he wrote to Joseph Sewall, the minister at Boston's Old South Church, reflecting on his duties. A governor "must be on his Watch and Guard in his own Life and conversation and to be constantly asking the aids of divine Grace to Assist him to some Reformation" of the people's religious life. Rulers, he concluded, could be "more substantial and Extensive Blessings to a People by their Example than in any other way—Precipta docent Exempla cogunt."[34]

Soon after taking office, Belcher began to transplant New England's conventions to his Nova Caesarea. In one of his first meetings with the legislature, he addressed the lawmakers as the provincial "General Court." His form of address was unfamiliar to the ears of Jerseymen. Perhaps the innovation was merely the unconscious slip of a foreigner, but it proved to be a symptom of what became a deliberate attempt to impose the ways of Massachusetts on this wilderness society. Belcher recalled the annual cycle of Puritan rituals with the governor designating a day for fasting and prayer each spring and in the fall summoning the people to give thanks for their blessings. The practice was unknown to Jerseymen. When Belcher proposed to set aside a day of thanksgiving, he won hearty support from the transplanted New Englanders in the Newark-Elizabethtown region. As he had in Boston, he consulted with the clergyman of these communities on the proper day and on the wording of the proclamation. His proclamations were less elaborate than the New England models, perhaps because he hoped to avoid offending other denominations. But his intentions were clear. His proclamation of 1750 noted that the people had reason to give thanks to the "supreme Governor of the World." Although the season had begun with signs of drought, the harvest had been bountiful. God has "in his great Mercy defended us from those numberless judgements that our Iniquities have deserved." The people lived secure in their civil and religious privileges. They also had reason to give thanks for the college.[35]

When Belcher issued a proclamation for a day of fasting in the spring of 1749, he invited Gilbert Tennent to preach before the provincial Council. When the sermon appeared in print, the public learned that the governor had chosen the minister's text. The event corresponded to the model of the public lectures given by New England's divines. Tennent invoked the political principles heard so often in Boston. Fasting, he explained, was a "Duty" required by the almighty for the preservation of the common welfare. Later that fall the minister returned to deliver a sermon of thanksgiving. "It is the Duty of GOD's professing People, to Praise or Thank him publickly for Benefits receiv'd, and to evidence the Sincerity thereof by the Performance of their Vows, or by a Conversation becoming the Gospel of CHRIST." The public welfare depended on good rulers: "It is a just and general Maxim, that Example has more Efficacy than Precept, and that by the Example of Princes in particular, their Subjects are form'd. . . . When the Righteous, saith Solomon, are in Authority, the People rejoice! But when the wicked bear Rule, the People mourn."[36]

Tennent summoned the people to be thankful for such a pious governor. He prayed "That the Almighty would be pleased to vouchsafe all Covenant Mercies upon the GOVERNOR of this Province . . . and particularly, that Jehovah would support his EXCELLENCY and Comfort him in the Wane of Life." Belcher's "pious Desires, Projects and Attempts for the lasting Benefit of this Colony, in Regard of both its religious and civil Interests" made his presence a "publick Blessing." In an appendix to the printed version of the fast sermon, the minister recalled the moment when the governor "expressly" called upon the ministers to lead the people in prayer for rain. It was a "dry Season." The people's "Supplications were speedily answer'd by seasonable and refreshing Showers. For this Instance of unmerited and condescending Mercy, in hearing the Crys of the Poor, may all Praises be ascribed to a gracious God."[37]

Tennent expounding political doctrine before a Council composed of Quakers and Anglicans is a scene difficult to imagine. Indeed, the silences in the record suggest that the event did not happen. Normally, proclamations were issued by the governor in Council, but there is no note of such a vote in the Council minutes. Nor do the records whisper the slightest hint that the councilors assembled to hear the sermon—at least in an official capacity. Perhaps the silence is due to poor record keeping. But there is a pattern of such omissions. For example, Belcher's proclamation summoning the people to give thanks for the college was issued as if on the advice of the Council. The text of the proclamation that appears in the *New-York Weekly Journal* suggests as much.[38] Again the Council's proceedings make no reference to such a decision. In his efforts at provincial reformation, Belcher strained conventions, often rankled sensibilities, sometimes constructed illusions.

Belcher was not oblivious to political realities, especially when it came to promoting the college. He quickly realized that the college's founders and advocates had erred by presenting their project principally as a seminary for training Calvinist clergymen. They had made little effort to placate denominational jealousies. If the college were to be built, it would need broad public support and government sponsorship. Belcher, therefore, proposed to expand the college's functions so that it would "Instruct the Rising Generation in a better knowledge of this World & of the Next." In his mind the "infant college" became something more than Tennent's seminary. Like Harvard it would train a future generation of leaders and bring civilization to this "unpolisht ignorant part of the World." By promoting and disseminating an appreciation of "Good literature," the college would become the foundation for New Jersey's future prosperity and tranquillity. Noting that this "Young Countrey" was "plagued with Quacks and Blundering (Man Slayers)," he promised "to trye at having a Professor of Physick and Chirgery establish[ed] in the College." All Jerseymen would benefit. As he explained to the West Jersey proprietors, land values would increase. By expanding the Board of Trustees to include Quakers and Anglicans, he expected to allay suspicions, win broad support, and persuade the legislature to lend its aid.[39]

Richard Smith, like most Quakers, dismissed Belcher's appeals. He knew the governor both as friend and neighbor and as a political ally, and he read his heart correctly. The college remained a device for remodeling the province into a society of Calvinist enthusiasts. Its true purpose was to convert the rising generation into Presbyterians. The governor's reforms were a ruse designed "to Decoy the [Anglican] Church and . . . the Quakers." Anglicans agreed. One described the college as a "Seminary of Sedition" and an engine for seducing the young and unsuspecting. If it succeeded, he asked, "What becomes of the Church[?]" Eventually, Belcher found a Quaker and an Anglican to sit on the Board of Trustees. But the college could not disguise its denominational identity. When the governor and the trustees petitioned the legislature for permission to raise money by public lottery, Belcher was already prepared for defeat. "As many in the Government are Quakers . . . I don't expect Any thing will be done" for the college. The petition was submitted repeatedly and each time rejected.[40]

The defeat, though disappointing, could not quash Belcher's enthusiasm. The college, he confessed, had become his "Child," his "dear little Daughter." The lawmakers' hostility to the college confirmed his initial opinion that this was a "wilderness" people in dire need of "societies for Learning." Convinced that funding must be found elsewhere, Belcher began a letter-writing campaign that extended from his home in Burlington north to New England and across the Atlantic to England and Scotland. He appealed to the governor of Connecticut and to old acquaintances such as Thomas Prince in New England. He wrote to Philip Doddridge and the Protestant Dissenting Deputies in London asking for their contributions.[41]

Aaron Burr spoke for the colony's evangelicals when he gave thanks for Belcher's appointment. "It pleased God at this difficult Juncture to send Mr. Belcher to be Our Governor, a Gentleman of many excellent Accomplishments & one that appears an hearty Friend to ye Cause & Kingdom of Christ." Tennent concurred. It was unusual to find a royal official favorably disposed to the evangelicals' cause. In an address thanking the governor for his aid, the college's trustees predicted that the college would become "a flourishing Seminary of Piety and Literature," "a lasting Foundation for the future Prosperity of Church and State," and "a perpetual Monument of Honour to your Name, above the Victories of renowned Conquerors." In November 1748, the board voted to confer the degree of Master of Arts upon the governor.[42]

Belcher found fulfillment as the American Nehemiah. The pleasures he had once derived from playing the servant of the king became dim memories tucked away in the recesses of his imagination. The vocabulary of royalty echoed faintly in his writings. The obsequious courtier appeared less often in his letterbooks. He seemed to let go his obsessions with cultivating interests in London and with punishing his enemies. Yet Jerseymen continued to intrude upon his life with their factious concerns. Although the rioting seemed to subside, the issue of proprietary influence carried over to the legislature's debates on taxation. By 1750 the government was at deadlock over the Assembly's proposal to asses unimproved proprietary lands at the same rate as improved properties. The proprietors in the Council refused to accept any tax bill from the lower house until their lands were assessed at a lower rate. The treasury was empty, and the governor had not been paid. Meanwhile, Robert Hunter Morris had joined Ferdinand John Paris in London, where he was persuading the Board of Trade that the governor was nominating friends of the rioters to the Council. Despite Richard Partridge's objections, the board laid aside Belcher's nominations and named Morrisites to the Council. An infuriated Belcher complained that rejections of his nominations were a "great dishonour to Me & much weaken my hands in the Government." Rumors abounded that he would be replaced, most likely by Morris.[43]

Governor Belcher liked to think that he enjoyed the people's approval and that he was a victim of a selfish pack of miscreants. Even while the exchanges between the Council and Assembly grew hotter, he boasted that "a good harmony subsists between the Governor & the good People of the Province." Again he speculated that "were the Governor elective I believe I shou'd have 19 votes in 20 throughout the Province." If he was unable to move the government to an accord on taxation, the fault lay with the proprietors. These landed magnates "are so partial in managing the Affairs of the Legislature I expect nothing but Confusion in the Government." Their allies in the Council blocked tax legislation "which shall in any measure subject their vast Estates in Land to bear any part of it."[44] Belcher's associations with the Smiths of Burlington and the evangelicals from the transplanted New England communities in the eastern section shaped his perspective. Although he enjoyed amicable relations with antiproprietors, he was repeatedly reminded that he had little influence with them.

Again he was frustrated by the disparity between the prestige of his office and its ineffectiveness. As he had in New England, he confronted a legislature composed of disparate and unorganized local oligarchs who formed and then reformed political associations. The governor's powers of appointment were circumscribed by the dictates of these assemblymen, and they in turn felt little reason to compromise their independence by following the governor's lead. Again, as he had in New Hampshire, Belcher resorted to the paper powers of office. In the summer of 1750, he ordered that John Coxe, a wealthy and prominent ally of the Morrisites, be expelled from the Council. Belcher explained that Coxe had "with insufferable insolence, traduced my Name and Character" and had in public called him a "Scoundrel" and an "Old woman." A year later when Lewis Ashfield, another prominent Morrisite, was appointed to the Council, Belcher refused him admission on the ground that Ashfield was under indictment for "Damning the King's Laws." When the Council accused the governor of defiling its integrity, Belcher retorted he was "Accountabel to the King my Royal Master but not any lower Rank or Order of Men."[45]

At the same time, Belcher was learning how little influence he had with the elected branch of government. In the winter of 1751, he had abandoned any hope of moving the rancorous debates on taxation to resolution and had dissolved the legislature. Hoping to change the Assembly's composition, he directly appealed to the public to consider the justice of his position. In his proclamation calling for elections, he explained that although he had "done every Thing . . . for the Advancement of the Welfare and Prosperity of the People under my Care," the lawmakers had demonstrated an insensitivity to the public welfare and had acted contrary to "the Sentiments of the good People of this Province." He also wrote to friends throughout the province to stand for election or to exert their influence on behalf of the administration. Although eleven of the twenty-four representatives were newcomers, Belcher could see that the changes had little to do with his exertions and that they did not alter the Assembly's position on taxation. "I have rarely observd even from great Britain, to the most Petite Government, The King has in America, that dissolutions of Assemblies have brot others together better disposed, bono publico."[46]

During the fall session, the Assembly passed another tax bill, which the Council again found "repugnant" and returned with its amendments. The lower house responded by tearing the amendments from the bill and returning them to the Council without comment and then proposed to bypass the upper house and send its bill directly to the governor for his approval. At first Belcher was intrigued with the stratagem. Councilor Alexander vigorously volunteered his objections to such an unprecedented maneuver. Belcher backed down and adjourned the lower house.[47] But when the legislature reconvened three months later, a majority of assemblymen rapidly moved toward passing a bill that satisfied the Council. Belcher was ecstatic when he signed the tax bill. The session "turned out the best of any since my Arrival," he declared. "I really find patience and Moderation of Excellent use in publick Affairs." Notwithstanding his boast, credit for the settlement lay with a majority of assemblymen, who had grown weary of the squabbling and had joined to endorse a settlement that was of their own making.[48]

Belcher was preoccupied by his move to Elizabethtown. He had never been happy at Burlington. His health had declined steadily. "This Town and my Situation in it have for 4 years past so subjected me to Fever & Ague," he wrote during the summer of 1751. His wife Louisa had visited Elizabethtown during the spring to find a new home. She had settled on a two-story brick house, which with some improvements could be made worthy of the province's chief magistrate. Two rooms were to be added—a dining room and a large bedroom. That fall the Belchers made their move.[49]

Elizabethtown's attraction was not just its healthy clime. From the moment of his arrival in the province, Governor Belcher had been drawn to the Calvinist communities of Newark and Elizabethtown. He sought solace for his exile in the companionship of these transplanted New Englanders. There was Aaron Burr, the son-in-law of Edwards, at Newark. Belcher took special pleasure in Jonathan Dickinson's ministry at Elizabethtown, and he mourned the news of his death. When the church turned to Elihu Spencer, a Yale graduate and protege of Jonathan Edwards, Belcher rejoiced. Elizabethtown's Presbyterians were equally elated on learning that the governor had chosen to live with them. Soon after he joined the church and settled into the town's social life. Belcher spent his days happily consulting with the evangelicals. He regularly met with Burr and wrote frequently to Edwards. He sent few letters to his friends in Burlington, and he troubled himself with governmental affairs only when they intruded upon him.[50]

The move did not stem the aging process. Belcher spent three weeks in bed during his first winter in residence. The decrepitudes of age advanced steadily. The paralysis in his hand prevented him from writing and caused him to rely on his wife's secretarial services. Gilbert Tennent prescribed rattlesnake root but to no avail. Benjamin Franklin offered an electrical therapy. After being "electrifyd several times," Belcher reported that "at present" he felt no change in his "Nervous disorder." His "Paralytic disorder" with the "other decays of nature" reminded him to become more diligent "in working at my Salvation" and in "preparing for the last Awful hour." The deaths of Richard Waldron, Paul Dudley, and so many other "Great Personages" reminded him to be ready.[51]

His thoughts turned to his family, especially his sons. Andrew and Jonathan were in their forties; Belcher still doubted that they would ever be able to support themselves. He scolded them incessantly. "I will not go on to bear your sluggishness and Indolence," he wrote Andrew. He continued in a later letter: "If you were of the Bee Species you know your fate would be to be stung out of the Hive." Andrew's behavior was "Intolerable." Nor did Belcher spare his other son. He regularly berated Jonathan, Jr., for his "Useless pride & Coyness," his dismal progress, and his "rude and ungrateful behavior." His letters seemed ineffective. He tried to rouse the jealousy of one by pretending to favor the other but to no avail. His sons did not reply. "Neither my love—my just anger—nor my good Example," Belcher raged, could stir them.[52]

Andrew declined to visit. In 1754 he received an urgent invitation to come so that he might discuss the family's affairs with his father. Andrew balked again, perhaps because he sensed a special eagerness in his father's letter. Perhaps he suspected the cause. For some time his father had been fretting that he was nearly fifty and still a bachelor. Belcher had concocted a stratagem that would keep his wife's wealth in the family and simultaneously secure Andrew's future. Louisa Teale had brought her daughter to New Jersey with her, and Belcher had decided that Andrew must marry her. Belcher was resolute and would not tolerate his son's willfulness. That spring Andrew complied and arrived in Elizabethtown; the marriage took place soon after. The father was overjoyed by the joining of the families' fortunes. When the couple departed for Boston, he bestowed several Boston properties valued at nearly £1000, a packet of bonds and notes worth over £4000, and the Milton estate upon his son. For the first time he wrote to Andrew as "My dear Son."[53]

Jonathan, Jr.'s, move to Dublin had given him only temporary respite from his father's wrath. "All I have done for you," Belcher wrote to his errant son, "turns out but an Abortion." He reminded Jonathan that many who began life with fewer advantages and privileges had accomplished much more than he had. "How many Templars much your juniors (void of the many Advantages you have Enjoy'd) are now in good Bread?" Jonathan's failure to gain an important position was inexplicable: "how many (without money & without price) daily get into Posts of Profit?" The son had not found a wealthy wife: "How many young Gentlemen (without your considerable pretensions) Marry daily to great Advantage?" Jonathan's apostasy could not be forgotten. "Your own silly pride and Unthinkingness have brought you into your present distress." Jonathan had been indulged to the tune of £3600. It would have been better had he been apprenticed to "some good honest Tradesman" in Boston. Jonathan did not answer, and his silence earned him only additional censures. In 1754, however, Belcher learned that his son was appointed chief justice of the Superior Court of Nova Scotia. He wrote to express his approval. Soon father and son were writing regularly. After Jonathan settled in Halifax, he came to visit. And in 1756, he married Abigail, the daughter of Jeremiah Allen, at Boston's King's Chapel.[54]

As Belcher watched the "Oyl in my Earthly Lamp" burn low, he found fulfillment in the company of the evangelicals at Elizabethtown and Newark.

Vicariously he joined with George Whitefield as the great itinerant took his crusade against Satan's forces to the far reaches of the English empire. Jonathan Edwards's struggles to awaken the people of Northampton became his own. He was happiest when visiting Aaron Burr and his family; sometimes one of the Edwardses was visiting. He prayed that with his declining energies he might still serve the cause of religious reformation. He often wrote to allies in the crusade against ignorance and heresy.[55]

Increasingly his letterbooks echoed with the rhetoric of spiritual decay and declension. Belcher painted the depravity of New Jersey society in the starkest terms. The people in his charge were "too much immerst" in "follies and Vices"; the laws are "too lean and too much in favor of Dilinquents of all sorts" to be able to stem the "Rapid Tide of Vice and Wickedness." The people were "too Ignorant and too indifferent and Negligint in Civil matters." Even more alarming, they were "too Cold & in a manner void of Real Vital Piety." Ministers were scarce, and there were too many who "pretend to be the Ministers of the Glorious Jesus" but, in fact, were "Traducing Him and His Doctrines by Endeavouring to lead the people into the dreadful Errors of Arianism Antinomianism Pelagianism &c: & so are decoying poor Souls into Eternal ruin." "O tempora! O mores!"[56]

Like New England's Jeremiahs, he did not descend into fatalism. Instead, he was defining his task as a Nehemiah for a benighted people. Belcher prayed for strength so that he might rekindle the spirit of reformation among the people. "With good Old Mordecai," who had saved the children of Israel in times of peril, he labored to build the foundations for peace and prosperity. He summoned the "Lovers of Virtue and Religion" to exert themselves with him, and he called upon the province's lawmakers to "become a Terror to Evil Doers and a Praise & Encouragement to those that do well.'" By doing so he promised that they would "draw down Blessings from Heaven, on this People, and on your Selves & Families." For his part he set for himself the special task of enlightening the people by promoting the college. In writing to Edwards, he prayed that though he was "so worthless a worm," he might be made "one of the least Instruments of Advancg the Kingdom of the blessed God our Saviour in this World."[57]

The college had become his favorite project. "I am sometimes afraid my little Daughter takes up too much Room in my Heart," he wrote to Burr. "And yet I must & will repeatedly praise God that . . . we have a reasonable Prospect that she may in Time to come (through the Mercy of God in Christ) be made a pure Fountain from whence may issue such Streams as shall make glad the City (or Church) of God." The college trustees had received permission from the government of Connecticut, largely with Belcher's aid, for running a lottery. When they appointed two agents, Samuel Davies and Gilbert Tennent, to tour the British Isles, Belcher provided them with a packet of letters introducing them to leading dissenters in London and Edinburgh.[58]

From his home in Elizabethtown Belcher watched the cause of "sincere Religion" on both sides of the Atlantic. He lamented when he learned that a prominent English dissenter had "taken ordrs in the Church of England." He dismissed reports that Anglicans were working toward reforming their church. He doubted that the church could tear down its "Hierarchical" forms of government and cleanse its worship service of the "Superstitous Trifles . . . derived from the Church of Rome." It seemed that the "Religion of the blessed Jesus is at so low an Ebb among the Nations that are called reformed." Even New England's ministers were lured by the corruptions of the age. In a letter congratulating Samuel Niles for his efforts to check the spread of heresy in New England, Belcher reflected on the declining times. He was "grievd that many profess & stile themselves Ministers of the Gospel" but appear to be "almost Ashamd of the Cross of Christ" and studiously avoid "even the mention of the name of Jesus Christ thro their whole discourses."[59]

The itinerants, especially Whitefield, were never far from his thoughts. Wherever Whitefield went, "the presence of Christ goes with him." Belcher prayed that he might see Whitefield once again and was disappointed to learn that the evangelical had taken his crusade to Ireland. He regularly wrote to the itinerant and through his letters participated vicariously in the crusade for a reformed and vital religion. "Go on—in the Strength of Christ," he wrote, "to pull down the strong holds of Sin & Satan." He rejoiced on receiving reports of Whitefield's well-being: "these things," he wrote in ecstasy, "I receive as the Panting Hart does Water from the cool Brook." In the fall of 1754, Whitefield did come. Arrangements were made for him to attend the college's commencement exercises at Newark. He received the M.A. degree and later in the day preached in the open air to the assembled throng.[60]

Of all the champions of reformation, Jonathan Edwards had become the governor's favorite. Belcher was grieved to learn that the minister had fallen out with his congregation at Northampton and had been dismissed. He congratulated Edwards on his appointment to the Indian mission at Stockbridge. "God has lifted up the light of His Countinance upon you. . . . In the strength of Christ may you go on Conquering & to Conquor & be instrumental in the hands of the great head of the Church for pullg down the strongholds of Sin & Satan & more especially for takg off the Scales from the Eyes of the benighted Indians who have been so long held in Chains by the Prince of Darkness." Soon after, when Edwards fell out with the local magnates of Hampshire County who oversaw the mission's finances, Belcher rushed to his defense and wrote urging friends in New England and in England to support the missionary.[61]

Belcher's letters sparked with urgency and expectation as he attended to the evangelical cause. While visiting Aaron Burr's family, he listened to the minister reflect upon imminent millennium. In the spring of 1754, Anglo-America began to prepare for war with France. Belcher received reports that the French were massing their forces in the Ohio Valley in preparation for an assault on the western frontiers. The governor of Virginia wrote requesting a contingent of New Jersey troops to join an expedition to repulse the enemy. Soon after Belcher received notice from London that a conference of delegates from the northern colonies was to assemble at Albany to make plans for war. While meeting with the legislature, Belcher listened to the evangelicals debate whether this conflagration signified God's plan for redeeming the world. Though they were not in agreement, their discussion quickened Belcher's imagination.[62]

In mid-summer of 1755 news arrived at Elizabethtown that a combined force of English and colonial troops under the command of General Edward Braddock had blundered into an ambush on the banks of the Monongahela River and had suffered grievous losses, including the general. The frontiers were exposed, and Belcher feared that skirmishing parties would soon be harassing New Jersey. The signs were clear: "God is plainly teaching us that we must not Put our Trust in an Arm of Flesh but, in the Practice of our Duty, in the Living God." Though "a Gloom at Present hangs over his Majestys Colonies on this Continent," he summoned the people and their lawmakers to redouble their efforts. America had become "the Seat of War," and the colonies must join in patriotic resolve to rid themselves finally of their papist foe. The imperative was simple: *"Carthago est delenda."* He envisioned a grand venture of thirty thousand colonials with five thousand English troops sailing up the St. Lawrence River and finally laying siege to Quebec. "If we wou'd hew the Tree down effectually the sacred Pages tell us we must lay the Ax to the root."[63]

The legislature was unimpressed. It voted troops and supplies but less than he requested; it approved support for the war on condition that it be allowed to print amounts of paper money in excess of limits set by London; and it often seemed more interested in pressing long-standing grievances over the governor's appointments than in prosecuting the war. Sometimes the lawmakers reprimanded the governor for refusing to call elections more frequently. Belcher was often livid. Aaron Burr strove to rouse the public: "Had we but the Spirit of our brave Ancestors . . . I doubt not, by the Smiles of Heaven, we should soon make our Enemies flee before us, and again sit quietly under our Vines and Fig-trees, and eat the Good of the Land."[64]

In the spring of 1756, Belcher issued a proclamation for a day of fasting so that the people might "humble themselves before GOD, for the crying

Sins of the Day, and return to him by Repentance and Reformation." This "sinful Land," the governor explained, lay under the "angry Resentments of an offended God." The people wallowed in "Infidelity, Prophaneness, Immorality, and a Disregard to the glorious Gospel of Christ." Thus their armies had suffered "total Defeat" and "Dissappointment" in their efforts to drive "our perfidious Enemies from their unrighteous Encroachments." He pointed to the "numerous Depredations and cruel Murders" that had been endured on the frontiers by the "many barbarous Nations of Indians." And recent "terrible Earthquakes" were more reminders of "Divine Providence." Only "Humiliation, Repentance and Reformation" would restore the people to God's favor and secure victory on the fields of battle.[65]

Though surrounded by a public that was indifferent and even hostile to his summons, Belcher found a receptive audience among the evangelicals. Aaron Burr and his clerical cohorts had come to depend on the governor to protect and promote their schemes. Indeed, he seemed to be the only royal governor on the continent deserving of such trust. In 1755 the college trustees addressed Jonathan Belcher. They were laying plans for establishing the college at the town of Princeton and proposed to name the first building in the governor's honor: "when your Excellency is translated [to his other worldly reward] let Belcher Hall proclaim your beneficent Acts, Advancement of Christianity, and Emolument of the Arts and Sciences to the latest Ages."[66]

Belcher savored the moment. In his reply he posed as he wanted to be remembered. He had governed three colonies and had made it his policy to act with moderation and with an eye on the king's honor and the welfare of the people. His administration had brought "Peace and Tranquility" to a people so long beset by "many Tumults and Riots." He thanked God that he had been given the strength and opportunity to promote this "Seminary for Religion & Learning." But he could not accept the offer. He had made it his motto to "be useful rather than attract attention." Instead of Belcher Hall, he proposed Nassau Hall "to the immortal Memory of the glorious King William the 3d. who was a Branch of the illustrious House of Nassau." Lest he be forgotten, however, he gave the college a portrait of himself "at full length in a gilt Frame" to be hung in the college library.[67]

Jonathan Belcher spent more of his days in bed. "I know," he wrote to Edwards, "my Dissolution is near at hand." He had sold his pew at Boston's Old South Church, dictated his will, which gave his large library to the College of New Jersey, and made arrangements that his body would be returned to Massachusetts for burial at Cambridge. He thought that he had governed well. He believed the people loved him: "were this Government Elective, nineteen in twenty would give me their Voices." He prayed that "with some measure of Grace I have sincerely endeavoured to contribute what I cou'd for Building up the Kingdom of the great Redeemer in this World, and which I humbly pray may be the happy Fruit of the incorporation of New Jersey College. . . . amen."[68]

Jonathan Belcher died on August 31, 1757, at his Elizabethtown home. The evangelicals were stunned. When the news came to Newark, Aaron Burr was out of town. His wife Esther grieved when she received the "Blacken news." She knew that her husband had been worrying for the governor's health. In preparation for the governor's death, he and his cohorts had sought out a successor but had failed to find a worthy candidate. While waiting for her husband's return, she reflected on the moment. "This is such a loss that we can't expect to have made up in [another] governor." As if anticipating her husband's reaction, she interpreted the event as a presage of dark times: "The Righteous are taken from the Evil to come." Two days later, Burr arrived stricken with fever. Though visibly weak, he agreed to deliver the funeral sermon on September 4. Three weeks later Burr died from the fever.[69]

When Jonathan Belcher's body was returned to Massachusetts, Thomas Hutchinson paused to take note of his first patron's passing. He was already compiling materials for his *History of Massachusetts-Bay* and would soon be composing his account of the Belcher administration. Hutchinson's history of the salary and treasury controversies, of the complicated border dispute with New Hampshire, of the currency debates that led to the Land Bank crisis, of the factional divisions and personalities that racked provincial government, and of the political maneuverings by which Belcher won his commissions and then lost them became a principal source for understanding these years. The portrait he painted of the governor was essentially sympathetic. Though sometimes overbearing in his relationship with his associates, Belcher governed well. His policies, especially with regard to currency questions, were sound, and he refrained from turning his office to personal profit. His fall from office was not due to his own failings but to the machinations of unscrupulous opponents.[70]

Hutchinson gave Belcher good marks. But the story he told fell flat by Belcher's standards. The history focused on constitutional relationships, monetary affairs, imperial conflicts, and factional disputes. Religious affairs, specifically the evangelicals' arrival in Massachusetts-Bay, vanish from the narrative. Jonathan Belcher is presented as a royal official and as a faction leader. He is remembered for his interpretations of the executive power and for his stand against inflation. The Jonathan Belcher who sought to nurture "vital piety," cared for the Puritan heritage, sponsored the missions to the

Indians, and shielded the Congregational way from Anglican assault disappears from history.

In contrast, Aaron Burr painted a portrait that captured the governor on his own terms. Belcher was a "Servant of God" first. Burr turned to the Book of Daniel for his text. Though Daniel served the king of Babylon, he had not forgotten his God. Though he thrived amidst courtly vices, he kept his virtue intact. So, too, Belcher went to Europe and learned the "Customs and Manners of the World." Unlike "too many of the young Gentry of the present Age, (who return from their Travels, replenished with the corrupt Principles, and Proficient in the scandalous Vices, and debauched Practices of the Places they have visited) . . . he preserved his Morals unsullied" and kept his "sacred Regard to the holy Religion" intact. As governor he acted selflessly and always with the interest of the people at his heart. Though crippled by the infirmities of age when he came to New Jersey, Governor Belcher proved to be a blessing to the people. He was a "Minister of God for Good unto his People," and a "Terrour to Evil Doers, and a Praise to those that did well." His piety, his faithful observation of the Sabbath, was an example to all. His support for the College of New Jersey was reminder that the "Welfare of Zion lay near his Heart" and that "he long'd for the Prosperity of Jerusalem." Like "pious Governor Nehemiah," Jonathan Belcher vowed not to "forsake the House of God, so long as he lived."[71]

Abbreviations

B.Ltrs   Belcher Letterbooks, Massachusetts Historical Society.

BP(MHS)   *Belcher Papers*, in Massachusetts Historical Society, *Collections*, 6th ser., VI-VII (Boston, 1893-94).

BP(NHHS)   Belcher Papers, New Hampshire Historical Society.

Cal.St.Pprs   *Calendar of State Papers, Colonial Series* (London, 1860-).

Col.Cur.Rprnts   *Colonial Currency Reprints, 1682-1751*, ed. Andrew McFarland Davis (Boston, 1910-11).

CR   Massachusetts Council Records (Legislative), microfilm at the Library of Congress, listed in Lillian A. Hamrick, ed., *A Guide to the Microfilm Collection of Early State Records* (Washington, D.C., 1950), 89-95.

Docs.NH   *Documents and Records Relating to the Province of New Hampshire*, ed. Nathaniel Bouton et al. (Concord and Manchester, 1867-1941).

Hrvrd Grads   Clifford K. Shipton, *Biographical Sketches of those who attended Harvard College. . .* (Cambridge, Mass., 1933-).

JHR   *Journals of the House of Representatives of Massachusetts...*, (Boston, 1919-).

NJ.Archs   *Archives of the State of New Jersey . . .* , ed. William A. Whitehead et al. (Newark, 1880-).

Swll Dry   *The Diary of Samuel Sewall, 1674-1729*, ed. M. Halsey Thomas (New York, 1973).

W-B   Waldron-Belcher Papers, Library of Congress.

WP   Waldron Papers, New Hampshire Historical Society.

Notes

Preface

1. *The Serviceable Man. A Discourse Made unto the General Court of the Massachusetts Colony* . . . (Boston, 1690), 2.

2. Jonathan Mitchel, *Nehemiah on the Wall in Troublesome Times* . . . (Cambridge, Mass., 1671); Cotton Mather, *Magnalia Christi Americana*, ed. Kenneth B. Murdock (Cambridge, Mass., 1977 [1702]), 213-28; Jonathan Edwards, *Some Thoughts Concerning the Present Revival of Religion* . . . in *The Great Awakening*, ed. C. C. Goen (*The Works of Jonathan Edwards*, ed. Perry Miller, et al. [New Haven, 1957-], 4:370-80; John Murray, *Nehemiah; or, The Struggle for Liberty* (Newburyport, Mass., 1779).

3. *The Religious Regards we owe to our Country, and the Blessing of Heaven assured thereunto* (Boston, 1718).

4. *A Servant of God dismissed from Labour to Rest* (New York, 1757), 17. For Belcher's reputation see Alan Heimert, *Religion and the American Mind from the Great Awakening to the Revolution* (Cambridge, Mass., 1966), 297, 302.

5. For example, see William Cooper, *The Honours of Christ demanded of the Magistrate* (Boston, 1740). For analysis of political thought, see T. H. Breen's *The Character of the Good Ruler: A Study of Puritan Political Ideas in New England, 1630-1730* (New Haven, 1970) which makes reference to the importance of the Nehemiah (2, 100, 102).

6. *Serviceable Man*, 27, 32.

7. Bernard Bailyn, *The Origins of American Politics* (New York, 1968); Philip Greven, *The Protestant Temperament: Patterns of Child-Rearing, Religious Experience, and the Self in Early America* (New York, 1977).

8. In addition to Greven's *Protestant Temperament*, see his *Spare the Child: The Religious Roots of Punishment and the Psychological Impact of Physical Abuse* (New York, 1991); "'Some Root of Bitterness': Corporal Punishment, Child Abuse, and the Apocalyptic Impulse in Michael Wigglesworth," in *The Transformation of Early American History: Society, Authority, and Ideology*, ed. James A. Henretta, Michael Kammen, and Stanley N. Katz (New York, 1991), 93-122; and *Four Generations: Population, Land, and Family in Colonial Andover, Massachusetts* (Ithaca, 1970). Also see John Demos's "Developmental Perspectives on the History of Childhood," *Journal of Interdisciplinary History* 2 (Autumn 1971): 315-27; *Entertaining Satan: Witchcraft and the Culture of Early New England* (New York, 1982); and "Underlying Themes in the Witchcraft of Seventeenth-Century New England," *American Historical Review* 75 (June 1970): 1311-26. Kenneth A. Lockridge's *The*

Diary, and Life, of William Byrd II of Virginia, 1674-1744 (Chapel Hill, 1987) was also helpful.

9. Greven, *Spare the Child*, 65-66.

10. Edmund S. Morgan, *The Puritan Family: Religion & Domestic Relations in Seventeenth-Century New England* (1944; New York, 1966), 143.

11. Michael Zuckerman, *Peaceable Kingdoms: New England Towns in the Eighteenth Century* (New York, 1970).

12. Greven, *Spare the Child*, 133-42.

13. Several studies begin to link family and political history: Melvin Yazawa, *From Colonies to Commonwealth: Familial Ideology and the Beginnings of the American Republic* (Baltimore, 1985); Edwin G. Burrows and Michael Wallace, "The American Revolution: The Ideology and Psychology of National Liberation," *Perspectives in American History* 6 (1972): 167-306; N. E. H. Hull, Peter C. Hoffer, and Steven L. Allen, "Choosing Sides: A Quantitative Study of the Personality Determinants of Loyalist and Revolutionary Political Affiliation in New York," *Journal of American History* 65 (September 1978): 344-66; and Jay Fliegelman, *Prodigals and Pilgrims: The American Revolution against Patriarchal Authority, 1750-1800* (New York, 1982). Some studies focus on individuals: John J. Waters, "James Otis, Jr.: An Ambivalent Revolutionary," *History of Childhood Quarterly*, 1 (Fall 1973): 142-50; Kenneth S. Lynn, *A Divided People* (Westport, Conn., 1977).

1. The Puritan in a Whiggish Age

1. [Boston] *Weekly News-Letter*, Aug. 6-13, and Aug. 13-20, 1730; *New-England Weekly Journal*, Aug. 11, 17, and Sept. 7, 1730.

2. Benjamin Colman, *Government the Pillar of the Earth* (Boston, 1730), appendix.

3. Ibid., 17; Ebenezer Gay, *The Duty of People to pray for and praise their Rulers* (Boston, 1730), 32-33.

4. For a discussion of Massachusetts's relationship to the crown, see Richard L. Bushman, *King and People in Provincial Massachusetts* (Chapel Hill, 1985), 11-54.

5. Thomas Foxcroft, *Observations Historical and Practical on the Rise and Primitive State of New-England* (Boston, 1730); Thomas Prince, *The People of New-England . . .* (Boston, 1730).

6. Belcher to Council and House of Representatives, Sept. 9, 1730, *JHR*, IX, 238-39; Belcher to Bishop of Lincoln, Nov. 18, 1731, *BP*(MHS) I, 54.

7. Belcher to James Belcher, Aug. 25, 1732, *BP*(MHS), 175.

8. Sumner Chilton Powell, *Puritan Village: The Formation of a New England Town* (Middletown, Conn., 1963), 165; W. H. Whitmore, "Notes on the Belcher Family," *New England Historical and Genealogical Register* 27 (July, 1873): 239-40.

9. Belcher to Prince, June 7, 1748, in Whitmore, "Notes on the Belcher Family," 240.

10. J. Wingate Thornton, "The Gilbert Family," *New England Historical and Genealogical Register* 4 (July and October, 1850): 229-32; Charles Henry Stanley Davis, *History of Wallingford . . .* (Meriden, Conn., 1870), 17-20.

11. Benjamin Church, *Entertaining Passages Relating to Philip's War*, in *So Dreadful a Judgment: Puritan Responses to King Philip's War, 1676-1677*, ed. Richard Slotkin and James K. Folsom (Middletown, Conn., 1978), 416.

12. *The Public Records of the Colony of Connecticut* . . . (Hartford, 1850-1890), II, 279, 284, 285, 292, 322, 379, 409.

13. Belcher to Blagrove, Mar. 18, 1734/5, B.Ltrs, IV, 534, for a rare letter in which Belcher recalls his childhood.

14. Sewall to Edward Hull, July 10, 1688, *Letter-Book of Samuel Sewall* (Massachusetts Historical Society, *Collections*, 6th Series, I-II [1886-88]), I, 85-86; Sewall to Bridget Usher, July 10, 1688, ibid., 110; Memorandum, Mar. 2, 1699/1700, ibid., 219; Robert Livingston to Robert Treat, Jan. 27, 1692/3, Connecticut Archives, Colonial Wars, II, 164; Francis Nicholson to [Povey], Aug. 31, 1688, *Documents Relative to the Colonial History of the State of New York* . . . , ed. John Romeyn Brodhead and E. B. O'Callaghan (Albany, 1856-87), III, 552; A. Belcher to Gov. Bellomont, Sept. 23, 1700, *Cal.St.Pprs.*, XVIII, 596; A. Belcher to Gov. Bellomont, Oct. 14, 1700, Ibid., 597. For merchant life in late seventeenth-century New England see Bernard Bailyn, *The New England Merchants in the Seventeenth Century* (Cambridge, Mass., 1955), 112-97; and Bernard and Lotte Bailyn, *Massachusetts Shipping, 1697-1714: A Statistical Study* (Cambridge, Mass., 1959).

15. Perry Miller, *The New England Mind: From Colony to Province* (Cambridge, Mass., 1953); and Richard R. Johnson, *Adjustment to Empire: The New England Colonies, 1675-1715* (New Brunswick, 1981).

16. *Swll Dry*, I, 152.

17. "The Declaration of . . . ," May 24, 1689, *Edward Randolph*, ed. Robert N. Toppan and Thomas S. Goodrich (Boston, 1898-1909), II, 95; CR, Apr. 20, 1689.

18. Thornton, "Gilbert Family," 346; Massachusetts Council Records (Executive), 25 June 1700, Massachusetts Archives; Governor Bellomont to Lords of Admiralty, Apr. 25, 1700, *Cal.St.Pprs.*, XVIII, 201; William Stoughton to Captains Timothy Prout . . . A. Belcher . . . , July 28, 1696, Massachusetts Archives, LXX, 286-87; Belcher account, Mar. 15, 1702, ibid., 575; *Swll Dry*, I, 394, 409.

19. Belcher to Prince, June 7, 1748, in Whitmore, "Notes on the Belcher Family," 240-41.

20. *Hrvrd Grads*, IV; James W. Schmotter, "Ministerial Careers in Eighteenth-Century New England: The Social Context, 1700-1760," *Journal of Social History* 9 (Winter, 1975): 249-67.

21. CR, May 31 and Sept. 8, 1703; Joseph Dudley to Board of Trade, Dec. 10, 1702, *Cal.St.Pprs.*, XXI, 39; Samuel Sewall to brother, June 3, 1704, Curwen Papers, I, 3, American Antiquarian Society.

22. Massachusetts Archives, VII, 144-62, 233-258.

23. For sketches of Dudley, Colman, and Dummer, see *Hrvrd Grads*, IV, 42-54, 120-37, 454-68. Also for Dummer, see Charles L. Sanford, "The Days of Jeremy Dummer, Colonial Agent" (Ph.D. diss., Harvard University, 1952).

24. Ebenezer Pemberton, *Advice to a Son* (London, 1705), 12-13, 20-25.

25. Jonathan Belcher to John White, Dec. 27, 1704, Belknap Papers, VII, 7, Massachusetts Historical Society.

26. Jonathan Belcher, "A Journal My Intended Voyage, & Journey to Holland, Hanover etc . . . ," 2-36, 99-110, 120, Massachusetts Historical Society.

27. Ibid., 19, 30.

28. Ibid., 26, 99.

29. Ibid., 35-39, 54-55, 110.

30. Ibid., 41-42; Belcher to White, Dec. 27, 1704, Belknap Papers, VII, 7.

31. Belcher, "Journal," 55.

32. Ibid., 56-68.

33. Ibid., 73-78.

34. Ibid., 118-21.

35. Ibid., 52-53, 108-9; Belcher to Bishop of Lincoln, Nov. 18, 1731, *BP*(MHS), I, 54; Belcher to White, Dec. 27, 1704, Belknap Papers, VII, 7.

36. Belknap Papers, VII, 7; Belcher, "Journal," 110-11, 120.

37. J. Belcher to Jonathan Belcher, Jr., Nov. 5, 1737, B.Ltrs, V, 391; Joseph Dudley to J. Belcher, Feb. 6, 1705, Stowe Manuscripts, CCXXII, 352, British Museum.

38. *Swll Dry*, I, 539-41.

39. Massachusetts Archives, VII, 268.

40. A. Belcher to governor and Council, [June 24, 1708], Massachusetts Archives, LXXI, 456; A. Belcher to Boston Assessors, Aug. 20, 1714, Miscellaneous Manuscripts, Boston Public Library.

41. For the war years, see Philip S. Haffenden, *New England in the English Nation* (Oxford, 1974), 204-90; G. M. Waller, *Samuel Vetch: Colonial Entrepreneur*, (Chapel Hill, 1960), 68-260.

42. A. Belcher to governor and Council, [June 20, 1706], Massachusetts Archives, LXXI, 219; William Keen to Privy Council, Mar. 1, 1711, *Acts of the Privy Council in England, Colonial Series*, ed. W. L. Grant and James Munro (London, 1908-1912), 2:634-35; CR, July 29 and Nov. 11, 1710, and June 13, 1711; Massachusetts, *Acts and Resolves, Public and Private, of the Province of the Massachusetts Bay* (Boston, 1869-1922), 9:65.

43. J. Belcher to "Dear Brother," Nov. 16, 1708, Belcher Miscellany, Princeton University Library.

44. J. Belcher to John White, Nov. 16, 1708, Belknap Papers, VII, 8.

45. *Swll Dry*, II, 618.

46. Belcher to Prince, June 7, 1748, in Whitmore, "Notes on the Belcher Family," 240.

47. A. Belcher accounts, Oct. 12, 1709, *Cal.St.Pprs*, XXV, 29-30; CR, Feb. 3 and 14, 1709[/10].

48. Proceedings of New London Congress, June 21, 1711, *Documents . . . of New York*, V, 257; Gerald S. Graham, *The Walker Expedition to Quebec, 1711* (*Publications of the Navy Records Society* 94 [London, 1953]): 24, 101, 103, 108-9, 123, 192.

49. Dudley to General Court, Oct. 17, 1711, CR; Fast Proclamation, Feb. 11, 1711/12, *Boston Weekly News-Letter*, Feb. 18-25, 1711[/12].

50. *Lex Mercatoria. Or, the Just Rules of Commerce Declared* (Boston, 1705), 11.

51. *The Deplorable State of New-England . . .* (London, 1708 [Boston, 1721]), 1, 25.

52. Petition from Massachusetts troops, Nov. 12, 1705, *Acts and Resolves*, VIII, 547-48; "Vindication" of A. Belcher, July 12, 1706, CR.

53. *Swll Dry*, II, 637-38; Carl Bridenbaugh, *Cities in the Wilderness: The First Century of Urban Life in America, 1625-1742* (New York, 1938), 196-97.

54. *Swll Dry*, II, 685, 715.

55. *Swll Dry*, II, 637-38.

56. Ebenezer Pemberton, *The Divine Original and Dignity of Government Asserted* (Boston, 1710), 4, 15, 69, 80-85, 98.

57. For the political scene, see Gary B. Nash, *The Urban Crucible: Social Change, Political Consciousness, and the Origins of the American Revolution*

(Cambridge, Mass., 1979), 26-101; William Pencak, *War, Politics, & Revolution in Provincial Massachusetts* (Boston, 1981), 45-53; and G. B. Warden, *Boston, 1689-1776* (Boston, 1970), 60-79.

58. [Paul Dudley], *Objections to the Bank of Credit Lately Projected at Boston* . . . (Boston, 1714), in *Col.Cur.Rprnts*, I, 248, 254-55; *A Letter, From One in Boston, To his Friend in the Country* . . . ([Boston], 1714), in ibid., 281, 285.

59. Nathaniel Byfield's petition to king, [nd], Egerton Manuscripts, CMXXIX, 146, British Museum; William Tailer to Jeremiah Dummer, July 1, 1715, Tailer Letterbook, Belknap Papers, Massachusetts Historical Society; J. Dummer to John White, June 25, 1715, Belknap Papers, VII, 13; J. Dummer to Maj. Sewall, Apr. 21, 1714, Curwen Papers, I, 51; *Swll Dry*, 783-86, 786, 788-89, 791, 799, 810.

60. Andrew Belcher to Jonathan Belcher, Oct. 7, 1715, *Letter-Book of Samuel Sewall*, II, 88-89.

61. Dummer to John White, May 9, 1716, Massachusetts Historical Society, *Proceedings*, 2d ser., IV (1887-89), 192-93; Belcher to Colman, May 31, 1716, Colman Papers, I, Massachusetts Historical Society; Dummer to White, Apr. 30, 1716, Belknap Papers, VII, 16.

2. The Perils of Public Life

1. J. Belcher to Prince, June 7, 1748, in W. H. Whitmore, "Notes on the Belcher Family," *New England Historical and Genealogical Register* 27 (July, 1873): 239-40; *Swll Dry*, II, 866.

2. A. Belcher's will, Oct. 9, 1717, Suffolk County Probate Court, no. 3874; *Swll Dry*, II, 881, 883; J. Belcher to "Hond Mother," Mar. 16, 1723/4, B.Ltrs, I, 34-35, Massachusetts Historical Society.

3. Massachusetts Archives, VII, 293-305, 365; A. Belcher to Governor and Council, [June 24, 1708], ibid., LXXI, 456; J. Belcher to Gov. Saltonstall, Oct. 4, 1714, Connecticut Archives, Towns and Lands, 1st ser., III, 31; Petition of J. Belcher, Oct. 14, 1714, ibid., Industry, I, 270; *Boston News-Letter*, Feb. 11-18, 1711[/12], May 11-18, 1713, Apr. 18-25, 1715; A. Belcher to Boston Assessors, Aug. 20, 1714, Miscellaneous Manuscripts, Boston Public Library.

4. *Swll Dry*, II, 872.

5. Ibid., II, 883-84; Sewall to Samuel Shute, Feb. 11, 1717/8, *Letter-Book of Samuel Sewall* (Massachusetts Historical Society, *Collections*, 6th ser., I-II [Boston, 1886-88]), II, 89-90.

6. Benjamin Colman, *The Religious Regards we owe to our Country* . . . (Boston, 1718), 32.

7. Ibid., 47-48.

8. William Ashurst to S. Sewall, July 21, 1716, Company for the Propagation of the Gospel in New England, Letterbook, 147, University of Virginia Library; Minutes of the New England Company, July 5, 1717, Guildhall (London). William Kellaway, *The New England Company, 1649-1776: Missionary Society to the American Indians* (London, 1961).

9. Hamilton Andrews Hill and George Frederich Bigelow, *An Historical Catalogue of the Old South Church (Third Church) Boston, 1669-1882* (Boston, 1883), 1:398, 421-22, 428, 429-30; *Swll Dry*, II, 879, 909, 970-71.

10. Arthur H. Cole, "The Tempo of Mercantile Life in Colonial America," *Business History Review* 33 (Autumn 1959): 277-99.

11. Average attendance for the 1719 Council stood at 18.6 and for 1720 at 19.7. It dropped to 10.6 in 1721, no doubt due to a smallpox epidemic. But attendance returned to 19.5 in 1722. In 1723 it stood at 19.9, in 1724 at 18.7, in 1725 at 19.7, in 1726 at 21.4, and in 1727 at 19.3. See CR. See Edward M. Cook, Jr., *The Fathers of the Towns: Leadership and Community Structure in Eighteenth-Century New England* (Baltimore, 1976), 147-54; and Robert Zemsky, *Merchants, Farmers, and River Gods: An Essay on Eighteenth-Century American Politics* (Boston, 1971), 216-29.

12. See Massachusetts Council Records (Executive), Jan. 7, 1718/9; Feb. 20; 1718/9; Mar. 24, 1718/9; July 9, 1719; Mar. 28, 1720; Sept. 5, 1720; Massachusetts Archives.

13. CR, Feb. 20. 1718/9; Apr. 19, 1719; June 1 and 30, 1719; Nov. 6, 1719; July 29, 1720; Feb. 4, 1720/1.

14. John Hancock, *Rulers should be Benefactors* (Boston, 1722), 16; John Webb, *A Sermon, Preached at the Thursday Lecture . . .* (Boston, 1722), 12; Peter Thacher, *Wise & Good CIVIL RULERS* (Boston, 1726), 18-23.

15. *Boston News-Letter*, Mar. 27-Apr. 3, 1721.

16. CR, June 3, 1725; Mather's Memorial, May 27, 1725, *JHR*, VI, 257-58.

17. Massachusetts Council Records (Executive), Feb. 5, 1718/9; *Swll Dry*, II, 916-17; Shute to Board of Trade, Sept. 29, 1718, *Cal.St.Pprs.*, XXX, 357-58; Bridger to Popple, July 17, 1719, ibid., XXXI, 162.

18. House of Representatives to Shute, Apr. 11, 1717, *JHR*, I, 171. For reviews of the Shute administration, see William Pencak, *War, Politics, & Revolution in Provincial Massachusetts* (Boston, 1981), 61-76; Gary B. Nash, *The Urban Crucible: Social Change, Political Consciousness, and the Origins of the American Revolution* (Cambridge, Mass, 1979), 76-88, 129-40; and T. H. Breen, *The Character of the Good Ruler: A Study of Puritan Political Ideas in New England, 1630-1730* (New Haven, 1970), 240-69.

19. See Zemsky, *Merchants, Farmers, and River Gods*; Pencak, *War, Politics, & Revolution*; Cooke, *Fathers of the Towns*, 143-63; Michael Zuckerman, *Peaceable Kingdoms: New England Towns in the Eighteenth Century* (New York, 1970); and John M. Murrin, "Review Essay," *History and Theory: Studies in the Philosophy of History* 11 (1972): 226-75.

20. Shute to Council and House of Representatives, Nov. 7, 1716, *JHR*, I, 129; Shute to Council and House of Representatives, June 22, 1717, ibid., 220-21; Sewall to J. Belcher, July 28, 1716, *Letter-Book of Samuel Sewall*, II, 54-55; *Swll Dry*, II, 833-34, 901, 916-17; William Tailer to Sandford, Oct. 8, 1716, Tailer Letterbook, Belknap Papers, Massachusetts Historical Society; Aaron Porter to [Stephen Sewall], Oct. 9, 1716, Curwen Papers, I, 55, American Antiquarian Society; Massachusetts Council Records (Executive), Feb. 5, 1718/9, June 2, 1720, Apr. 4, 1721; *A Letter from a Gentleman in Mount Hope . . .* ([Boston, 1721]), in *Col.Cur.Rprnts*, II, 263; William G. McLoughlin, *New England Dissent, 1630-1833: The Baptists and the Separation of Church and State* (Cambridge, Mass., 1971), I, 203-4.

21. *JHR*, II, 228-33.

22. Elisha Cooke, *Mr. Cooke's Just and Seasonable VINDICATION . . .* (Boston, 1720), 9, 19-20; *Reflections upon Reflections: Or, More NEWS from Robinson Cruso's Island . . .* ([Boston], 1720), in *Col.Cur.Rprnts*, II, 118; *New NEWS from Robinson Cruso's ISLAND . . .* (Boston, 1720) in ibid., 127; *The Distressed State of the Town of Boston . . .* (Boston, 1720), in ibid., I, 404, 408.

23. *Boston Town Records* in *Records Relating to the Early History of Boston* (Boston, 1876-1909), VIII, 155; *JHR*, II, 99-100.

24. Dec. 1-19, 1722, CR.

25. *Swll Dry*, II, 999.

26. *JHR*, IV, 173 and V, 280-81.

27. William Waldron to Richard Waldron, May 11, 1724, Gratz Autograph Collection, Colonial Clergy, case 8, box 25, Historical Society of Pennsylvania; John Colman to Benjamin Colman, May 18, 1724, Davis Papers, II, 48, Massachusetts Historical Society; William Waldron to Richard Waldron, Nov. 4, 1723, Jan. 6 and Feb. 24, 1723/4, Waldron Papers, Massachusetts Historical Society.

28. *Swll Dry*, II, 1001-2; Belcher to Stephen Stephens, May 5, 1724, B.Ltrs, I, 69; Belcher to John Pettigrew, May 7, 1724, ibid., 76.

29. For biographical sketches of Belcher's sons, see *Hrvrd Grads*, VII, 305-11, VIII, 343-64.

30. Cotton Mather, *Concio ad Populum* . . . (Boston, 1719), 5-8.

31. Philip Greven, *Spare the Child: The Religious Roots of Punishment and the Psychological Impact of Child Abuse* (New York, 1990), 133-42.

32. Belcher to John Colman, May 8, 1724, B.Ltrs, I, 79-80; Belcher to Cotton Mather, [1722], Curwen Papers, II, 111.

33. Belcher to Jonathan Belcher, Jr., May 7, 1737, B.Ltrs, V, 197.

34. Belcher to Richard Partridge, Nov. 1, 1731, *BP*(MHS) I, 39; Belcher to Horace Walpole, Jan. 21, 1739/40, ibid., II, 264-65; Belcher to Stevens, July 30, 1751, B.Ltrs, IX, 189.

35. Massachusetts Council Records (Executive), July 7 and Aug. 14, 1727; John Boydell to John Yeamans, May 9, 1728, Greenough Papers, I, Massachusetts Historical Society; J. Hammond Trumbull and Charles J. Hoadley, eds., *The Public Records of the Colony of Connecticut* . . . (Hartford, 1850-1890), 7:185-86, 191, 218-19; J. Talcott to Belcher, May 29, 1728, *Talcott Papers, 1724-1741*, (*Collections* of the Connecticut Historical Society [Hartford, 1892-96]), IV, 116-17.

36. Belcher to J. Belcher, Jr., Oct. 27, 1732, B.Ltrs, II, 529. Also Belcher to Richard Waldron, Apr. 18, 1734, ibid., IV, 88; Belcher to Waldron, Feb. 13, 1734/5, ibid., 496.

37. Samuel Sewall to Stephen Williams, Nov. 15, 1727, Gratz Collection, American Prose, case 6, box 10; William Douglass to C. Colden, Nov. 20, 1727, *The Letters and Papers of Cadwallader Colden* (New York Historical Society *Collections* [New York, 1918-19]) I, 238-39; Douglass to Colden, Apr. 22, 1728, ibid., 257-58; Burnet to Council and House of Representatives, July 24, 1728, *JHR*, VIII, 245-47; House of Representatives to Burnet, Aug. 15, 1728, ibid., 279-81.

38. House of Representatives' address to the towns, Sept. 11, 1728, ibid., 315-18. Douglass to Colden, Sept. 9, 1728, *Letters and Papers of Cadwallader Colden*, I, 270; Burnet to Board of Trade, Oct. 26, 1728, *Cal.St.Pprs.*, XXXVI, 225-26; *New-England Weekly Journal*, July 7, 1729.

39. *The Public Records of the Colony of Connecticut*, VII, 185-86; Belcher to Talcott, Nov. 11, 1728, *Talcott Papers*, IV, 136-38; Belcher to Benjamin Colman, July 7, 1729, Davis Papers, II.

40. *JHR*, VIII, 391; Belcher to Sewall, Mar. 10, 1728/9, *Letter-Book of Samuel Sewall*, II, 265-66.

41. For the London scene, see James A. Henretta, *"Salutary Neglect": Colonial Administration under the Duke of Newcastle* (Princeton, 1972), 3-106; Jack P. Greene, *Peripheries and Center: Constitutional Development in the Extended Polities of the*

British Empire and the United States, 1607-1788 (Athens, Ga., 1986), 55-76; and Alison Gilbert Olson, *Making the Empire Work: London and American Interest Groups, 1690-1790* (Cambridge, Mass., 1992), 94-125.

42. Wilks and Belcher to House of Representatives, Apr. 25, 1729, *JHR*, IX, 15-16. Wilks and Belcher to House of Representatives, June 7, 1729, ibid., 54-55.

43. Shute to Privy Council, [1728], Additional Manuscripts, Newcastle Papers, 33057, 435, British Museum; Board of Trade to Lords Justices, Sept. 3, 1723, Additional Manuscripts, 35908, 50; Newcastle to Burnet, June 26, 1729, Colonial Office Papers 5/10, New Hampshire, 19.

44. Wilks and Belcher to House of Representatives, Oct. 8, 1729, *JHR*, IX, 167-69; Wilks and Belcher to House of Representatives, Oct. 8 and Oct. 24, 1729, ibid., 312-16; Report of Board of Trade, Sept. 27, 1729, Colonial Office Papers 5/177; *Journals of the Commissioners for Trade and Plantations . . .* (London, 1920-38), VI, 65-66.

45. [John Cushing] to ?, Aug. 11, 1729, Miscellaneous Manuscripts, IX, Massachusetts Historical Society; *Boston Town Records*, XII, 10. *JHR*, IX, 45.

46. CR, Dec. 13, 1728, and Apr. 18, 1729. Average daily attendance dropped to 17.2 in 1728 and to 13.7 in 1729, which with the exception of 1721 was the lowest rate since the arrival of Governor Dudley in 1702. The average for the period 1702 to 1735 was 18.2.

47. House of Representatives to Burnet, Aug. 30, 1729, *JHR*, IX, 68-69.

48. *Cal.St.Pprs.*, XXXVI, 522-23; *Acts of the Privy Council*, ed. W. L. Grant and James Munro (London, 1908-12), III, 253-56.

49. Shute to ?, Oct. 24, 1729, Gratz Collection, Colonial Governors, case 2, box 31; Shute to John Yeamans, Oct. 27, 1729, Greenough Papers, I; Belcher to Richard Partridge, Feb. 18, 1733/4, B.Ltrs, IV, 47; Belcher to Jonathan Belcher, Jr., June 17, 1741, ibid., VII, 309. Philip Haffenden, "Colonial Appointments and Patronage under the Duke of Newcastle, 1724-1739," *English Historical Review* 78 (July 1963), 417-35.

50. Belcher to Benjamin Colman, Feb. 7, 1729/30, Colman Papers, I, Massachusetts Historical Society. London merchants to king, Dec. 2, 1729, Belcher Miscellany, Princeton University Library; Henry Newman to John Wentworth, Dec. 1, 1729, Newman Papers, Massachusetts Historical Society.

51. Belcher to Newcastle, Dec. 31, 1729, Bancroft Transcripts, American, II, 193-97, New York Public Library; Belcher to Talcott, Apr. 23, 1730, *Talcott Papers*, IV, 198; Charles L. Sanford, "The Days of Jeremy Dummer, Colonial Agent" (Ph.D. diss., Harvard University, 1952), 403-8.

52. "Belcher the Apostate," Bancroft Transcripts, 4-5, 32-36, 41-44.

53. Isaac ? to Sister Rebecca, Apr. 11, 1730, Avery Papers, I, Massachusetts Historical Society; John Boydell to John Yeamans, May 26, 1730, Greenough Papers, I.

54. Dunbar to Newcastle, Feb. 4, 1730, *Cal.St.Pprs.*, XXXVII, 25.

3. Interpreting the Role of Governor

1. Belcher to Jonathan Belcher, Jr., Aug. 7, 1734, in "Jonathan Belcher: Notes on a Recently Acquired Portrait of an Early Benefactor of the Princeton Library," *Princeton University Library Chronicle* 14 (Summer 1953): 169-76.

2. Belcher to Richard Waldron, Apr. 18, 1734, B.Ltrs, IV, 88.

3. Belcher to Francis Harrison, Nov. 15, 1731, ibid., II, 83; Belcher to Edward and Jonathan Mayne, Aug. 23, 1734, ibid., IV, 246.

4. Belcher to Fisher Jackson, Feb. 6, 1733/4, ibid., 24; Belcher to Parminter and Barrow, Aug. 23, 1734, ibid., 245; Belcher to Switzer, July 21, 1740, ibid., VI, 452-53; Belcher to Andrew Belcher, Oct. 9, 1747, ibid., 118; Belcher to Andrew Belcher, Nov. 6, 1747, ibid., 138. Albert K. Teele, *The History of Milton, Mass., 1640-1887* (Boston, 1887), 111-12.

5. Belcher to Partridge, Jan. 23, 1732/3, B.Ltrs, III, 120.

6. Belcher to Partridge, Oct. 20, 1732, ibid., II, 510; Belcher to Jonathan Belcher, Jr., Feb. 5, 1732/3, *BP*(MHS), I, 258; Belcher to Partridge, Apr. 25, 1733, ibid., 271.

7. Belcher to Jonathan Belcher, Jr., May 7, 1737, B.Ltrs, V, 197. For Byfield Lyde, see *Hrvrd Grads*, VII, 206-14.

8. Belcher to Partridge, Apr. 30, 1733, *BP*(MHS), I, 275; *Hrvrd Grads*, VII, 308.

9. Belcher to Onslow, Oct. 29, 1731, *BP*(MHS)., I, 21; Belcher to Harrison, Apr. 17, 1732, ibid., 254.

10. Belcher to Jonathan Belcher, Jr., Oct. 27, 1732, ibid., II, 530; Belcher to Jonathan Belcher, Jr., Dec. 11, 1732, ibid., III, 29-32; Belcher to Jonathan Belcher, Jr., Apr. 28, 1732, *BP*(MHS), I, 128; Belcher to Jonathan Belcher, Jr., Oct. 20, 1732, ibid., I, 204. And Belcher to Jonathan Belcher, Jr., Apr. 23, 1733, ibid., 264; Belcher to Jonathan Belcher, Jr., Aug. 23, 1734, B.Ltrs, IV, 244-45; Belcher to Jonathan Belcher, Jr., Nov. 5, 1734, ibid., 339-40; Belcher to Jonathan Belcher, Jr., June 2, 1740, ibid., VI, 369.

11. Belcher to Jonathan Belcher, Jr., Nov. 11, 1731, *BP*(MHS), I, 49-52; Belcher to Jonathan Belcher, Jr., Dec. 6, 1731, ibid., 79-80.

12. Belcher to Partridge, Sept. 19, 1732, B.Ltrs, II, 473; Belcher to Jonathan Belcher, Jr., June 30, 1733, ibid., III, 282; Belcher to Partridge, May 25, 1734, ibid., IV, 147; Belcher to Jonathan Belcher, Jr., Oct. 20, 1732, *BP*(MHS), I, 197-205.

13. Belcher to Jonathan Belcher, Jr., Oct. 20, 1732, *BP*(MHS), I, 200; Belcher to Jonathan Belcher, Jr., Oct. 27, 1732, B.Ltrs, II, 529; Belcher to Jonathan Belcher, Jr., Dec. 19, 1732, ibid., III, 40-41.

14. Belcher to Partridge, Nov. 23, 1733, B.Ltrs, 499; Belcher to Partridge, May 25, 1734, ibid., 148

15. Belcher to Jonathan Belcher, Jr. Apr. 7, 1735, *BP*(MHS), 198-99; Belcher to Sharp, Oct. 29, 1731, B.Ltrs, II, 42-43; Belcher to Shute, Nov. 1, 1731, ibid., 55-56; Belcher to Henry Bendish, Nov. 20, 1731, ibid., 95; Belcher to Mrs. William Partridge, Apr. 2, 1733, ibid., III, 154.

16. Belcher to Jonathan Belcher, Jr., May 7, 1734, B.Ltrs, V, 195; Belcher to Jonathan Belcher, Jr., Oct. 16, 1739, *BP*(MHS), II, 214; Belcher to Jonathan Belcher, Jr., May 8, 1740, ibid., 292.

17. Belcher to Jonathan Belcher, Jr., May 19, 1740, *BP*(MHS), 300; Belcher to Richard Partridge, Jan. 13, 1736/7, B.Ltrs, V, 122-23; Belcher to Newman, Jan. 13, 1736/7, ibid., 123; Belcher to Partridge, May 20, 1740, ibid., VI, 352; Belcher to Jonathan Belcher, Jr., July 21, 1740, ibid., 447-48.

18. Belcher to Sherburne, Jan. 19, 1740/1, ibid., VII, 149; Belcher to Holden, May 25, 1734, ibid, IV, 146-47.

19. Belcher to Richard Waldron, Oct. 30, 1739, *BP*(MHS), II, 240.

20. Belcher to Lord Egmont, Aug. 1, 1737, B.Ltrs, V, 321; Belcher to Thomas Coram, Oct. 6, 1733, *BP*(MHS), I, 392.

21. Ebenezer Gay, *The Duty of People to pray for and praise their Rulers* (Boston, 1730), 13; Thomas Foxcroft, *Observations Historical and Practical on the*

Rise and Primitive State of New-England (Boston, 1730), 13-17; Thomas Prince, *The People of New-England* . . . (Boston, 1730); Edward Holyoke, *Integrity and Religion to be principally regarded, by such as design others to Stations of publick Trust* (Boston, 1736), 10; Samuel Wigglesworth, *An Essay for Reviving Religion* (Boston, 1733), 27-28. Also Nathan O. Hatch, *The Sacred Cause of Liberty: Republican Thought and the Millenium in Revolutionary New England* (New Haven, 1977).

22. Belcher to Watts, Nov. 8, 1734, B.Ltrs, IV, 352-53.

23. Belcher to John Pettigrew, May 7, 1724, B.Ltrs, I, 76; Belcher to Benjamin Colman, July 7, 1729, Davis Papers, II, Massachusetts Historical Society.

24. Belcher to Mrs. Partridge, Apr. 24, 1732, *BP*(MHS), I, 110-11; Belcher to Joseph Williams, May 25, 1734, ibid., II, 68; Belcher to Warham Mather, Jan. 20, 1734/5, ibid., 186-87.

25. Belcher to Whittlesey, Dec. 20, 1731, ibid., I, 89; Belcher to George Bunker, Oct. 3, 1732, ibid., 190-91; Wigglesworth, *Essay for Reviving Religion*, 27-28.

26. Belcher to Council and House of Representatives, Sept. 9, 1730, *JHR*, IX, 238-39.

27. Ibid.; Belcher to Partridge, Dec. 7, 1731, *BP*(MHS), I, 82.

28. See William G. McLoughlin, *New England Dissent, 1630-1833: The Baptists and the Separation of Church and State* (Cambridge, Mass., 1971), I, 165-243; Arthur J. Worrall, *Quakers in the Colonial Northeast* (Hanover, N.H., 1980); Carl Bridenbaugh, *Mitre and Sceptre: Transatlantic Faiths, Ideas, Personalities, and Politics, 1689-1775* (New York, 1962), 3-82.

29. Belcher to Council and House of Representatives, Dec. 2, 1731, *JHR*, X, 300; Belcher to Partridge, Apr. 29, 1732, B.Ltrs, II, 295; Belcher to Partridge, Dec. 7, 1731, *BP*(MHS), I, 82.

30. Belcher to Grafton, Dec. 12, 1730, Fulham Palace Collections, Massachusetts, II, 75; Belcher to Bishop of London, Dec. 12, 1730, ibid., 86; Belcher to Bishop of London, Nov. 11, 1732, B.Ltrs, II, 549; Belcher to Bishop of London, Feb. 25, 1733/4, ibid., IV, 52.

31. Henry Wilder Foote, *Annals of King's Chapel: From the Puritan Age of New England to the Present Day* (Boston, 1882), I, 418-19; Harwood to Bishop of London, July 9, 1731, *Historical Collections relating to the American Colonial Church*, ed. William Stevens Perry (Hartford, Conn., 1870-78), 3:269. Cutler to Bishop of London, Feb. 4, 1729/30, ibid., 253-54; Dunbar to Belcher, Apr. 15, 1734, Colonial Office Papers, 5/10 New Hampshire, 47, Public Record Office (London); Dunbar to Bishop of London, Dec. 28, 1734, Fulham Palace Collections, New Hampshire, 53.

32. Belcher to Bishop of London, Dec. 4, 1731, *BP*(MHS), I, 72-73.

33. *Acts of the Privy Council*, ed. W. L. Grant and James Munro (London, 1908-12), 3:491-92.

34. Cutler to Bishop of London, Oct. 25, 1731, Fulham Palace, Massachusetts, II, 122; Bearcroft to Bishop of Oxford, Feb. 3, 1740, *Historical Collections*, ed. Perry, III, 337.

35. Lois Kimball Mathews, *The Expansion of New England: The Spread of New England Settlement and Institutions to the Mississippi River, 1620-1865* (Boston, 1909), 76-107; and John Frederick Martin, *Profits in the Wilderness: Entrepreneurship and the Founding of New England Towns in the Seventeenth Century* (Chapel Hill, 1991).

36. George Sheldon, *The Conference at Deerfield, Mass., August 27-31, 1735, Between Gov. Belcher and Several Tribes of Western Indians* (Boston, 1906).

37. Belcher to Sir Robert Clark, Mar. 6, 1729/30, New England Company Papers, 7956, Guildhall (London). William Kellaway, *The New England Company, 1649-1776: Missionary Society to the American Indians* (London, 1961), 269-70.

38. Belcher to Council and House of Representatives, Dec. 16, 1730, *JHR*, IX, 351-52; Belcher to John Stoddard, Mar. 31, 1732, B.Ltrs, II, 240; *A CONFERENCE of His Excellency Jonathan Belcher* . . . (Boston, 1732); Joseph Sewall, *Christ Victorious over the Powers of Darkness* . . . (Boston, 1733), 28-29.

39. Samuel Hopkins, *Historical Memoirs, Relating to the Housatunnuck Indians* . . . (Boston, 1753), 1-40. Patrick Frazier, *The Mohicans of Stockbridge* (Lincoln, 1992), 28-95.

40. Sheldon, *Conference at Deerfield*, 11-16.

41. Ibid., 19-20.

42. Belcher to Council and House of Representatives, Nov. 25, 1736, *JHR*, XIV, 107; Hopkins, *Historical Memoirs*, 47-57.

43. Belcher to Council and House of Representatives, Nov. 25, 1736, *JHR*, XIV, 107.

44. Belcher to Godfrey and Lloyd, Dec. 3, 1739, B.Ltrs, VI, 172; Belcher to Partridge, Dec. 1, 1741, ibid., VII, 400.

45. Belcher to Toppan, Aug. 14, 1732, ibid., II, 427. Belcher to Toppan, Apr. 16, 1733, ibid., 163-64; *Hrvrd Grads*, IV, 113-17.

46. Belcher to Council and House of Representatives, Nov. 2, 1732, *JHR*, XI, 85. Belcher to Council and House of Representatives, Aug. 15, 1733, ibid., 257-58; Belcher to Council and House of Representatives, Nov. 1, 1733, ibid., 322. Joseph J. Malone, *Pine Trees and Politics: The Naval Stores and Forest Policy in Colonial New England, 1691-1775* (Seattle, 1964), 100-102.

47. Belcher to Council and House of Representatives, Nov. 2, 1732, *JHR*, XI, 85. Belcher to Council and House of Representatives, Dec. 16, 1730, ibid., IX, 350-51; Belcher to Council and House of Representatives, Apr. 19, 1735, ibid., XII, 208; Belcher to Council and House of Representatives, Dec. 27, 1735, ibid., XIII, 191; *Acts and Resolves, Public and Private, of the Province of the Massachusetts Bay*, eds. Abner C. Goodwell and Melvin M. Bigelow (Boston, 1869-1922), XII, 221, 310. Victor S. Clark, *History of Manufactures in the United States* (New York, 1929), 1:33-43.

48. Belcher to Ellis Huske, June 11, 1733, B.Ltrs, III, 248; Belcher to Ellis Huske, June 18, 1733, ibid., 256; Henry Newman to Belcher, Sept. 28, 1726, Newman Papers, Massachusetts Historical Society.

49. Belcher to Council and House of Representatives, May 31, 1734, *JHR*, XII, 8-9.

50. "To the Publisher of the Weekly News-letter," Feb. 28, 1734, in *Col.Cur.Rprnts*, III, 81-82. And John Webb, *The Government of Christ considered and applied* (Boston, 1738), 30; John Barnard, *The Throne Established by Righteousness* (Boston, 1734), 28-30.

51. "A Modest Apology for Paper Money," *The Weekly Rehearsal*, Mar. 18, 1734, in *Col.Cur.Rprnts*, III, 91-100; "A few Remarks . . . ," Apr. 1, 1734, in ibid., 129-34; *Some Observations on the Scheme projected for emitting 60000 l.* . . . (Boston, 1738), in ibid., 179-216; [William Douglass], *An Essay Concerning Silver and Paper Currencies* (Boston, [1738]) in ibid., 217-54; *An Inquiry into the Nature and Uses of Money* . . . (Boston, 1740) in ibid., 365-479.

52. House of Representatives to Belcher, July 5, 1739, *JHR*, XVII, 102. Also House of Representatives to Belcher, Dec. 18, 1739, ibid., 178.

53. *Boston Weekly Post-Boy*, Mar. 31, 1740.

54. *The Melancholy State of this Province* . . . ([Boston], 1736) in *Col.Cur.Rprnts*, III, 139-40.

55. Barnard, *Throne Established by Righteousness*, 30-31; Webb, *Government of Christ considered and applied*, 30.

56. William T. Youngs, Jr., *God's Messengers: Religious Leadership in Colonial New England, 1700-1750* (Baltimore, 1976); G. B. Warden, *Boston, 1689-1776* (Boston, 1970), 80-126; Gary B. Nash, *The Urban Crucible: Social Change, Political Consciousness, and the Origins of the American Revolution* (Cambridge, Mass., 1979), 76-157, 198-232; John M. Murrin, "Anglicizing an American Colony: The Transformation of Provincial Massachusetts" (Ph.D. diss., Yale University, 1966); and Murrin, "The Legal Transformation: The Bench and Bar of Eighteenth-Century Massachusetts," in *Colonial America: Essays in Politics and Social Development*, ed. Stanley N. Katz (Boston, 1971), 415-49.

57. Bernard Bailyn, *The Ordeal of Thomas Hutchinson* (Cambridge, Mass., 1974).

58. Belcher to Council and House of Representatives, Aug. 8, 1741, *JHR*, XIX, 60.

59. Quotations in Warden, *Boston*, 122.

60. Council to House of Representatives, Dec. 13, 1728, CR. Also Council to Representatives, Apr. 18, 1729, ibid.; Council to House of Representatives, Dec. 17, 1729, ibid.

61. Belcher to Bunker, Oct. 3, 1732, *BP*(MHS), I, 190-91; Belcher to Jonathan Belcher, Jr., Dec. 25, 1733, ibid., 444; Belcher to Waldron, Jan. 21, 1739/40, ibid., II, 269.

62. Belcher to Watts, Dec. 10, 1737, ibid., V, 473; Belcher to Waldron, Oct. 20, 1740, ibid., VII, 15; Belcher to Waldron, Nov. 3, 1740, *BP*(MHS), II, 343; Belcher to Waldron, Feb. 9, 1740/1, ibid., 373-74.

63. Belcher to Waldron, May 5, 1737, B.Ltrs, V, 187; "Americanus," *A Letter to the Freeholders and other Inhabitants of the Massachusetts-Bay, relating to their approaching Election of Representatives* ([Newport], 1739).

64. Belcher to Waldron, May 6, 1734, B.Ltrs, IV, 117-18. Belcher to Sherburne, Aug. 21, 1732, ibid., II, 438-39.

65. Belcher to Waldron, June 11, 1733, *BP*(MHS), I, 301. And Belcher to Waldron, July 2, 1733, ibid., 317.

66. Belcher to Waldron, Apr. 18, 1734, B.Ltrs, IV, 88.

67. Belcher to Waldron, Aug. 6, 1737, ibid., V, 334; and Waldron's account of Belcher's trip dated Oct. 14 and 25, 1737, WP.

68. Whitefield to Belcher quoted in Hamilton Andrews Hill, *History of the Old South Church (Third Church), Boston, 1669-1884* (Boston, 1890), 1:513; Belcher to Mrs. Partridge, Nov. 24, 1734, B.Ltrs, IV, 378; Belcher to Mrs. Partridge, Apr. 24, 1732, *BP*(MHS), I, 111; Belcher to Martha Gerrish, Mar. 23, 1733/4, ibid., II, 30-31.

69. Belcher to Holden, May 25, 1734, B.Ltrs, IV, 146-47; Belcher to Nathaniel Stone, Aug. 18, 1740, ibid., VI, 493-95.

70. Belcher to Mrs. Partridge, Apr. 24, 1732, *BP*(MHS), 110-11; Belcher to Chandler, Nov. 12, 1739, B.Ltrs, VI, 130.

71. Belcher to Henry Sherburne, Apr. 2, 1733, ibid., III, 155; Belcher to Mrs. Partridge, Nov. 25, 1734, ibid., IV, 378; Belcher to Whittlesey, Dec. 20, 1731, *BP*(MHS), I, 89. And Belcher to Waldron, Aug. 30, 1736, ibid., III, 16; Belcher to New Hampshire Council and House of Representatives, Nov. 28, 1730, *Docs.NH*, IV,

580; Belcher to Council and House of Representatives, Dec. 16, 1730, *JHR*, IX, 350-52.

72. Belcher to Jonathan Belcher, Jr., June 17, 1741, B.Ltrs, VII, 312.

73. Thomas Hutchinson, *The History of the Colony and Province of Massachusetts-Bay*, ed. Lawrence Shaw Mayo (Cambridge, Mass., 1936), 3:213.

74. James West Davidson, *The Logic of Millennial Thought: Eighteenth-Century New England* (New Haven, 1977); Hatch, *Sacred Cause of Liberty*, 28-31.

4. The Art of Politics

1. Belcher to Council and House of Representatives, Sept. 9, 1730, *JHR*, IX, 238-42.

2. Ibid.

3. Quotation in T. H. Breen, *The Character of the Good Ruler: A Study of Puritan Political Ideas in New England, 1630-1730* (New Haven, 1970), 218.

4. J. Cotton to Willard, Oct. 8, 1730, Curwen Papers, III, 10, American Antiquarian Society; [John Cushing] to "the Secretary," Aug. 11, 1729, Miscellaneous Bound Manuscripts, IX, Massachusetts Historical Society; Thomas Hutchinson, *The History of the Colony and Province of Massachusetts-Bay*, ed. Lawrence Shaw Mayo (Cambridge, Mass., 1936), 2:281-85.

5. Hutchinson, *History of the Colony and Province of Massachusetts-Bay*, 2:284-85; Belcher to Waldron, Feb. 7, 1731/2, B.Ltrs, II, 202.

6. Belcher to Partridge, Nov. 1, 1731, *BP*(MHS), I, 39; Belcher to Horace Walpole, Jan. 21, 1739/40, ibid., II, 264-65.

7. Belcher to Waldron, Feb. 15, 1730/1, Belcher Papers, I, 19, BP(NHHS).

8. William Douglass to C. Colden, Nov. 20, 1727, *The Letters and Papers of Cadwallader Colden* (New York Historical Society *Collections* [New York, 1918-19]), I, 238-39; Richard Bushman, *King and People in Provincial Massachusetts* (Chapel Hill, 1985), 76-78.

9. *JHR*, XI, 163-66; Belcher to Partridge, Apr. 27, 1732, ibid., 122.

10. Dunbar to Popple, Sept. 15, 1730, *Cal.St.Pprs*, XXXVII, 278; Dunbar to Popple, Nov. 17, 1730, ibid., 344; Joseph J. Malone, *Pine Trees and Politics: The Naval Stores and Forest Policy in Colonial New England, 1691-1775* (Seattle, 1964), 91-110. And Belcher to Holden, Oct. 29, 1731, *BP*(MHS), 22.

11. Belcher to Newcastle, Oct. 29, 1731, *BP*(MHS), I, 11.

12. *A LETTER to a Gentleman* . . . ([Boston, 1731]); J. Cotton to Willard, Oct. 8, 1730, Curwen Papers, III, 10; *Boston Gazette*, Jan. 11-18, 1731; Dunbar to Popple, Jan. 12, 1731, *Cal.St.Pprs*, XXXVIII, 7-8.

13. Belcher to Council and House of Representatives, Oct. 28, 1730, *JHR*, IX, 348. See proceedings of Oct. 1 and 2 in ibid., 300-306; and CR, Oct. 27 and 28, 1730.

14. Extract from *The Political State of Great Britain* . . . ([Boston, 1731]), 14-15; Belcher to Board of Trade, Apr. 5, 1731, *Cal.St.Pprs*, XXXVIII, 84-85. *JHR*, X, 101-9.

15. House of Representatives to Council, Mar. 9, 1730[/1], *ibid.*, X, 62.

16. *Boston Town Records*, in *Records Relating to the Early History of Boston* (Boston, 1876-1909), 12:24; Belcher to Newcastle, Apr. 26, 1731, *Cal.St.Pprs*, XXXVIII, 99. John Boydell to John Yeamans, Apr. 8, 1731, David S. Greenough Papers, Massachusetts Historical Society.

17. Belcher to Jonathan Belcher, Jr., Nov. 1, 1731, *BP*(MHS), I, 34; Belcher to Partridge, Nov. 1, 1731, ibid., 38.

18. Belcher to Partridge, Nov. 1, 1731, ibid., 37-38; Belcher to Wilks, Nov. 1, 1731, ibid., 42; Belcher to Harrison, Nov. 15, 1731, B.Ltrs, II, 83.

19. *Acts of the Privy Council,* ed. W. L. Grant and James Munro (London, 1908-12), 3:261-62.

20. Belcher to Wilks, Nov. 1, 1731, *BP*(MHS), I, 42-43; Wilks to Josiah Willard, Aug. 25, 1731, Massachusetts Archives, LII, 411.

21. *JHR,* X, 411.

22. Ibid., 93; House of Representatives to Belcher, Apr. 11, 1733, ibid., XI, 183-92.

23. Belcher to Waldron, June 11, 1733, *BP*(MHS), I, 301; Belcher to Waldron, July 2, 1733, ibid., 317; *JHR,* XI, 216, 251. Belcher to Thomas Palmer, Dec. 26, 1733, B.Ltrs, III, 544-45.

24. [Boston] *Weekly Rehearsal,* June 25, 1733; Belcher to Waldron, July 2, 1733, *BP*(MHS), I, 317. William H. Whitmore, *The Massachusetts Civil List for the Colonial and Provincial Periods, 1630-1774* (Albany, 1870), 69, 78, 83, 100.

25. *Hrvrd Grads,* V, 96-118, VII, 301-33; Robert J. Taylor, *Western Massachusetts in the Revolution* (Providence, 1954), 11-51; Gregory H. Nobles, *Divisions throughout the Whole: Politics and Society in Hampshire County, Massachusetts, 1740-1775* (New York, 1983), 29-30.

26. John L. Brooke, *The Heart of the Commonwealth: Society and Political Culture in Worcester County, Massachusetts, 1713-1861* (New York, 1989), 17-40, 97-108.

27. Belcher to Waldron, June 11, 1733, *BP*(MHS), I, 301; Belcher to Waldron, June 18, 1733, ibid., 302; Belcher to Waldron, July 12, 1733, ibid., 324; Benjamin Pemberton to Charles Delafaye, Oct. 8, 1733, *Cal.St.Pprs*, XL, 210-11.

28. Belcher to Newcastle, June 28, 1733, B.Ltrs, 272-73; *Acts of the Privy Council*, III, 328-34; *Proceedings and Debates of the British Parliaments Respecting North America*, ed. Leo Stock (Washington, D.C., 1924-41), 4:214; Belcher to Jonathan Belcher, Jr., Sept. 18, 1733, *BP*(MHS), I, 371.

29. Belcher to Chandler, Aug. 27, 1733, ibid., 357-59; *JHR,* XI, 260; Belcher to Stoddard, Aug. 27, 1733, B.Ltrs, III, 359. And Belcher to Wilks, Oct. 5, 1733, ibid., 417.

30. *JHR,* XI, 297-311; Hutchinson, *History of the Colony and Province of Massachusetts-Bay,* 2:287. Belcher to Council and House of Representatives, Nov. 2, 1733, *JHR,* XI, 324-25.

31. Belcher to Newcastle, Nov. 13, 1733, *BP*(MHS), I, 407-10; Belcher to Delafaye, Nov. 13, 1733, B.Ltrs, III, 480-81. And Belcher to Partridge, Nov. 13, 1733, ibid., 471.

32. *Acts of the Privy Council,* III, 263.

33. Belcher to Royall, Nov. 16, 1736, B.Ltrs, V, 40.

34. Belcher to Board of Trade, Nov. 27, 1733, *BP*(MHS), I, 430-31; Belcher to Toppan, Dec. 3, 1733, B.Ltrs, III, 519; Gary B. Nash, *The Urban Crucible: Social Change, Political Consciousness, and the Origins of the American Revolution* (Cambridge, Mass., 1979), 138-39.

35. *JHR,* XIII, 55, 95, 205; Pemberton to Newcastle, Jan. 14, 1735, *Cal.St.Pprs*, XLI, 356; James A. Henretta, *"Salutary Neglect": Colonial Administration under the Duke of Newcastle* (Princeton, 1972), 247-49.

36. Hutchinson, *History of the Colony and Province of Massachusetts-Bay*, 2:297.
37. Belcher to Waldron, Nov. 16, 1733, *BP*(MHS), I, 415; Belcher to Waldron, June 3, 1734, ibid., II, 75; Belcher to Waldron, Sept. 16, 1734, ibid., 120-21. Belcher to Partridge, May 9, 1734, B.Ltrs, IV, 125; Belcher to Waldron, May 16, 1734, ibid., IV, 130-31; Belcher to Waldron, May 30, 1734, ibid., 152; John Boydell to John Yeamans, Feb. 26, 1733[/4], Greenough Papers, I; William Pencak, *War, Politics, & Revolution in Provincial Massachusetts* (Boston, 1981), 92-95.
38. Belcher to Stoddard, Apr. 15, 1734, B.Ltrs., IV, 87; Belcher to Stoddard, May 20, 1734, ibid., 131-32; Belcher to Stoddard, Feb. 25, 1734/5, ibid., 504; Belcher to Stoddard, Nov. 13, 1736, ibid., V, 33. Also Nobles, *Divisions throughout the Whole*, 29-30.
39. Belcher to Wilks, Nov. 13, 1733, B.Ltrs, III, 474; Belcher to Waldron, Feb. 7, 1736/7, ibid., V, 143-44. Belcher to Waldron, Nov. 15, 1736, ibid., 37; Belcher to Partridge, Jan. 8, 1736/7, ibid., 112; *Boston Weekly News-Letter*, Nov. 14-20, 1735.
40. Belcher to Jonathan Belcher, Jr., Dec. 19, 1732, B.Ltrs, III, 40-41; Belcher to Waldron, Aug. 15, 1734, ibid., IV, 242; Belcher to Partridge, Nov. 1, 1731, *BP*(MHS), I, 37-38; Belcher to Jonathan Belcher, Jr., Apr. 23, 1733, ibid., I, 264.
41. William Cooper, *The Honours of CHRIST demanded of the Magistrate* (Boston, 1740), 35-41.

5. The Soul of Politics

1. Belcher to Waldron, Apr. 29, 1734, *BP*(MHS), II, 43; Belcher to Partridge, May 26, 1732, B.Ltrs, II, 326-27; Belcher to Waldron, July 24, 1735, BP(NHHS), II, 161.
2. *Docs.NH*, IV, 561-84, 759-72; Belcher to Newcastle, Jan. 23, 1731, *Cal.St.Pprs*, XXXVIII, 26.
3. *Docs.NH*, IV, 569-70; Jeremy Belknap, *The History of New-Hampshire* (Dover, 1812), I, 224-26.
4. For a sketch of Waldron, see *Hrvrd Grads*, V, 653-57.
5. *Hrvrd Grads*, V, 156-66, VI, 220-23; *Docs.NH*, XVIII, 79.
6. Belcher to Waldron, Jan. 18, 1730/1, BP(NHHS), I, 19; Belcher to Waldron, Feb. 15, 1730/1, ibid., 51. Waldron to Belcher, Oct. 25, 1730, W-B, I, 15; Dunbar to Popple, Jan. 12, 1731, *Cal.St.Pprs*, XXXVIII, 7-8.
7. Henry Newman to John Wentworth, Dec. 1, 1729, Newman Papers, Massachusetts Historical Society; Belcher to Newman, Nov. 20, 1731, *BP*(MHS), I, 58.
8. Belcher to Waldron, Feb. 6, 1729/30, BP(NHHS), I, 1; Belcher to Waldron, Jan. 3, 1731/2, B.Ltrs, II, 184-85.
9. Belcher to Waldron, Apr. 29, 1734, *BP*(MHS), I, 42-43.
10. Waldron to Belcher, Aug. 15, 1735, W-B, I, 225; Belcher to Waldron, Sept. 7, 1730, BP(NHHS), I, 21.
11. Belcher to Board of Trade, Nov. 12, 1734, *BP*(MHS), II, 156. Bernard Bailyn, *The New England Merchants in the Seventeenth Century* (Cambridge, Mass., 1955), 196-97.
12. Waldron to Belcher, Apr. 2, 1731, WP, I, 16; Waldron to Belcher, Feb. 8, 1730/1, W-B, I, 31; Waldron to Belcher, Feb. 19, 1730/1, ibid., 36.
13. Belcher to Sherburne, Aug. 21, 1732, B.Ltrs, 438; Waldron to Belcher, Sept. 1, 1732, W-B, 105; Waldron to Belcher, Sept. 15, 1732, ibid., 117-18.

14. *Hrvrd Grads*, IV, 147-50, 655; William Henry Fry, *New Hampshire as a Royal Province* (New York, 1908), 459; Charles E. Clark, *The Eastern Frontier: The Settlement of Northern New England, 1610-1763* (New York, 1970), 308-9.

15. Waldron to Belcher, Jan. 15, 1730/1, W-B, I, 27. Waldron to Belcher, Jan. 1, 1730/1, ibid., I, 19; Waldron to Belcher, Feb. 8, 1730/1, ibid., 31; Waldron to Belcher, Feb. 19, 1730/1, ibid., 36; Dunbar to Popple, July 11, 1731, *Cal.St.Pprs*, XXXVIII, 175.

16. Belcher to Board of Trade, Oct. 29, 1731, *BP*(MHS), I, 17-18; Belcher to Waldron, June 7, 1731, BP(NHHS), I, 81; Waldron to Belcher, June 11, 1731, WP, I, 18.

17. Dunbar to Popple, July 11, 1731, *Cal.St.Pprs*, XXXVIII, 177; Jere R. Daniell, "Politics in New Hampshire under Governor Benning Wentworth, 1741-1767," *William and Mary Quarterly*, 3d ser., 23 (January 1966): 76-105.

18. *Docs.NH*, IV, 594-95, 598-99; Petition to Board of Trade, July 10, 1731, Peter Force Transcripts, New Hampshire Boundary, Library of Congress.

19. Petition to king, October 1731, *Docs.NH*, IV, 613-15; Belcher to Waldron, May 14, 1739, BP(NHHS), III, 50; Waldron to Belcher, June 27, 1735, W-B, I, 210.

20. Belcher to Sherburne, Oct. 25, 1731, B.Ltrs, II, 22. Belcher to Waldron, Nov. 1, 1731, BP(NHHS), I, 46.

21. Waldron to Belcher, Apr. 16, 1731, WP, I, 16; Dunbar to Popple, July 11, 1731, *Cal.St.Pprs*, XXXVIII, 176-78. Belcher to Waldron, Nov. 2, 1730, BP (NHHS), I, 3.

22. Dunbar to Belcher, Aug. 16, 1731, Colonial Office Papers, 5/10, New Hampshire, 44, Public Record Office (London); Waldron to Belcher, July 2, 1731, WP, I, 19; Waldron to Belcher, July 9, 1731, ibid., 20; Waldron to Belcher, July 30, 1731, ibid., 23.

23. Belcher to Waldron, Dec. 10, 1733, B.Ltrs, III, 529; Belcher to Waldron, Sept. 29, 1735, BP(NHHS), II, 193; Dunbar to Popple, July 11, 1731, *Cal.St.Pprs*, XXXVIII, 174-75.

24. Belcher to Partridge, Nov. 11, 1731, B.Ltrs, II, 76-78.

25. Belcher to Popple, Apr. 27, 1732, B.Ltrs, II, 281; Board of Trade to Belcher, Oct. 10, 1732, *Cal.St.Pprs*, XXXIX, 234.

26. Proclamation, Jan. 1, 1733, BP(NHHS), I, 233n; Belcher to House of Representatives, Mar. 10, 1732/3, *Docs.NH*, IV, 644-45; Belcher to Board of Trade, May 21, 1733, BP(NHHS), I, 294-95; Belcher to Partridge, Aug. 14, 1732, B.Ltrs, II, 414.

27. Belcher to Waldron, Nov. 15, 1731, B.Ltrs, II, 83-84; Belcher to Huske, Nov. 15, 1731, ibid., 85; Belcher to Waldron, Jan. 3, 1731/2, ibid., 185; Belcher to Waldron, July 3, 1732, ibid., 384; Belcher to Waldron, Feb. 15, 1730/1, BP(NHHS), I, 51. Belcher to Sherburne, Nov. 15, 1731, *New England Historical and Genealogical Register* 17 (October 1863): 306.

28. Belcher Proclamation, Mar. 12, 1732/3, Peter Force Transcripts, New Hampshire Governors, Library of Congress; *Hrvrd Grads*, V, 162-63.

29. Belcher to Partridge, Sept. 19, 1732, B.Ltrs, II, 472; Belcher to Dunbar, July 4, 1733, ibid., III, 293; Belcher to Shadrach Walton, July 9, 1733, ibid., 299; Belcher to Dunbar, July 9, 1733, BP(NHHS), I, 318-19.

30. Belcher to Waldron, Oct. 1, 1733, BP(NHHS), 373; Belcher to Waldron, Nov. 16, 1733, ibid., 415; Belcher to Waldron, Dec. 21, 1733, ibid., 439; Belcher to Sherburne, July 30, 1733, B.Ltrs, III, 336. Dunbar to Council, Dec. 6, 1733, Weare Papers, I, 34, New Hampshire State Archives.

31. Dunbar to Belcher, Apr. 26, 1734, Colonial Office Papers, 5/10, New Hampshire, 48; Dunbar to Belcher, June 20, 1734, ibid., 50.

32. Waldron to Belcher, Apr. 29, 1734, W-B, I, 171. Dunbar to Belcher, Apr. 29, 1734, Colonial Office Papers, 5/10, New Hampshire, 49; Waldron to Belcher, Apr. 26, 1734, WP, I, 37; Dunbar to William Shirley, Apr. 29, 1734, Admiralty Papers, 3817, 13-15, Public Record Office (London).

33. Dunbar to Shirley, Apr. 29, 1734, ibid., 31-32; Dunbar to Belcher, June 20, 1734, ibid., 37-42; Belcher Proclamation, May 6, 1734, Force Transcripts, New Hampshire Governors.

34. Belcher to Waldron, May 9, 1734, BP(NHHS), II, 61-62; Governor's orders to justices of the peace, Oct. 24, 1734, Admiralty Papers, 3817, 43-45; Belcher to Sheriff Greely, Nov. 2, 1734, ibid., 47-8; Greely to Belcher, Nov. 6, 1734, ibid., 48; Jaffrey to Belcher, Nov. 11, 1734, ibid., 49.

35. Belcher to Waldron, Dec. 21, 1733, BP(NHHS), I, 439; Belcher to Waldron, May 23, 1734, ibid., II, 66; Belcher to Board of Trade, July 1, 1734, ibid., 78-85; Belcher to Waldron, May 6, 1734, B.Ltrs, IV, 116-18.

36. Waldron to Belcher, Sept. 1, 1732, W-B, I, 105-6; Waldron to Belcher, Mar. 17, 1732/3, ibid., 165-66.

37. Waldron to Belcher, May 30, 1735, ibid., 188-89; Waldron to Belcher, June 6, 1735, ibid., 195. And Waldron to Belcher, May 26, 1735, ibid., 185; Waldron to Belcher, June 2, 1735, ibid., 191-2; Belcher to Waldron, Aug. 15, 1734, B.Ltrs, IV, 242-3.

38. House of Representatives to Belcher, May 10, 1732, Docs.NH, IV, 617-18. Belcher to Council and House of Representatives, Jan. 2, 1733/4, ibid., 647-48; House of Representatives to Belcher, Jan. 11, 1733/4, ibid., IV, 653-4; Belcher to House of Representatives, Jan. 23, 1733/4, ibid., 666-67.

39. Waldron to Belcher, Mar. 24, 1732, WP, I, 30. Waldron to Belcher, Feb. 26, 1730/1, W-B, I, 41; Belcher to Loan Committee, Mar. 4, 1733/4, Docs.NH, IV, 668; executive orders to call in loans, May 26, 1732, and Mar. 4, 1733/4, Force Transcripts, New Hampshire Governors; Belcher to Waldron, Jan. 3, 1731/2, B.Ltrs, II, 185.

40. House of Representatives to Belcher, May 8, 1735, Docs.NH, IV, 688; Belcher to Waldron, Nov. 14, 1734, BP(NHHS), II, 158-59; Belcher to Waldron, Jan. 27, 1734/5, ibid., 188; Belcher to Waldron, Mar. 17, 1734/5, B.Ltrs, IV, 532. Belcher to Sherburne, Mar. 3, 1734/5, ibid., 515; Belcher to Waldron, July 14, 1735, BP(NHHS), II, 157; Andrew McFarland Davis, "New Hampshire Merchants' Notes, 1734-35," Colonial Society of Massachusetts, Publications, 14 (1913): 382-83.

41. Belcher to Waldron, Feb. 13, 1734/5, B.Ltrs, IV, 496; Belcher to Waldron, Feb. 24, 1734/5, ibid., 500; Belcher to Waldron, June 2, 1735, BP(NHHS), II, 125.

42. House of Representatives to Belcher, May 8, 1736, Docs.NH, IV, 709; "Address of Eight of Council to his Majesty," Jan. 28, 1733/4, Force Transcripts, New Hampshire Miscellaneous Records; Waldron to Belcher, Mar. 19, 1735/6, W-B, I, 269.

43. Waldron to Belcher, Feb. 1736/7, New Hampshire Miscellany, Library of Congress; Waldron to Belcher, Aug. 18, 1732, W-B, I, 99; Waldron to Belcher, ND, ibid., 104; House of Representatives to Belcher, May 2, 1735, Docs.NH, IV, 683. Belcher to Waldron, Aug. 15, 1734, B.Ltrs, IV, 241-42; Belcher to Waldron, May 2, 1737, ibid., V, 183-84; Fry, New Hampshire as a Royal Province, 150-52.

44. Belcher to Waldron, June 2, 1735, BP(NHHS), II, 125. Belcher to Waldron, Sept. 22, 1735, ibid., 189; Belcher to Waldron, Nov. 25, 1734, B.Ltrs, IV, 376-77; Belcher to Waldron, Mar. 17, 1734/5, ibid., 533.

45. Belcher to Wilks, Nov. 13, 1733, ibid., III, 473; Belcher to Wilks, Sept. 24, 1737, ibid., V, 368. Thomas Hutchinson, The History of the Colony and Province of

Massachusetts-Bay, ed. Lawrence Shaw Mayo (Cambridge, Mass., 1936), 2:292-93; *Acts of the Privy Council*, ed. W. L. Grant and James Munro (London, 1908-12), 3:128-30; "Account of the Proceedings of the Council for issuing a Commission to Settle the Boundarys between Massachusetts Bay and New Hampshire," Wilmington Papers, Library of Congress.

46. Atkinson to Thomlinson, Mar. 4, 1736/7, "Additional Belcher Papers, 1732-1749," ed. Barrett Wendell, Massachusetts Historical Society *Proceedings*, 3d ser., XLIV (1910-11), 191.

47. Waldron to Belcher, Feb. 1736/7, New Hampshire Miscellany, Library of Congress; Belcher to Council and House of Representatives, Aug. 4, 1737, *JHR*, XV, 121; Belcher to Waldron, July 7, 1737, B.Ltrs, V, 283. And Belcher to Waldron, Apr. 25, 1737, ibid., 179-80; Belcher to Waldron, July 18, 1737, ibid., 304-5.

48. *Docs.NH*, IV, 715-32. Belcher to Newcastle, June 1, 1737, B.Ltrs, V, 239.

49. Belcher to Waldron, Aug. 3, 1737, ibid., 330-31. Belcher to Board of Trade, July 11, 1737, ibid., 289; Belcher to Board of Trade, Aug. 10, 1737, ibid., 336; *JHR*, XV, 50; Belknap, *History of New Hampshire*, I, 241-47.

50. Ibid., 245-47; Fry, *New Hampshire as a Royal Province*, 259-61.

51. Belcher to Waldron, July 18, 1737, B.Ltrs, V, 304-5; Belcher to Waldron, Aug. 3, 1737, ibid., 330; *JHR*, XV, 168. *Docs.NH*, IV, 745-47, 755-56; Belcher to Waldron, Sept. 2, 1737, BP(NHHS), III, 28; Wiggin's Complaint [Mar. 15, 1738] and Belcher's answer, Wiggin Papers, New Hampshire Historical Society.

52. Belcher to Waldron, Aug. 15, 1734, B.Ltrs, IV, 241-42; Belcher to Waldron, Sept. 23, 1734, ibid., 269. Belcher to Waldron, May 15, 1738, Dreer Collection, Colonial Governors, Historical Society of Pennsylvania.

53. Belcher to Waldron, Jan. 30, 1735/6, BP(NHHS), III, 5; Belcher to Waldron, Aug. 15, 1734, B.Ltrs, IV, 241-42.

54. Belcher to Waldron, June 9, 1735, BP(NHHS), II, 137; Belcher to Waldron, July 24, 1735, ibid., 161; Belcher to Waldron, Apr. 12, 1739, ibid., III, 40.

55. Belcher to Waldron, Apr. 12, 1739, ibid., 40; Belcher to Waldron, Sept. 15, 1740, BP(MHS), II, 329-30. And Waldron to Belcher, May 30, 1735, W-B, I, 188-89; Waldron to Belcher, June 6, 1735, ibid., 195.

56. Complaint against Belcher [Mar. 15, 1738], Wiggin Papers. And Partridge to Belcher, Aug. 18, 1739, New Hampshire Miscellany, Library of Congress; Thomlinson to Jaffrey, Aug. 20, 1739, "Additional Belcher Papers," 199-201; Partridge to Wilmington, Dec. 1, 1738, Wilmington Papers, II, Library of Congress; Daniell, "Politics in New Hampshire under Governor Wentworth," 78-80.

57. Belcher to Partridge, Jan. 15, 1739/40, BP(NHHS), II, 262. And Belcher to Waldron, Jan. 21, 1739/40, ibid., 269-72.

58. Belcher to Waldron, Apr. 20, 1741, ibid., 376; Belcher to Waldron, Sept. 15, 1740, ibid., 329-30.

6. Servant to the King and People

1. Belcher to Jonathan Belcher, Jr., Oct. 29, 1739, B.Ltrs, VI, 106.

2. Belcher to Horace Walpole, Jan. 21, 1739/40, *BP*(MHS), II, 264-68. Newman to Belcher, Oct. 20, 1737, Newman Papers, Massachusetts Historical Society; Boydell to [Yeamans], June 5, 1737, Greenough Papers, II, Massachusetts Historical Society.

3. Waldo to Popple, July 9, 1736, *Cal.St.Pprs*, XLII, 247; Penobscot Indians to Belcher, July 22, 1736, ibid., 250; Shirley to Newcastle, Dec. 22, 1736, *Correspondence of William Shirley, Governor of Massachusetts and Military Commander*

in America, 1731-1760, ed. Charles Henry Lincoln (New York, 1912), 1:7-8; A. R. Cutter to Belcher, Dec. 3, 1737, Henry Knox Papers, XL, 19, Massachusetts Historical Society; Statement by William Woodside, May 10, 1738, ibid., 30; Shirley to Waldo, Nov. 16, 1738, ibid., 36; Massachusetts Council Records (Executive), July 23 and Aug. 3, 1736, Massachusetts Archives; Joseph J. Malone, *Pine Trees and Politics: The Naval Stores and Forest Policy in Colonial New England, 1691-1775* (Seattle, 1964), 114-15.

    4. Belcher to Partridge and Jonathan Belcher, Jr., Jan. 25, 1736/7, B.Ltrs, V, 137. Belcher to Partridge and Jonathan Belcher, Jr., Mar. 3, 1736/7, ibid., 167; Belcher to Lloyd, July 1, 1737, ibid., 277; *Hrvrd Grads*, VIII, 540-49.

    5. Belcher to Partridge, May 9, 1737, B.Ltrs, V, 202-7; Belcher to Coram, Nov. 7, 1737, ibid., 409.

    6. Belcher to Francis Harrison, Nov. 15, 1731, ibid., II, 83. Belcher to Jonathan Belcher, Jr., Nov. 12, 1740, ibid., VII, 59; Belcher to Wilks, May 11, 1741, ibid., 249.

    7. Belcher to Jonathan Belcher, Jr., Oct. 29, 1739, ibid., VI, 105-7.

    8. Belcher to Jonathan Belcher, Jr., Nov. 20, 1736, ibid., V, 49; Belcher to Jonathan Belcher, Jr., May 7, 1737, ibid., 196; Belcher to Queen Caroline, Dec. 5, 1737, ibid., 459-61.

    9. Belcher to Partridge, Feb. 18, 1733/4, ibid., IV, 47-48.

    10. Belcher to Jonathan Belcher, Jr., Jan. 27, 1740/1, BP(MHS), II, 367; Belcher to Partridge, Feb. 7, 1736/7, B.Ltrs, V, 145. J. H. Plumb, *Sir Robert Walpole: The King's Minister* (London, 1960), 97-98; Carl Bridenbaugh, *Mitre and Sceptre: Transatlantic Faiths, Ideas, Personalities, and Politics, 1689-1775* (New York, 1962), 35-43; Norman C. Hunt, *Two Early Political Associations: The Quakers and the Dissenting Deputies in the Age of Sir Robert Walpole* (Oxford, 1961), 18-112.

    11. Partridge to Josiah Foster, 6 month, 6 day, 1737, Miscellaneous Manuscripts, XLI, 34, Friends House (London); Partridge to Belcher, Aug. 18, 1739, New Hampshire Miscellany, Library of Congress; Belcher to English Friends, Nov. 10, 1737, B.Ltrs, V, 432-33; Belcher to English Friends, May 9, 1740, ibid., VI, 317. Minutes of Meetings for Sufferings, XXVII, 34, Friends House.

    12. Belcher to Barrington, Nov. 24, 1731, B.Ltrs, II, 113; Belcher to Barrington, Apr. 24, 1732, ibid., 272; Belcher to Alexander Spotswood, Oct. 9, 1732, ibid., 496-97.

    13. Belcher to Bladen, Jan. 8, 1732/3, ibid., III, 90.

    14. Waldron to Belcher, Nov. 5, 1731, WP, I, 28; Belcher to Huske, Nov. 8, 1731, B.Ltrs, II, 68-69; Belcher to Waldron, Nov. 8, 1731, BP(MHS), I, 47; Belcher to Bladen, Nov. 23, 1731, ibid., 61-63; Belcher to Bishop of Lincoln, May 25, 1732, ibid., 134-35.

    15. Belcher to Barrington, Oct. 5, 1733, B.Ltrs, III, 411-12; Belcher to Partridge and Jonathan Belcher, Jr., Dec. 3, 1734, ibid., IV, 402-3. Thomas C. Barrow, *Trade and Empire: The British Customs Service in Colonial America, 1660-1775* (Cambridge, Mass., 1967), 117-18.

    16. Shirley to Waldo, Apr. 21, 1739, Knox Papers, XL, 43; Belcher to Jonathan Belcher, Jr., Dec. 24, 1737, B.Ltrs, V, 521. Belcher to Holden, Nov. 25, 1737, ibid., 446-47; F. Shirley to Newcastle, Mar. 2, 1736/7, Additional Manuscripts, Newcastle Papers, 32690, 261, British Museum; Shirley to Admiralty, May 6, 1739, Admiralty Papers, 3817, 110-28, Public Record Office (London). John A. Schutz, *William Shirley: King's Governor of Massachusetts* (Chapel Hill, 1961), 3-43.

    17. Jonathan Belcher, Jr., to Partridge, Aug. 15, 1739, BP(NHHS), III, 66; Belcher to Jonathan Belcher, Jr., Feb. 23, 1731/2, B.Ltrs, II, 212.

    18. Thomlinson to Jaffrey, Atkinson, Rindge, and Packer, Aug. 20, 1739, Barrett Wendell, ed., "Additional Belcher Papers, 1732-1749," Massachusetts Historical

Society *Proceedings*, XLIV (1910), 199-200; Belcher to Harrington, Oct. 23, 1739, B.Ltrs, VI, 87-88.

19. Belcher to Wilks, Nov. 7, 1737, ibid., V, 404-5.

20. J. Gilman, G. Gerrish, J. Lord, and P. Thyng to Wager, [1738], *Docs.NH*, XVIII, 58-59; Thomas Hutchinson, *The History of the Colony and Province of Massachusetts-Bay*, ed. Lawrence Shaw Mayo (Cambridge, Mass., 1936), 2:301-2.

21. Shirley to Waldo, Apr. 15, 1739, Knox Papers, XL, 43; James A. Henretta, *"Salutary Neglect": Colonial Administration under the Duke of Newcastle* (Princeton, 1972), 212-13. And Hutchinson, *History of the Colony and Province of Massachusetts-Bay*, 2:302-3.

22. Partridge to Wilmington, Dec. 1, 1738, Wilmington Papers, Library of Congress; Partridge to Belcher, Aug. 18, 1739, New Hampshire Miscellany, Library of Congress; *Acts of the Privy Council in England, Colonial Series*, ed. W. L. Grant and James Munro (London, 1908-12), 3:592-600, 637-39.

23. Belcher to Wilmington, Oct. 22, 1739, B.Ltrs, VI, 75-77.

24. Newcastle to Shirley, Apr. 5, 1740, *Correspondence of William Shirley*, I, 18-19; Belcher to Waldron, Jan. 25, 1739/40, B.Ltrs, VI, 236.

25. Belcher to Neal, Aug. 14, 1732, B.Ltrs, II, 425; Belcher to Mascerene, Feb. 6, 1741/2, ibid., VII, 420-21; Belcher to Jonathan Belcher, Jr., Dec. 25, 1733, *BP*(MHS), I, 444; Belcher to Waldron, Jan. 21, 1739/40, ibid., II, 269; Belcher to Waldron, Aug. 12, 1736, BP(NHHS), III, 14.

26. John Barnard, *The Throne Established by Righteousness* (Boston, 1734), 54-55; William Cooper, *The Honours of CHRIST demanded of the Magistrate* (Boston, 1740), 34-38; William Williams, *God the Strength of Rulers and People . . .* (Boston, 1741), 40-41.

27. Samuel Wigglesworth, *An Essay for Reviving Religion* (Boston, 1733), 28; copies of Colman's address are in the Boston Public Library and in the Colman Papers, II, Massachusetts Historical Society.

28. Samuel Fiske, *The Character of the Candidates for Civil Government . . .* (Boston, 1731), 42.

29. For example, see *The Records of the First Church in Salem Massachusetts, 1629-1736*, ed. Richard D. Pierce (Salem, 1974); *Records of the First Church at Dorchester, in New England, 1636-1734*, eds. S. J. Barrows and William B. Trask (Boston, 1891); *Early Records of Dedham, Massachusetts, 1706-1736*, ed. Julius H. Tuttle (Dedham, 1936).

30. See chapter 2, note 19, and William Douglass, *A Summary, Historical and Political, Of the first Planting, progressive Improvements, and present State of the British Settlements in North-America* (Boston, 1749), 489-92, 501-16.

31. Belcher to Waldron, July 28, 1735, BP(NHHS), II, 163; Belcher to Shute, Apr. 24, 1732, *BP*(MHS), I, 114.

32. G. B. Warden, *Boston, 1689-1776* (Boston, 1970), 121-22; Belcher to Newcastle, June 1, 1737, ibid., 239-40.

33. Barnard, *Throne Established*, 30; John Webb, *The Government of Christ considered and applied* (Boston, 1738), 30.

34. Belcher to Board of Trade, Nov. 7, 1737, B.Ltrs, V, 414-16.

35. Belcher to Wilks, June 14, 1737, ibid., 258.

36. Belcher to Chandler, Nov. 12, 1739, ibid., VI, 130; House of Representatives to Belcher, Oct. 5, 1739, *JHR*, XVII, 145.

37. Belcher to Waldron, Oct. 30, 1739, *BP*(MHS), II, 240.

38. Newcastle to Belcher, Jan. 5, 1739/40, *Docs.NH*, V, 47; Belcher to Newcastle, July 15, 1740, *BP*(MHS), II, 312.
39. Belcher to Partridge, June 5, 1740, B.Ltrs, VI, 378; Belcher to W. Blakeney, July 21, 1740, ibid., 449-50; Belcher to Partridge, July 29, 1740, ibid., 479.
40. Belcher to Stoddard, July 22, 1740, ibid., VI, 453; Belcher to S. Denny, Aug. 18, 1740, ibid., 492-93.
41. House of Representatives to Belcher, Jan. 2, 1740[/1], *JHR*, XVIII, 184-85. New Hampshire House of Representatives to Belcher, Aug. 4, 1740, *Docs.NH*, V, 69-70.
42. Belcher to Partridge, Oct. 25, 1740, B.Ltrs, VII, 25. Belcher to H. Walpole, Nov. 25, 1740, ibid., 110-11; Newcastle to Shirley, Apr. 5, 1740, *Correspondence of William Shirley*, 1:17-19; Atkinson to Shirley, May 20, 1740, Colonial Office Papers, 5, 10 New Hampshire, 58.
43. Belcher to Board of Trade, Jan. 14, 1739/40, *BP*(MHS), 255-57; Belcher to Council and House of Representatives, Sept. 19, 1739, *JHR*, XVII, 115. Belcher to Partridge, Nov. 22, 1739, B.Ltrs, VI, 151.
44. George Athan Billias, *The Massachusetts Land Bankers of 1740*, in *University of Maine Studies* 2d ser., no. 74 (Orono, 1959); John L. Brooke, *The Heart of the Commonwealth: Society and Political Culture in Worcester County, Massachusetts, 1713-1861* (New York, 1989), 41-128.
45. *By His EXCELLENCY Jonathan Belcher. . . . A PROCLAMATION* [July 17, 1740] ([Boston, 1740]); Belcher to Board of Trade, Nov. 17, 1740, *BP*(MHS), II, 349.
46. Belcher to Council and House of Representatives, Nov. 22, 1740, *JHR*, XVIII, 132; Belcher to Jonathan Belcher, Jr., Nov. 19, 1740, B.Ltrs, VII, 96; Belcher to Chandler, Jan. 12, 1740/1, ibid., 144-45. Executive Proclamations, Nov. 5 and 6, 1740, "Calendar of the Papers and Records relating to the Land Bank of 1740," ed. Andrew McFarland Davis, *Publications of the Colonial Society of Massachusetts*, IV (1910), 7.
47. *Journal of the Commissioners for Trade and Plantations* (London, 1920-38), 273-74, 355-56; *Acts of the Privy Council*, III, 683; *Proceedings and Debates of the British Parliaments Respecting North America*, ed. Leo Stock (Washington, D.C., 1924-41), 5:97; *Boston Weekly News-Letter*, Nov. 6-14, 1740, and Jan. 22-29, 1740/1; Schutz, *William Shirley*, 32-33.
48. *Boston Weekly News-Letter*, Dec. 18-25, 1741; Massachusetts Council Records (Executive), Dec. 5, 19, 26, 1740, and Jan. 1, 9, 15, 1740[/1]; Letters of resignation from Stoddard, Choate, and Adams, Nov. 10, 1740, "Calendar of Papers and Records relating to the Land Bank," 8; Belcher to I. Plaisted, Jan. 26, 1740/1, B.Ltrs, VII, 155.
49. Massachusetts Council Records (Executive), Jan. 15, 1740[/1]; *Boston Weekly News-Letter*, Jan. 1-8, 1741; *JHR*, XVIII, 227-28; justice of the peace quoted in Andrew McFarland Davis, *Currency and Banking in the Province of the Massachusetts-Bay (Publications of the American Economic Association*, 3d ser., I-II [1900-1901]), II, 151.
50. Colman to Belcher, Jan. 26, 1741, Colman Papers, II.
51. Belcher to Hutchinson, May 11, 1741, *BP*(MHS), II, 388-90. Belcher to Waldron, Nov. 17, 1740, B.Ltrs, VII, 78.
52. Affidavit of Royall, May 11, 1741, "Calendar of Papers and Records relating to the Land Bank of 1740," 20. And affidavits by Crosby, et al., May 11-12, 1741, ibid., 19-20; arrest warrants, May 14, 1741, ibid., 20; Massachusetts Council Records (Executive), May 9-20, 1741.

53. Belcher to Waldron, May 25, 1741, B.Ltrs, VII, 286. William Pencak, *War, Politics, & Revolution in Provincial Massachusetts* (Boston, 1981), 106; Robert Zemsky, *Merchants, Farmers, and River Gods: An Essay on Eighteenth-Century Politics* (Boston, 1971), 247-48; John L. Brooke, *The Heart of the Commonwealth: Society and Political Culture in Worcester County, Massachusetts* (New York, 1989), 102-8.
54. Belcher to House of Representatives, May 28, 1741, *JHR*, XIX, 9.
55. Belcher to Waldron, Jan. 25, 1739/40, B.Ltrs, VI, 236.
56. Belcher to Partridge, Jan. 26, 1740/1, *BP*(MHS), II, 362-63. Memorial of Massachusetts and London merchants to Newcastle, [1741], Colonial Office Papers, 5/10 Massachusetts, 184.
57. Hutchinson, *History of the Colony and Province of Massachusetts-Bay*, 2:303; Henretta, "*Salutary Neglect*," 212-16.
58. Belcher to Partridge, Jan. 26, 1740/1, *BP*(MHS), II, 362; Belcher to Hutchinson, May 11, 1741, ibid., 387. Belcher to Partridge, May 7, 1741, ibid., 379; Belcher to Waldron, May 18, 1741, B.Ltrs, VII, 260.
59. Williams, *God the Strength of Rulers and People*, 40-43.
60. Allen to Colman, Dec. 1, 1740, John Davis Papers, II, Massachusetts Historical Society. Bridenbaugh, *Mitre and Sceptre*, 44-45.
61. Belcher to Partridge, July 3, 1741, *BP*(MHS), II, 402; Belcher to Jonathan Belcher, Jr., July 3, 1741, ibid., 404; Belcher to Jonathan Belcher, Jr., Nov. 29, 1740, B.Ltrs, VII, 115; Belcher to Sherburne, July 20, 1741, ibid., 350; Belcher to Sherburne, July 27, 1741, ibid., 355. R. Waldron, Jr., to R. Waldron, Sr., June 27, 1741, Miscellaneous Manuscripts, New-York Historical Society.
62. *The Diaries of Benjamin Lynde and of Benjamin Lynde, Jr.*, ed. Fitch E. Oliver (Boston, 1880), 114-15.
63. Belcher to Waldron, July 6, 1741, B.Ltrs.,VII, 341-42.

7. Exile and Fulfillment

1. Belcher to Watts, Jan. 15, 1741/2, B.Ltrs, VII, 413; Belcher to C. Dean, Mar. 10, 1741/2, ibid., 429-30.
2. Belcher to Sewall, Jan. 19, 1741/2, ibid., 417; Belcher to Greenleaf, July 22, 1742, ibid., 470.
3. Belcher to Coram, Aug. 31, 1742, ibid., 490.
4. Belcher to Jonathan Belcher, Jr., Oct. 26, 1741, ibid., 393; Belcher to Partridge, Aug. 31, 1742, ibid., 487; Belcher to Andrew Belcher, June 20, 1743, ibid., 549; Belcher to Jonathan Belcher, Jr., Dec. 1, 1741, *BP*(MHS), 417-19; Belcher to Andrew Belcher, Mar. 18, 1741/2, ibid., 420; Belcher to Partridge, May 27, 1742, ibid., 430-31; Belcher to Andrew Belcher, Apr. 20, 1743, ibid., 447-48; Belcher to Partridge, May 3, 1743, ibid., 451.
5. Belcher to Andrew Belcher, June 20, 1743, B.Ltrs, VII, 547; Belcher to Andrew Belcher, Dec. 6, 1742, ibid., 511; Belcher to Guyse, Mar. 2, 1742/3, ibid., 526.
6. Belcher to Wilks, Dec. 1, 1741, B.Ltrs, VII, 403; Belcher to Newman, Jan. 16, 1741/2, ibid., 414-15; Belcher to Partridge, Aug. 31, 1742, ibid., 487; Newman to Jonathan Belcher, Jr., May 17, 1743, Newman Papers, Massachusetts Historical Society.
7. Belcher to Waldron, Sept. 24, 1743, Gratz Autograph Collection, Colonial Governors, case 2, box 29, Historical Society of Pennsylvania.

8. Belcher to Willard, Oct. 20, 1747, B.Ltrs, VIII, 86; Belcher to Brattle, Jan. 18, 1747/8, ibid., 212-13.

9. Belcher to Hardwicke, July 2, 1744, Additional Manuscripts, Hardwicke Papers, 35909, 97, British Museum; Belcher to Brattle, Jan. 28, 1747/8, B.Ltrs, VIII, 212-13. Minutes of Meetings for Sufferings, 5 month, 27 day, and 6th month, 3rd day, 1744, XXVII, 449-51, Friends House (London).

10. Belcher to Newcastle, July 29, 1745, Newcastle Papers, Additional Manuscripts, 32704, 547, British Museum; Belcher to Newcastle, Mar. 12, 1745/6, ibid., 32707, 292.

11. Belcher to Waldron, Aug. 7, 1749, BP(NHHS), III, 152.

12. Belcher to Coram, Aug. 31, 1742, B.Ltrs, VII, 490. Belcher to Bradbury, Sept. 16, 1747, ibid., VIII, 41-42; Belcher to Avery, Sept. 27, 1747, ibid., 65.

13. Belcher to Hardwicke, June 10, 1746, Newcastle Papers, 32704, 298; Kilby to Hancock, July 18, 1746, *New-England Historical and Genealogical Register* 26 (January 1872): 47-48; Stanley Nider Katz, *Newcastle's New York: Anglo-American Politics, 1732-1753* (Cambridge, Mass., 1968), 223-24; James A. Henretta, *"Salutary Neglect": Colonial Administration under the Duke of Newcastle* (Princeton, 1972), 232-33.

14. Paris to J. Alexander, Feb. 10, 1746[/7], Rutherford Collection, New Jersey, 121, New-York Historical Society; Paris to Alexander, Feb. 13, 1746[/7], Paris Papers, X, 20, New Jersey Historical Society; R. Smith, Jr., to J. Smith, 3 month, 8th day, 1746, Smith Family Papers, chronological series, II, 211, Library Company of Philadelphia; Belcher to Newcastle, May 18, 1747, Newcastle Papers, 32711, 81.

15. Belcher to J. Belcher, Sept. 17, 1747, B.Ltrs, VIII, 43. Paris to Alexander, Feb. 17, 1746[/7], ibid., VI, 422-24; Paris to Alexander, Jan. 27, 1746, Statesmen Autograph Collection, New Jersey Historical Society; Alexander to [Paris], Dec. 1, 1746, Paris Papers, X, 21.

16. Belcher to Jonathan Belcher, Jr., Feb. 1, 1750/1, B.Ltrs, IX, 81-83.

17. Belcher to Beard, Sept. 27, 1747, ibid., 41; Belcher to Walley, Oct. 2, 1747, ibid., 85; J. Dickinson to Foxcroft, Nov. 24, 1746, Foxcroft Correspondence, Princeton University Library; Hatfield and Crane to Avery, Mar. 20, 1747, Miscellaneous Manuscripts, Princeton University Library; Avery to Dickinson, Apr. 25, 1747, ibid.

18. Belcher to Willard, Oct. 2, 1747, B.Ltrs, VIII, 88-89; Belcher to Winslow, Oct. 3, 1747, ibid., 92; Elizabethtown mayor and aldermen address Belcher, *Pennsylvania Gazette*, Aug. 27, 1747.

19. Belcher to Peagrum, Sept. 27, 1747, B.Ltrs, VIII, 63-64. Belcher to Willard, Oct. 2, 1748, ibid., 88; Belcher to Caswall, Feb. 10, 1747/8, ibid., 242; Belcher to Sergeant, Feb. 23, 1747/8, ibid., 254-55.

20. Belcher to Byles, Jan. 26, 1747/8, ibid., 207. Belcher to Andrew Belcher, Nov. 6, 1747, ibid., 136-37; Belcher to Andrew Belcher, Dec. 4, 1747, ibid., 163.

21. [William Livingston], *Philosophic Solitude . . .* (New York, 1747), ix, 17; Belcher to Byles, Jan. 26, 1747/8, B.Ltrs, VIII, 207.

22. Alexander to R. H. Morris, May 30, 1749, *NJ.Archs*, VII, 262-63; *A Letter to B. G.* ([Philadelphia, 1739]).

23. John Smith Diaries, 6th month, 22-24th days, 1747, Library Company of Philadelphia; Alexander to [Paris], Dec. 6, 1746, Paris Papers, X, 21; Paris to Alexander, Feb. 10, 1746[/7], Rutherford Collection, New Jersey, 121.

24. Alexander to Murray, Dec. 3, 1747, *NJ.Archs*, VII, 77-78; R. H. Morris's "Representation" to Belcher, 1747, Morris Papers, I, Rutgers University Library.

25. Belcher to Sergeant, Feb. 23, 1747/8, B.Ltrs, VIII, 253. Alexander to Ogden, Mar. 9, 1747/8, Rutherford Collection, New Jersey, 141; P. Collinson to Alexander, Oct. 14, 1747, ibid., IV, 81; T. Penn to Peters, June 10, 1747, Thomas Penn Letterbooks, II, 199, Historical Society of Pennsylvania; T. Penn to Alexander, Sept. 1, 1748, ibid., 246.

26. Belcher to J. Wendell, Oct. 5, 1747, B.Ltrs, VIII, 100-101; C. Read to R. H. Morris, Apr. 16, 1748, Morris Papers, II; Coxe to Alexander, May 2, 1748, Alexander Papers, VII, 7, Princeton University Library; Coxe to Alexander, May 30, 1748, *NJ.Archs*, VII, 127-30.

27. Memorandum of Council meeting, Dec. 16, 1748, ibid., VII, 183-4; Council to Belcher, Dec. 22, 1748, ibid., 185-88; Council Records, Dec. 16, 1748, ibid., XVI, 64-68. Alexander to Coxe, Sept. 5, 1748, ibid., VII, 155.

28. Belcher to Andrew Belcher, Oct. 6, 1748, B.Ltrs, VIII, 485-86; Belcher to Brattle, Oct. 12, 1748, ibid., 495.

29. Allison B. Olson, "The Founding of Princeton University: Religion and Politics in Eighteenth-Century New Jersey," *New Jersey History* 87 (Autumn 1969): 133-50; Thomas Jefferson Wertenbaker, *Princeton, 1746-1896* (Princeton, 1946), 3-47.

30. Belcher to West Jersey Society, Sept. 18, 1747, B.Ltrs, VIII, 52-53; Belcher to Dickinson, Oct. 8, 1747, ibid., 116; Belcher to J. Edwards, May 31, 1748, ibid., 342-43.

31. J. Logan to Belcher, May 18, 1748, Logan Letterbook, 4, Historical Society of Pennsylvania; Burr to Doddridge, Nov. 24, 1748, Miscellaneous Manuscripts, Boston Public Library; S. Hazard to R. Cary, Feb. 27, 1753, Hazard Letterbook, Princeton University Library; S. Johnson to Bishop of London, Apr. 27, 1747, Princeton University Archives; The Minutes of the Proceedings of the Board of Trustees of the College of New Jersey, I, 18, 19, Princeton University Archives.

32. Carl Bridenbaugh, *Mitre and Sceptre: Transatlantic Faiths, Ideas, Personalities, and Politics, 1689-1775* (New York, 1962), 129. Belcher to Edwards, May 31, 1748, B.Ltrs, VIII, 342-43.

33. Belcher to Pemberton, June 20, 1748, ibid., 373. And Belcher to Pemberton, Apr. 2, 1748, ibid., 285-86; Belcher to Tennent, June 18, 1748, ibid., 371-72.

34. Belcher to Sergeant, Feb. 23, 1747/8, ibid., 254-55; Belcher to Sewall, Apr. 8, 1748, ibid., 290-91. And Belcher to Brattle, Jan. 28, 1747/8, ibid., 214; Belcher to Edwards, Feb. 5, 1747/8, ibid., 227-29.

35. *Weekly New-York Journal*, Oct. 22, 1750. Also Proclamation for Thanksgiving, Oct. 14, 1749, *NJ.Archs*, XVI, 98-99; Belcher to Burr, Feb. 22, 1750/1, B.Ltrs, IX, 103.

36. Gilbert Tennent, *Two Sermons Preach'd at Burlington* . . . (Philadelphia, [1749]), 10, 27; Tennent, *A Sermon Preach'd at Burlington*. . . (Philadelphia, 1749), 6. Tennent to Doddridge, July 20, 1751, Miscellaneous Manuscripts, Presbyterian Historical Society, Philadelphia.

37. Tennent, *Two Sermons*, 40.

38. *Weekly New-York Journal*, Oct. 22, 1750.

39. Belcher to ?, Nov. 14, 1748, Belcher Manuscripts, Princeton University Library; Belcher to John Belcher, June 29, 1748, B.Ltrs, VIII, 401.

40. R. Smith to J. Smith, Nov. 23, 1748, Smith Family Papers, Chronological Series, III, 72; W. Skinner to Secretary of Society for the Propagation of the Gospel, Jan. 9, 1748/9, Princeton University Archives; Belcher to W. Belcher, June 29, 1748, B.Ltrs, VIII, 402-3.

41. Belcher to Edwards, July 6, 1754, ibid., X, 420-21. Belcher to Edwards, May 31, 1748, ibid., VIII, 340-43; Belcher to Doddridge, Dec. 24, 1750, ibid., IX, 53-54; Belcher to High Commissioners of the Church of Scotland, Oct. 10, 1753, ibid., 240-42; Belcher to Avery, Oct. 11, 1753, ibid., 246; Belcher to Whitefield, Oct. 11, 1753, ibid., 256-57; Minutes of the Protestant Dissenting Deputies, I, 316, 358, 369, 397, Guildhall (London).

42. Burr to Doddridge, Apr. 1748, Burr Collection, Princeton University Library; Trustees to Belcher, Oct. 13, 1748, *Pennsylvania Gazette*, Nov. 3, 1748. G. Tennent to Doddridge, July 20, 1751, Miscellaneous Manuscripts, Presbyterian Historical Society; M. Hatfield and S. Crane to Avery, Mar. 7, 1747/8, Miscellaneous Manuscripts, Princeton University Library; Minutes of the Proceedings of the Board of Trustees of the College of New Jersey, I, 13.

43. Belcher to Hardwicke, Nov. 12, 1750, B.Ltrs, IX, 25-27. Belcher to Partridge, June 3, 1751, ibid., 145-46; Paris to Alexander, July 4, 1749, Alexander Papers, VIII, 73; Board of Trade to Belcher, Mar. 27, 1751, *NJ.Archs*, VII, 585-86.

44. Belcher to Peagrum, Nov. 7, 1750, B.Ltrs, IX, 16; Belcher to Partridge, Nov. 11, 1751, ibid., 262-63.

45. Belcher to Board of Trade, July 31, 1750, *NJ.Archs*, VII, 540-50; Belcher to Council, Oct. 23, 1751, ibid., 634; Belcher to Ashfield, Sept. 24, 1751, B.Ltrs, IX, 223.

46. Belcher's Proclamation, Feb. 25, 1751, *New-York Gazette*, Mar. 4, 1751, in *NJ.Archs*, XIX, 30-32; Belcher to Oliver, May 4, 1751, B.Ltrs, IX, 123. Belcher to Kearney, Feb. 25, 1750/1, ibid., 105; Belcher to Woodruffe, Feb. 25, 1750/1, ibid., 105-6; Belcher to Morris, Feb. 25, 1750/1, ibid., 106. And Michael C. Batinski, *The New Jersey Assembly, 1738-1775: The Making of a Legislative Community* (Lanham, Md., 1987), 147-53.

47. Council to Assembly, Oct. 22, 1751, *NJ.Archs*, XVI, 341-43. Belcher to Assembly, Oct. 22, 1751, ibid., VII, 625; Alexander to Morris, Oct. 27, 1751, ibid., 627.

48. Belcher to Brattle, Feb. 22, 1752, B.Ltrs, IX, 359.

49. Belcher to Partridge, July 3, 1751, *NJ.Archs*, VII, 601; Belcher to Walley, Feb. 1, 1747/8, B.Ltrs, VIII, 222.

50. Belcher to Edwards, Feb. 5, 1747/8, ibid., VIII, 227-29. Theodore George Thayer, *As We Were: The Story of Old Elizabethtown* (Elizabeth, N.J., 1964), 2, 69, 80.

51. Belcher to Franklin, Jan. 20, 1752, *The Papers of Benjamin Franklin*, ed. Leonard W. Labaree et al. (New Haven, 1959-), 4:255; Belcher to Brown, June 3, 1752, B.Ltrs, IX, 448. Belcher to Andrew Belcher, Mar. 8, 1747/8, ibid., VIII, 264.

52. Belcher to Andrew Belcher, Jan. 25, 1747/8, B.Ltrs, 200-201; Belcher to Andrew Belcher, May 18, 1748, ibid., 317-18; Belcher to Jonathan Belcher, Jr., Feb. 1, 1750/1, ibid., IX, 83.

53. Belcher to Andrew Belcher, May 14, 1754, ibid., 378-80; Belcher to Andrew Belcher, July 12, 1754, ibid., 426.

54. Belcher to Jonathan Belcher, Jr., Dec. 24, 1753, ibid., 304-5. Belcher to Partridge, Nov. 29, 1753, ibid., 287.

55. Belcher to Foxcroft, Oct. 7, 1755, ibid., XI, 406. Belcher to New England Company, Mar. 8, 1753, ibid., X, 106; Belcher to Whitefield, Nov. 3, 1755, ibid., XI, 429-31.

56. Belcher to Lady Huntington, July 2, 1753, ibid., X, 160; Belcher to Niles, Nov. 10, 1753, ibid., 274-75; Belcher to Warrell, Dec. 29, 1753, ibid., 308.

57. Belcher to Council and Assembly, Feb. 12, 1752, *NJ.Archs*, XVI, 364-65; Belcher to Edwards, Jan. 22, 1752, B.Ltrs, IX, 338-39; Belcher to Warrell, Dec. 29, 1753, ibid., X, 308; Belcher to Huntington, July 2, 1753, ibid., 160; Belcher to Walter, Jan. 4, 1754, ibid., 309.

58. Belcher to Burr, July 9, 1754, ibid., 423. And Belcher to Prince, Aug. 23, 1753, ibid., 203-5; Belcher to Wolcott, Sept. 27, 1753, ibid., 228; Belcher to Marquis of Lothian, Oct. 10, 1753, ibid., 242-43.

59. Belcher to Doddridge, Dec. 24, 1750, B.Ltrs, IX, 52-53; Belcher to Niles, Oct. 10, 1752, ibid., X, 30; Belcher to Noyes, July 24, 1754, ibid., 438.

60. Belcher to Moody, Oct. 8, 1751, ibid., IX, 231; Belcher to Whitefield, Aug. 5, 1754, ibid., X, 444; Belcher to Whitefield, Nov. 3, 1755, ibid., XI, 429-30.

61. Belcher to Edwards, Jan. 22, 1752, ibid., IX, 339. Belcher to Edwards, May 31, 1748, ibid., VIII, 342-43; Belcher to New England Company, Mar. 8, 1753, ibid., X, 106.

62. Alan Heimert, *Religion and the American Mind: From the Great Awakening to the Revolution* (Cambridge, Mass., 1966), 86-87.

63. Belcher to Brattle, July 31, 1755, B.Ltrs, XI, 334; Belcher to St. Clair, Sept. 3, 1755, *NJ.Archs*, VIII, pt. 2, 133-34; Belcher to Shirley, Nov. 20, 1755, ibid., pt. 2, 168-69.

64. Aaron Burr, *A DISCOURSE . . . on Account of the late Encroachments of the French . . .* (New York, 1755), 39-41.

65. Belcher's Proclamation, Apr. 3, 1756, *The New York Mercury*, Apr. 12, 1756, in *NJ.Archs*, XX, 20-22.

66. Trustees to Belcher, Sept. 24, 1755, Minutes of the Proceedings of the Board of Trustees of the College of New Jersey, I, 42.

67. Belcher to Trustees, May 29, 1756, ibid., 44, 49.

68. Belcher to Oliver, Nov. 27, 1755, B.Ltrs, XI, 483; Belcher to Edwards, Dec. 30, 1755, ibid., 565; Belcher to Edwards, Dec. 8, 1756, Bamberger Autograph Collection, New Jersey Historical Society.

69. E. Burr to Fedelia, [Aug. 31, 1757], *The Journal of Esther Edwards Burr, 1754-1757*, ed. Carol F. Karlsen and Laurie Crumpacker (New Haven, 1984), 273. Aaron Burr, *A Servant of GOD dismissed from Labour to Rest* (New York, 1757).

70. Thomas Hutchinson, *The History of the Colony and Province of Massachusetts-Bay*, ed. Lawrence Shaw Mayo (Cambridge, Mass., 1936), 2:280-304.

71. Burr, *A Servant of God Dismissed*, 13, 15-18.

Sources

Primary Sources

The rich manuscript collections at the Massachusetts Historical Society, Boston, provided the basic materials for this study. In addition to Jonathan Belcher's eleven letterbooks and his "Journey My intended Voyage, & a Journey to Holland, Hanover etc, . . . 1704," there were the Amory Papers, the Belknap Papers, the Colman Papers, the John Davis Papers, the Dolbeare Papers, the Greenough Papers, the Jeffries Papers, the Henry Knox Papers, the Henry Newman Papers, the Pepperrell Papers, the John Rindge Letterbooks, the Saltonstall Collections, the Smith-Carter Papers, the Waldron Papers, and the Miscellaneous Manuscript Collections both bound and unbound.

Also in Boston were the Miscellaneous Manuscript Collections and the Belcher-Wilmington Papers at the Public Library. The Massachusetts Archives has several bound manuscript collections containing an invaluable registry of ship owners (VII), records of government business (LII, LXX-LXXII), and the Records of the Massachusetts Council (executive sessions). The Suffolk County Probate Court provided a copy of Andrew Belcher's will.

Several Belcher letterbooks have been lost, but fortunately the Belcher Papers at the New Hampshire Historical Society, Concord, fill some of the gaps. The Waldron Papers at the society are an especially rich collection. The Wiggin Papers were also consulted. The Weare Papers at the New Hampshire State Archives provided some important details.

Important materials relating to Belcher's business activities in Connecticut were found at the Connecticut State Archives in the series marked Colonial Wars, Industry, and Towns and Lands.

The New Jersey Historical Society's collections in Newark were indispensable for Belcher's last years. Especially helpful were the Papers of Ferdinand John Paris. The Bamberger Autograph Collection and the Statesmen Autograph Collection were also consulted, along with the collections at the New-York Historical Society: the Rutherford Collection, the Alexander Papers, and the William Alexander Papers. The Robert Morris Papers at the Rutgers University Library aided in the understanding of the political background for the Belcher administration. The Miscellaneous Manuscript Collections at the Princeton University Library were rich in material. Especially important was the small but illuminating collection of Belcher papers. Also helpful were the James Alexander Papers, the Aaron Burr Collection, the Thomas Foxcroft Papers, and the Samuel Hazard Letterbook. The Proceedings of the Trustees of the College of New Jersey in the Princeton University Archives helped with Belcher's connection to the founding of the college.

The Gratz and Dreer Autograph Collections at the Historical Society of Pennsylvania in Philadelphia were filled with surprising and important materials. Also at the historical society were the James Logan Letterbook and the Thomas Penn Letterbooks, which provided background for Belcher's years in New Jersey. And for the same reason, the Smith Family Papers at the Library Company of Philadelphia were worth consulting. The Miscellaneous Manuscript Collections at the Presbyterian Historical Society in Philadelphia yielded a few interesting pieces.

The Library of Congress holds a small and rich collection of Waldron-Belcher Papers. In addition there are the Peter Force transcripts, New Hampshire Miscellaneous Papers, and the Wilmington Papers. The Library of Congress also has prepared an invaluable edition of the minutes of the Massachusetts Council (legislative sessions), which are listed in Lillian A. Hamrick, ed., *A Guide to the Microfilm Collection of Early State Records* (Washington, D.C., 1950), 89-95.

Other collections were helpful. The Curwen Papers at the American Antiquarian Society in Worcester, Massachuetts, helped to fill in many important gaps in the record. The George Bancroft transcripts at the New York Public Library include the interesting play, "Belcher the Apostate." The Thomas Moffat Letterbook at the library was also helpful. The Miscellaneous Manuscript Collections at the Clements Library, the University of Michigan, yielded a few bits of information. The Account Books of Francis Browne, 1706-14, at Yale University's library aided in understanding the Belchers' business activities. The Letterbook of the Company for the Propagation of the Gospel in New England at the University of Virginia Library was also consulted.

The Colonial Office Papers and the Admiralty Papers in the British Public Record Office, London, provided important details. But more important were the holdings of the British Museum, especially the Hardwicke Papers, the Newcastle Papers, and the Stowe Papers. For religious affairs the collections of letters in the Massachusetts and New Hampshire series at Fulham Palace, the minutes of the Protestant Dissenting Deputies and the papers of the New England Company at Guildhall (London), and the collections of Miscellaneous Manuscripts and the Minutes of the Meetings for Sufferings at Friends House were invaluable.

Printed Primary Sources

This work rests on a systematic and thorough reading of all publications, including pamphlets, sermons, tracts, newspapers, and even almanacs printed in Boston between 1690 and 1742 and in New York and Philadelphia between 1745 and 1758. The reading was guided by Charles Evan's invaluable *American Bibliography: A Chronological Dictionary of All Books, Pamphlets and Periodical Publications in the United States of America, 1639-1800* and the supplements compiled by Roger P. Bristol (New York, 1903-59). The American Antiquarian Society's microcard publications of "Early American Imprints" and of newspapers through Redex made these materials readily available. *Colonial Currency Reprints, 1682-1751*, ed. Andrew McFarland Davis (Boston, 1910-11) was helpful especially because of the editorial comments.

The *Collections* of the Massachusetts Historical Society include *Belcher Papers*, 6th ser., VI-VII (Boston, 1893-94). These two valuable volumes contain selections from the letterbooks during the time of Belcher's government in Massachusetts. Because they are more accessible than the letterbooks, they have been cited in the reference notes. Discrepancies with the original material appear on occasion in these volumes. In those cases the quotations were taken from the original letterbooks. The *Letter-Book of Samuel Sewall* (Massachusetts Historical Society *Collections*, 6th ser., I-II [Boston, 1886-88]) was also invaluable for Belcher's early years. The Historical Society's edition of the Sewall diary has been replaced in recent years by M. Halsey Thomas' edition of *The Diary of Samuel Sewall, 1674-1729*, 2 vols. (New York, 1973).

The *Collections* and the *Proceedings* of the Massachusetts Historical Society, as well as the *Publications* of the the Colonial Society of Massachusetts and the *New England Historical and Genealogical Register*, contain so much valuable primary as well as secondary material that the time spent perusing these series in their entirety was well spent.

The *Journals of the House of Representatives of Massachusetts* . . . (Boston, 1919-) were indispensable. Also valuable were *The Acts and Resolves, Public and Private, of the Province of the Massachusetts Bay* (Boston, 1869-1922) and the *Boston Town Records* in *Records Relating to the Early History of Boston* (Boston, 1876-1909). The legislative records of New Hampshire, as well as other valuable primary materials, are in *Documents and Records Relating to the Province of New-Hampshire* . . . , ed. Nathaniel Bouton et al. (Concord, 1867-1943). Legislative records in *The Public Records of the Colony of Connecticut* . . . (Hartford, 1850-90) document Belcher's early business and political ventures. For helpful details relating to Belcher's rise to power see the *Talcott Papers, 1724-1741*, in the *Collections* of the Connecticut Historical Society (Hartford, 1892-96), and *Documents Relative to the Colonial History of the State of New York* . . . , ed. John Romeyn Brodhead and E. B. O'Callaghan (Albany, 1856-87). For William Douglass's valuable perspective on Massachusetts politics, see *The Letters and Papers of Cadwallader Colden* in the New-York Historical Society *Collections* (New York, 1918-19). The *Archives of the State of New Jersey* . . . , ed. William A. Whitehead et al. (Newark, 1880-) contain legislative records, important collections of correspondence, and relevant abstracts from Philadelphia and New York Newspapers. *The Votes and Proceedings of the General Assembly* . . . of New Jersey are on microfilm at the Library of Congress (see Hamrick, ed., *A Guide to the Microfilm Collections of Early State Records*, 144-48).

An indispensable source for politics in London is the *Calendar of State Papers, Colonial Series* (London, 1860-). Also see the *Acts of the Privy Council*, ed. W. L. Grant and James Munro (London, 1908-12) and *Proceedings and Debates of the British Parliaments Respecting North America*, ed. Leo Stock (Washington, D.C., 1924-41).

Secondary Sources

Perry Miller's magisterial *The New England Mind: From Colony to Province* (Cambridge, Mass., 1953) remains after forty years an essential, indeed indispensable, starting point for the study of New England in the first half of the eighteenth century. Both social and intellectual historians have made important revisions in that work. The bibliography of recent work on this era is summarized and discussed in many of the essays in Jack P. Greene and J. R. Pole, eds., *Colonial British America: Essays in the New History of the Early Modern Era* (Baltimore, 1984). In addition see Jack P. Greene's *Pursuits of Happiness: The Social Development of Early Modern British Colonies and the Formation of American Culture* (Chapel Hill, 1988) for an unmatched synthesis and discussion of recent work on social developments. Also important is John J. McCusker and Russell R. Menard, *The Economy of British America, 1607-1789* (Chapel Hill, 1985).

Several works stand out as worthy of special notice. Bernard Bailyn's *The New England Merchants in the Seventeenth Century* (Cambridge, Mass., 1955) and Bernard and Lotte Bailyn's *Massachusetts Shipping, 1697-1714: A Statistical Study* (Cambridge, Mass., 1959) are essential for understanding the merchant community. Numerous local studies proved important for writing this study: Michael Zuckerman's *Peaceable Kingdoms: New England Towns in the Eighteenth Century* (New York, 1970), Christine Leigh Heyrman, *Commerce and Culture: The Maritime Communities of Colonial Massachusetts, 1690-1750* (New York, 1984); Gary B. Nash, *The Urban Crucible: Social Change, Political Consciousness, and the Origins of the American Revolution* (Cambridge, Mass., 1979); and Edward M. Cook, Jr., *The Fathers of the Towns: Leadership and Community Structure in Eighteenth-Century New England* (Baltimore, 1976). John M. Murrin's "Review Essay" of the early work by John Demos (*A Little Commonwealth: Family Life in Plymouth Colony* [New York, 1970]), Philip J. Greven, Jr. (*Four Generations: Population, Land, and Family in Colonial Andover, Massachusetts* [Ithaca, 1970]), Kenneth A. Lockridge (*A New England Town, The First Hundred Years: Dedham, Massachusetts, 1636-1736* [New York, 1970]), and Michael Zuckerman in *History and Theory: Studies in the Philosophy of History* 11 (1972): 226-75, remains an important and suggestive discussion, which should be read with James A. Henretta's review essay, "The Morphology of New England Society in the Colonial Period," *Journal of Interdisciplinary History* 2 (Autumn 1971): 379-98.

Several works were indispensable for guiding this exploration into the inner world of Jonathan Belcher. John Demos' "Developmental Perspectives on the History of Childhood," *Journal of Interdisciplinary History*, 2 (Autumn 1971): 315-28, pointed toward an explanation of Belcher's hobgoblins. Also see John F. Walzer, "A Period of Ambivalence: Eighteenth-Century American Childhood," in *History of Childhood*, ed. Lloyd deMause (New York, 1974), 351-82; John J. Waters, "James Otis, Jr.: An Ambivalent Revolutionary," *History of Childhood Quarterly* 1 (Summer 1973): 142-50; and J. M. Bumsted, "Religion, Finance, and Democracy in Massachusetts: The Town of Norton as a Case Study," *Journal of American History* 57 (March 1971): 817-31. Finally, this study owes much to Philip Greven's insightful *The Protestant Temperament: Patterns of Child-Rearing, Religious Experience, and the Self in Early America* (New York, 1977). Greven's book has been criticized severely. Although Jay Fliegelman (*Prodigals and Pilgrims: The American Revolution against Patriarchal Authority, 1750-1800* [New York, 1982]) finds it "severely hampered by his insistence on viewing the primary data of American family history apart from the intellectual and cultural history of the period," Fliegelman's decision to examine the intellectual history without regard for Greven's primary data does not permit such quick dismissal. Professor Greven does not agree with the interpretation of Belcher that is presented in this study, perhaps because he did not have the time to spend poring over the personal papers of Jonathan Belcher. But his analysis of three "distinctive forms of self" or "temperaments" guided the analysis and writing of this biographical study. Indeed, Belcher life's seems to confirm Greven's overall thesis. Also see Greven's *Spare the Child: The Religious Roots of Punishment and the Psychological Impact of Child Abuse* (New York, 1991).

Richard L. Bushman's *From Puritan to Yankee: Character and Social Order in Connecticut, 1690-1765* (Cambridge, Mass., 1967) and Richard S. Dunn's *Puritans* and Yankees: The Winthrop Dynasty of New England, 1630-1717 (Princeton, 1962) remain important treatments of cultural shifts in the age of Belcher. For the influence of the marketplace and for the transition from the traditional and republican to the liberal worldview, see the collected essays by Joyce Appleby in *Liberalism and Republicanism in the Historical Imagination* (Cambridge, Mass., 1992). But the collection by James Henretta in *The Origins of American Capitalism: Collected Essays* (Boston, 1991) remained the more compelling. John Frederick Martin's recent work *Profits in the Wilderness: Entrepreneurship and the Founding of New England Towns in the Seventeenth Century* (Chapel Hill, 1991) provides an important perspective on commerce in this world.

Although economic historians have written much on colonial money, few have attended to the ways Americans thought about money, especially paper currency. Joseph Dorfman's *The Economic Mind in American Civilization, 1606-1865* (New York, 1946), vol. 1, remains a helpful summary of the debates over paper money. Perry Miller's short discussion in *From Colony to Province* is an invaluable starting point. Elizabeth Elaine Dunn's "'The Power of a Wise Imagination': Studies in Value Conflict in Early America" (Ph.D. diss., University of Illinois at Champaign-Urbana, 1990) signals the beginning of a fruitful rereading of Andrew McFarland Davis's seemingly impenetrable *Colonial Currency Reprints, 1682-1751.* Patricia Cline Cohen's *A Calculating People: The Spread of Numeracy in Early America* (Chicago, 1982) presents an important perspective for understanding the cultural shifts within which these debates were conducted.

While the "new" social historians have produced an impressive corpus of scholarship, Puritan studies have also continued to flourish. Several works are worthy of special note. Alan Heimert's *Religion and the American Mind: From the Great Awakening to the Revolution* (Cambridge, Mass., 1966) has endured despite the initial reviews and indeed seems to have gained the recognition that it deserves. The work of Sacvan Bercovitch, especially *The American Jeremiad* (Madison, 1978), cannot be ignored. The most impressive recent synthesis that deserves to stand on the shelf next to Perry Miller's is Harry S. Stout's *The New England Soul: Preaching and Religious Culture in Colonial New England* (New York, 1986). And while David D. Hall's *Worlds of Wonder, Days of Judgment: Popular Religious Beliefs in Early New England* (New York, 1989) does not appear in the footnotes of this study, it provided important, stimulating, and critical perspective for placing Belcher's intellectual world in context. So too did the work of Jon Butler that is summarized in his *Awash in a Sea of Faith: Christianizing the American People* (Cambridge, Mass., 1990).

Understanding London's influence in the lives of New Englanders like Jonathan Belcher was aided by several works, including Michael Kraus's *The Atlantic Civilization: Eighteenth-Century Origins* (New York, 1949) and Ian Kenneth Steele's *The English Atlantic, 1675-1740: An Exploration of Communication and Community* (New York, 1986). The ideas of gentility have been explored by Edwin H. Cady, *The Gentleman in America: A Literary Study in American Culture* (Syracuse, 1949), and most recently by Richard L. Bushman, *The Refinement of America: Persons, Houses, Cities* (New York, 1992). The relevant sections of Howard Mumford Jones's *O Strange New World. American Culture: The Formative Years* (New York, 1964) are invaluable for richness of detail and sensitivity to the classical tradition.

T. H. Breen's *The Character of the Good Ruler: A Study of Puritan Political Ideas in New England, 1630-1730* (New Haven, 1970) and the relevant chapters in his *Puritans and Adventurers: Change and Persistence in Early America* (New York, 1980) are indispensable for understanding the political culture of early eighteenth-century New England. For another and complementary perspective that explores the meaning of the imperial relationship and the significance of the monarchical connections, see Richard L. Bushman's *King and People in Provincial Massachusetts* (Chapel Hill, 1985). And see his essay "Corruption and Power in Provincial America," in *Library of Congress Symposia on the American Revolution: The Development of a Revolutionary Mentality* (Washington, D.C., 1972), 62-91. Bernard Bailyn's work has left a clear imprint on the study of early American politics. Although *The Ideological Origins of the American Revolution* (Cambridge, Mass., 1967) is most often cited in current scholarship, *The Origins of American Politics* (New York, 1968) remains invaluable for linking political beliefs with behavior. Indeed, Belcher's New England seems to confirm Bailyn's interpretation of early American politics. Gordon S. Wood's "Conspiracy and the Paranoid Style: Causality and Deceit in the Eighteenth Century," *William and Mary Quarterly* 3d ser., 39 (July 1982): 401-41 (perhaps one of the most impressive essays to appear in that journal), will continue to inspire and haunt historians as they seek to penetrate the vocabulary of early American politics.

John L. Brooke's *The Heart of the Commonwealth: Society and Political Culture in Worcester County, Massachusetts, 1713-1861* (New York, 1989) is an outstanding analysis of conflict and change in political culture, which must not be neglected by any serious student of this slippery subject.

The relationship of leaders to the public was a critical subject in this study. Helpful were Emory Elliott, *Power and the Pulpit in Puritan New England* (Princeton, 1975); Donald M. Scott, *From Office to Profession: The New England Ministry, 1750-1850* (Philadelphia, 1978); and William T. Youngs, Jr., *God's Messengers: Religious Leadership in Colonial New England, 1700-1750* (Baltimore, 1976). And Edmund Morgan's *Inventing the People: The Rise of Popular Sovereignty in England and America* (New York, 1988) appeared at an important time in the writing of this study. Like many of Professor Morgan's works, this study defines an important subject, which will no doubt attract the attention of other scholars. For another perspective, see Alison G. Olson, "Eighteenth-Century Colonial Legislatures and their Constituents," *Journal of American History*, 79 (September 1992): 343-67.

The study of Massachusetts politics must begin with Thomas Hutchinson, *The History of the Colony and Province of Massachusetts-Bay*, 3 vols, ed. Lawrence Shaw Mayo (Cambridge, Mass., 1936). Robert Zemsky, *Merchants, Farmers, and River Gods: An Essay on Eighteenth-Century American Politics* (Boston, 1971), and William Pencak, *War, Politics, & Revolution in Provincial Massachusetts* (Boston, 1981) present two excellent analyses of the political system. In addition to Gary Nash's analysis of Boston politics in *The Urban Crucible*, see G. B. Warden, *Boston, 1689-1776* (Boston, 1970). For the years between the Glorious Revolution and the end of Queen Anne's War, see Philip Haffenden, *New England in the English Nation* (Oxford, 1974), which is rich in detail, and Richard R. Johnson, *Adjustment to Empire: The New England Colonies, 1675-1715* (New Brunswick, 1981), which is a masterful example of narration and analysis. And no student of Massachusetts political culture can overlook John M. Murrin's "Anglicizing an American Colony: The Transformation of Provincial Massachusetts" (Ph.D. diss., Yale University, 1966).

Perspective for analysis of the legislature first came by comparing the data in Pencak's *War, Politics, & Revolution*, Zuckerman's *Peaceable Kingdom's*, and Murrin's "Review Essay" with data in Jack P. Greene, "Legislative Turnover in British America, 1696 to 1775: A Quantitative Analysis," *William and Mary Quarterly*, 3d ser., vol. 38 (July 1981): 442-63, and Nelson W. Polsby, "The Institutionalization of the U.S. House of Representatives," *American Political Science Review*, 62 (March 1968): 144-68.

David J. Rothman's *Politics and Power: The United States Senate, 1869-1901* (Cambridge, Mass., 1966) also lent perspective for understanding the distance that separated modern politics from early eighteenth-century America. The works of Erving Goffman, especially his *Frame Analysis: An Essay on the Organization of Experience* (Cambridge, Mass., 1974), and Victor Turner in his *Dramas, Fields, and Metaphors: Symbolic Action in Human Society* (Ithaca, 1974) were helpful for developing the discussion of competing scenarios in legislative politics. Also helpful was Jack P. Greene's essay "Character, Persona, and Authority: A Study of Alternative Styles of Leadership in Revolutionary Virginia," in *The Revolutionary War in the South: Power, Conflict, and Leadership. Essays in Honor of John Richard Alden*, ed. W. Robert Higgins (Durham, 1979).

Jeremy Belknap, *The History of New-Hampshire* (Dover, 1812), remains the starting point for the study of Belcher's administration in that colony. Jere R. Daniell's *Colonial New Hampshire: A History* (Millwood, N.Y., 1981) provides an analysis of the social and political scene based on both primary and secondary sources. His bibliography is an indispensable source for the literature. In addition, see E. Van Deveneter, *The Emergence of Provincial New Hampshire, 1623-1741* (Baltimore, 1976), and Charles E. Clark, *The Eastern Frontier: The Settlement of Northern New England, 1610-1763* (New York, 1970).

An excellent introduction to the political narrative in New Jersey is Donald L. Kemmerer's *Path to Freedom: The Struggle for Self-Government in Colonial New Jersey, 1703-1776* (Princeton, 1940). Peter O. Wacker's *Land and People: A Cultural Geography of Preindustrial New Jersey* (New Brunswick, 1975) is indispensable for understanding the social scene that Governor Belcher confronted. Also see Thomas Jefferson Wertenbaker's *The Founding of American Civilization: The Middle Colonies* (New York, 1938). Two studies of New Jersey's political system have appeared recently. In addition to my own *The New Jersey Assembly, 1738-1775: The Making of a Legislative Community* (Lanham, Md., 1987), see Thomas L. Purvis's outstanding analysis in the *Proprietors, Patronage, and Paper Money: Legislative Politics in New Jersey, 1703-1776* (New Brunswick, 1986).

The empire continues to attract historians' attention. James A. Henretta's *"Salutary Neglect": Colonial Administration under the Duke of Newcastle* (Princeton, 1972) was invaluable for this study. See also Philip Haffenden, "Colonial Appointments and Patronage under the Duke of Newcastle, 1724-1739," *English Historical Review* 77 (July 1963): 417-35. For the interests at play in the working of the imperial machinery, see Michael Kammen, *Empire and Interest: The American Colonies and the Politics of Mercantilism* (Philadelphia, 1970), and Alison Gilbert Olson, *Making the Empire Work: London and American Interest Groups, 1690-1790* (Cambridge, Mass., 1992). Finally, the relevant sections of Jack P. Greene's *Peripheries and Center: Constitutional Development in the Extended Polities of the British Empire and the United States, 1607-1788* (Athens, Ga, 1987) helped to put the ideological issues into the discussion of imperial politics in the age of Newcastle.

Index